A THEORY OF PLANNING

For Maria with much love

NIVERSITY OF BIRMINGHAM
MAIN LIB

A Theory of Planning

HT 65
107868

JOHN SILLINCE
Senior Lecturer in Urban and Regional Planning, Coventry (Lanchester) Polytechnic

Gower

© J.A.A. Sillince, 1986

All rights reserved. No part of this publication may be reproduced, stored in a retrieval system, or transmitted in any form or by any means, electronic, mechanical photocopying, recording, or otherwise, without the prior permission of Gower Publishing Company Limited.

Published by

Gower Publishing Company Limited
Gower House, Croft Road, Aldershot, Hampshire, England

and

Gower Publishing Company
Old Post Road, Brookfield, Vermont 05036, USA

British Library Cataloguing in Publication Data

Sillince, John
A theory of planning.
1. Regional planning -----Political aspects
I. Title
361.6'1 HT931

ISBN 0 566 05231 8

18071457

Printed and bound in Great Britain by
Paradigm Print, Bungay, Suffolk.

Contents

Preface

A central theme of this book is that planning is a political activity raising and arguing about social and environmental issues which have a direct ethical relevance to us all. While this theme is largely accepted today, the manner in which planning policies are formulated often tends to obscure these issues and ethical values. Rationality and scientific methodology are often used to make policies seem self-evidently justified and to hide questionable assumptions.

Yet to understand why this paradox exists one needs to search beyond the planner's tactics in cleverly presenting policies to doubtful politicians and public. Both politicians and the public need many of the illusions and reassurance that planning provides. And departmental rivalry and bureaucratic conflict force the planners onto the defensive and into an attitude more prepared to adopt a technical role. This role is largely a fiction. In a government system where the various agencies are notoriously myopic and territorial, the planner's vision of comprehensiveness is a clarion call to rationality and order amidst partiality and 'muddling through'. Yet for such a vision to be effective requires just the opposite of technique. Comprehensive vision implies the ability to weigh the ethical questions involved from all sides, and to adopt an attitude of curiosity about the effects of decisions. Unfortunately the defensive language of planning policies means that such issues are not addressed. The possibilities of comprehensive investigation of important social and environmental questions are obscured. Only the techniques and language use a rationalist costume.

This is the real meaning of rationality in current planning.

Rationality is widely trusted, so long as it avoids questions of value. The planning profession is supported by this public trust, but also imprisoned by it.

I would like to thank my past students in Planning Theory for ideas and questions that have shaped the course over the years. I would also like to thank colleagues for their helpful comments. In particular Tim Coupe, Richard Farnell, and George Goodall have made many useful comments.

PART I
EIGHT PLANNING CASE STUDIES

1 Roads planning in Oxford

In the early 1950s the first modern town plans for Oxford appeared: [1]. Their objectives were aesthetics, neatness, and tidiness. These objectives seem very different from more recent planning objectives. So we must ask ourselves why were these objectives considered to be so important? One reason is that after the 1947 Town and Country Planning Act there was a shortage of town planners, and town planning in its early years was carried out by other professionals - mainly architects, surveyors, and civil engineers, with their mainly physical view of civic design and engineering solutions to problems. The chief planner in Oxford at that time was an architect, and in fact the early town plans for Oxford were produced in the City Architects Department. Also the objectives of aesthetics, tidiness, and neatness were largely those of the middle class preservation groups in Oxford. The majority of Oxford residents, more concerned with jobs and housing, were at that time indifferent to planning. Wide coverage of planning issues had not yet begun in the media, and there was as yet no tradition of widespread public participation in planning.

Three rings of roads had been proposed for Oxford. The outer ring road was completed between the late fifties and early sixties, and the inner ring road was approved in 1959. It was the third road, the inner relief road, which caused widespread public controversy, and it is this road that we consider here.

The inner relief road was favoured by shopkeepers in Oxford, who wanted more access for private cars in central Oxford, in the belief that increasing such access would lead to more prosperity for the city. There indeed was increasing congestion in the city centre. The main opposition to the inner relief road came from the University community which was generally, though not unanimously, against the proposal. The University occupied large sections of the city centre and would be directly affected by the proposal.

There were three alternative routes for the inner relief road. But all, in the south, passed through Christ Church Meadow, an open space next to Christ Church College (part of the University), and through St Ebbes, a working class area of terraced housing.

It was opposition by the University which delayed the planning process on this issue. The opposition led to four public inquiries and debates in both Houses of Parliament. An early argument used by the University was that inner relief roads do not relieve traffic - they merely redistribute it.

The 1953 Development Plan did not propose a road through Christ Church Meadow, but did propose one through St Ebbes. The inner relief road was therefore not a complete circuit. So in 1955 the minister asked the city council to propose a complete system of inner relief roads.

The Oxford Preservation Trust wanted the road to go through Christ Church Meadow, since it would have no effect directly on historic buildings. The Oxford Ratepayers Association was also in favour of a road through Christ Church Meadow, because it was the least expensive route (no buildings would be demolished) and wanted the road to continue through St Ebbes. Redevelopment in St Ebbes would increase rateable values here. Thus the Oxford Ratepayers Association viewed the road very much in terms of the benefits to the council's finances.

A debate began in the Times newspaper, and it became clear that the University was divided over the issue of the Christ Church Meadow road.

The minister had secret meetings in the Council House with the various groups. However the residents of St Ebbes were not invited to these meetings. They had remained silent or indifferent, had not organised any opposition, and were therefore considered politically unimportant.

In 1956 the first Public Inquiry was held. Afterwards the University issued a writ against the minister. The debate was taken up in the House of Lords.

In 1960 a second Public Inquiry was held. This stimulated a traffic survey. But the survey made the earlier assumptions that there was a need for more access for cars in the city centre, and accepted the need for improved radial routes. The University now began to develop a new argument - that the inner relief road plan went against plans for the development of Cowley as a counter-centre to Oxford, intended to take pressure off central Oxford.

In 1963 a plan for a sunken route through the Meadow was put forward. Opponents regarded this as merely cosmetic treatment of an unwise proposal.

New traffic statistics were collected as a result of so much controversy. It was found that between 1958 and 1964 there had been a 2½ times <u>less</u> increase in central business traffic in Oxford than in other town centres.

In 1965 the third Public Inquiry was held. Colin Buchanan was brought in as an expert witness for the opposition. He put forward, on the basis of research done for his book 'Traffic in Towns' a new concept. This was that total access to historic town centres led to their complete destruction as historic places, and that instead public transport should be improved as an alternative to private cars.

In 1967 the St Ebbes redevelopment and the inner relief road there were approved by the minister, Richard Crossman - a graduate of Oxford University. The route of the inner relief road through Christ Church Meadow was refused. The opposition from the University and others had eventually won. In 1968 an alternative route (a more expensive one) south of the Meadow was put forward. This was approved after a fourth Public Inquiry in 1970.

THEORETICAL POINTS

(i) Opposition to planning proposals is effective if opponents are conversant with letter-writing and argument, and if opponents have 'friends in high places'. This was true of the University. It was not true of the residents of St Ebbes.

(ii) Opposition can only come about if the people affected perceive that alternatives exist. The residents of St Ebbes were unaware of any alternatives.

(iii) Because the St Ebbes residents did not organise any opposition, they were considered to be unimportant.

(iv) Over such a long period the crucial change in traffic philosophy (developed by Buchanan) was able to have a decisive influence. This change could not have been anticipated in 1955.

NOTES

[1] The material for this chapter comes from J. Simmie, <u>Power, Property and Corporation</u>, London, Macmillan, 1981, pp.164-88.

2 The Bedfordshire structure plan

The planners and others who worked on the 1976 Bedfordshire Structure Plan found that the power to anticipate and influence changes during the plan period was extremely limited: [1]. So limited was this power that the influence could credibly be drawn that Structure Planning serves less to anticipate and control future environmental changes than to act as a forum for debate. Such debate is not worthless, since it is surely right that development companies, government, and the concerned public should have some forum for discussing and learning about Structure Planning issues. But it is a much less ambitious aim for a Structure Plan to have, than to aim at anticipating and influencing change.

What were the limits to the power of the Structure Plan and the County Planning Authority responsible for it? Here are some of them.

(i) Influential future development processes were outside the control of the County Planning Authority. While it wished to develop a coherent policy towards future population and housing, it could not control the actions of District Councils on the provision or non-provision of District Council public housing. Thus while the Structure Plan may have anticipated (or encouraged) fast employment growth in one area, such growth could potentially be slowed down, or even aborted, by lack of council house provision by the District Council in which that employment centre was located. District Councils sometimes jealously guard their right to have a housing policy (or lack of one) unaffected by the wishes of Structure Planners.

Another important future environmental process outside the control of the County Planning Authority was the development of Luton Airport.

Any future large-scale growth here was likely to have major repercussions upon the County's employment and housing growth targets. Yet decisions about the future expansion of the airport lay with the Minister of Transport, and not the County.

This limited power of the County was general to employment matters. The County could not control (through Planning Law) the rate of job-formation inside its borders, since many firms expand and contract without the need for planning permission - almost-empty factories becoming fully utilised and vice-versa. Moreover expanding employment outside the County boundary could always create extra demand within the County for commuter homes.

Many workplaces in the County were controlled by multi-national companies, whose plans for expansion and contraction might be made elsewhere, unconstrained by perception of local policies and by local loyalties.

(ii) The Structure Planners faced many constraints on their decision-making. Many areas were already earmarked for development. Many sites already had planning permission. Other areas had commitments created by promises by local councillors. Also many areas were affected by industrial pollution. And many areas were good quality agricultural land. All these factors limited the planners' freedom to make policies which departed from what had gone before.

(iii) Development decisions are made by many public agencies, often with little reference made to planning policies. The Anglian Water Authority pre-empted the planners by announcing a large expansion of sewerage capacity (thereby creating a large amount of surplus capacity) in part of the County. This announcement was made without first consulting the County Council. Also the St Pancras to Bedford railway line was electrified by British Rail without consultations with the County.

This fragmentation of decision-making is also shown by the need by District Councils, making day-to-day development control decisions, for plans emphasising more short-term and localised objectives than dealt with in the Structure Plan.

(iv) The lack of discretion felt by the planners working on the Structure Plan was reflected in a low-growth strategy which aimed at concentrating growth near existing centres. But this ran against the preferences of home-buyers and industrialists for rural or semi-rural locations in attractive, 'green', areas.

(v) The Structure Plan excluded issues which were felt to be too contentious, such as the issue of brickfields pollution and transportation policy. Thus several important areas of control were not directly confronted. It was therefore not a comprehensive plan. Transportation policy was a source of much disagreement between the Labour-controlled County Council, who favoured public transport subsidies, and the District Councils, who favoured more urban accessibility for cars.

(vi) The County was only one government organisation among many concerned with development processes in Bedfordshire. The fact that land already enjoying urban zonings or planning permissions was in the wrong place (not around Luton, for example, where development pressures were high) often meant little to the District Councils. And any Structure Plan policy requiring housing for low-paid workers could easily be prejudiced by future cutbacks of central government housing funds. The policy of neighbouring Hertfordshire was at least more certain - it had a restrictive policy on housing development. But it was unknown how much of its growth would spill over into Bedfordshire.

Sometimes this fragmentation of control led to compromises. For example the County Council threatened to revoke a planning permission for a multi-storey car park in central Bedford, granted by the District Council. Faced with the enormous cost of such a revocation it eventually backed down after getting an assurance from the District Council on the elimination of a certain amount of road-side car parking to balance the increase in off-street parking.

(vii) Another problem faced by the Structure Planners was that little consensus existed about what the issues were. The only consensus coming out of the public participation exercise was for low growth. On many other issues the local public was divided.

THEORETICAL POINTS

What sort of planning process was followed in this case study? Here is the 'rational-comprehensive' planning process:

<u>Step 1</u> : Define goals

<u>Step 2</u> : Disaggregate goals into objectives

<u>Step 3</u> : Generate a large array of alternatives

<u>Step 4</u> : Evaluate alternatives

<u>Step 5</u> : Implement the preferred alternative

But in this case study, means influenced ends, that is, resources, lack of powers, constraints, all determined goals. This contradicts step 1.

Also there was a restricted number and variety of alternatives which were generated, due to political conflict and due to the desire to get a plan that most would agree to. This contradicts step 3.

Also it was uncertain how implementation would proceed. Perhaps the preferred alternative would not be the one which the Districts eventually were influenced by. This contradicts step 5.

The real process followed shows more the characteristics of the 'disjointed-incremental' strategy. Here are some of those characteristics.

(i) A restricted variety of alternatives was considered.

(ii) Objectives were made to suit the available powers and resources.

(iii) A discrete series of time-steps was not followed.

(iv) The aims were remedial rather than profound, such as easing congestion, and switching the balance of development slightly.

(v) There were many power centres. These included the County, the Districts, the regional planners, the Water Authority, British Rail, private developers, and central government departments.

NOTES

[1] Material for this chapter comes from A. Blowers, 'The Politics of Consensus - The Bedfordshire Structure Plan', pp.136-79 in A. Blowers, The Limits to Power, Pergamon, London 1978.

3 Air pollution in Bedfordshire

Bedfordshire is a major source of bricks. 20 per cent of the country's cheap bricks are made there: [1]. There is one producer there - the London Brick Company. The planning permissions for the many brickworks in Bedfordshire were given in the period 1947-1952 when there was a national shortage of bricks. Because of this the planning conditions were vague - 'the land shall be filled and restored' - (this applied to the clay pits) and in practice such conditions were unenforceable. The minister at the time of making these planning conditions had admitted that materials to fill the clay pits were not cheaply available.

The brick industry in Bedfordshire is also a cause of much air pollution there. Sulphur dioxide is one gas emitted, and this gives rise to fears of human health. Fluorides cause fluorosis (a bone disease) in local cattle. And mercaptans create the particularly unpleasant smell noticeable in the brick-producing areas.

In 1960 there was a small local survey of doctors, to try to find if the brick industry had harmful effects on residents' health. The study was inconclusive. In 1968 the County Council called a Brickfields Conference. This produced much discussion about air pollution and health but led to little action.

There are several reasons why no action was taken. There was a national need for cheap bricks. Public opinion in Bedfordshire was not sufficiently aroused. The opposition was unorganised. There was a lack of information about the dangers. And the company prevented the release of any information which might promote discussion.

Much of the land around the various brickworks was owned by the company. Every farming tenant had to sign an agreement to waive any right to claim compensation from the company for the effects of air pollution.

This picture suddenly changed in the late seventies when the company needed new planning permissions. The issue moved from a 'dormant' phase to an 'active' phase, where public opinion locally became sufficiently aroused for air pollution to become a major political issue.

One of the exhausted clay pits was used by the London Brick Company for its profitable waste disposal business. It proposed moving the dumping of toxic waste from another of its pits to this one. Local residents became afraid of the effects of dumping toxic waste nearby. The County Council reacted sympathetically to such fears, and the Leader of the County Council described the company as the 'unacceptable face of capitalism'.

Shortly afterwards the company proposed building two large new works with four chimneys 400 feet high. Air pollution, though not reduced by more filters, would be spread more thinly over a wider area. The company argued that because this reduced the concentration of air pollution that it would be an improvement. Also the company proposed the demolition of many old buildings and of 98 old chimneys, and the cleaning up and landscaping of many of its sites.

These proposals were met by public suspicion. Public opinion by now had become much more environmentally conscious.

At the start of this proposal the major issue seemed to be that of dereliction but after a while air pollution emerged as the major issue about which the public was concerned.

At the start of the proposal the major party involved were the planners who used negotiation with the company. After a while the public became the major force, and conflict became the main process. The influence of the planners declined.

THE PHASE OF NEGOTIATION

The planners were anxious to achieve environmental gains. They urged the councillors to 'be nice to the Company to win concessions'. But as time went on, the documents prepared by the planners showed increasing concern with air pollution, as they began to react to public pressure.

At the start of negotiations, the planners argued for one of the two new works being sited at an old clay pit in the south of the county on environmental grounds. This provoked much local opposition. Lacking any support, the planners had to back down.

From this point on, opposition grew. Seven village groups were formed, and a County-wide opposition group, PROBE, was formed, chaired by the Marquis of Tavistock from nearby Woburn Abbey. The group had 3

MPs, and the leader of the County Council amongst its members. The County Council itself was divided on the issue.

The planners lacked the necessary expertise to evaluate the costs and benefits of alternative methods of reducing air pollution. They did not know about the technological possibilities or difficulties of pollution abatement. So they recommended that this task be carried out by consultants. The planners' main interest had been to obtain an agreement with the company (a Section 52 agreement) to get the company to restore and improve the landscape.

THE PHASE OF CONFLICT

The consultants reported in 1979. They thought the health risks were low but also said that not enough data existed to enable them to be conclusive on this question. They suggested deferring or even refusing permission for the new works while more air pollution data was collected.

Meanwhile the Section 52 Agreement was drawn up by the planners. It was at this point that the company formally made its application for planning permission for reconstruction and resiting of its operations in Bedfordshire.

Three options presented themselves to the County Council.

(i) It could refuse permission.

(ii) It could approve, get a Section 52 Agreement for landscape improvements, but surrender any future opportunity to put pressure on the company to reduce air pollution.

(iii) It could grant a part-permission for a first phase, with a Section 52 Agreement for first phase landscape improvements, giving it the flexibility to toughen up later on air pollution control.

The County Planning Committee was at that time in favour of the third option of granting part-permission only. Before it could recommend this however, the Department of the Environment carried out its own review of brickmaking. The review was, like the consultants report, inconclusive. But it was important in that it delayed matters.

The delay gave time for the opposition to form. The local branch of the National Farmers Union lent its weight to the opposition. By the time the issue reached the Council again the issue was very politically sensitive.

This time the County Council was more critical of the company and decided that air pollution was the main danger. So when it finally decided on the application, it gave part-permission but included very strict air pollution conditions. The brick kilns would have to be so designed as to be capable of removing the pollutants - the sulphur dioxide and the fluoride - and the odours given off. This was not what the company had wanted.

The chairman of the London Brick Company reacted by personally meeting the County Councillors. He said present technology to reduce air pollution was limited. He suggested that if such technology became available at a later date the company would be prepared to install it. And he hinted that the company had other permissions outside the county.

Immediately after the meeting the company announced publicly that it would not now proceed with its investment plans in Bedfordshire but would invest in Cambridgeshire and Buckinghamshire where it had obtained acceptable planning permissions. This was followed in 1981 by an announcement that one of its Bedfordshire brick factories would close with the loss of 1,100 jobs.

Trade union officials at the threatened factory persuaded County Councillors to meet with the company again. The company gave assurances that if the County Council dropped its planning conditions on air pollution, it would make Bedfordshire its top priority area for investment.

So finally the County Council granted permission without pollution conditions.

THEORETICAL POINTS

(i) Planning's strength does not come from expertise or from its rationality. The planners had to rely on consultants on the question of the costs and benefits of pollution abatement technology, and on lawyers to draw up the Section 52 Agreement.
(ii) Planning is a political activity. It reflects the political environment determined by power relations.
(iii) Planning can exert influence on issues which do not arouse political conflict. It cannot exert influence on issues which arouse political conflict. It is therefore in planners' interests to work well away from the public limelight in many cases.

NOTES

[1] A. Blowers, 'Much Ado About Nothing - a Case Study of Planning and Power', pp.140-60 in P. Healey, G. McDougall and M.J. Thomas, (Eds) Planning Theory : Prospects for the 1980s, Pergamon, London, 1982.

4 Local planning in 4 English cities

This chapter draws upon a study of local plan preparation in Birmingham, Leicester, Leeds, and Bristol: [1]. The study identified two types of local plan being drawn up during the 1970s. These were firstly local plans aimed primarily at facilitating development, and secondly local plans aimed primarily at investigating problems. We will look at each type of plan in turn.

(i) LOCAL PLANS FOR FACILITATING DEVELOPMENT

Within this category there were two subcategories. Some local plans were concerned with allocating new development land within more strategic plans. These were usually for areas on the urban fringe. Other plans were intended to stimulate the development of commercial or service centres.

Local plans aiming at facilitating development were usually concerned with 'working up the detail'. They tended to be map-based, and were generally physical in orientation, being concerned with making provision for land needs, solving infrastructure problems, increasing accessibility and so on.

For example, the Abbey District Plan, on the edge of Leicester, concerned the allocation of 170 hectares of housing land. It was a detailed implementation document for the second phase of the town expansion plan, under which an extra population of 30,000 was to be provided. The plan was concerned mainly with spatial relationships between different land uses, and with programming problems. Also it was concerned with the problem of metal contamination of some areas, and with the need to retain the separate identity of nearby villages. The town expansion had started in 1967 when development took place at Beaumont Leys, as a 'departure' from the 1956 Development Plan for Leicester. The approach was subsequently confirmed by the Leicestershire Sub-Regional Study of 1969 and by the 1975 Leicestershire Structure Plan. Implementation was assured since the City Council had owned the land since 1900 and due to the fact that the local authority was prepared to pay for infrastructure provision. By 1979 a development brief for the centre of the expansion area was being drawn up. General, earlier commitments were thus being made more specific.

Other plans to facilitate development away from the urban fringe were usually in commercial centres. They were intended either to put a local authority's central area more 'on the map' (for example the Leeds Central Area Plan, the Bristol City Docks Plan) or to protect environments attractive to investment (for example the Jewellery Quarter and Harborne, both in Birmingham).

Plans to facilitate development were legitimate because they worked with existing town and country planning legislation. They were feasible in that they were concerned only with proposing things which were known to be highly likely to be implemented. They had support, because both the private and public sector development agencies needed them to carry out their programmes.

(ii) LOCAL PLANS TO INVESTIGATE PROBLEMS

These plans had more widely-ranging and difficult objectives. Firstly they aimed at appreciating the inter-related nature of environmental and social problems. They also aimed at encouraging a 'corporate' view of problems, so that the many relevant council departments and other public agencies would be able to cooperate more effectively. They also aimed at encouraging public participation in the hope that here lay much of the support that was necessary to prise the necessary funds away from other, competing, programmes.

For example, the Chapeltown Local Plan in Leeds was concerned with social, educational, and housing problems in a run-down area of nineteenth century housing. It was begun in 1972. The initiative came from Leeds Housing Committee. The plan aimed to get a number of city council committees and other agencies committed to providing facilities in their capital programmes. These bodies included the housing, education, and social services committees of the City Council, the County Transportation Committee, and the regional and area Health Authorities. But in only a few cases were its recommendations implemented - the problem of getting these different bodies to adopt a common view in the end proved unsolvable. Because of the plan's limited success, the participation of residents was small, many residents gradually becoming cynical about the ineffectiveness of the Local Plan.

This Local Plan is representative of the lack of success of local plans which have attempted to investigate problems during the 1970s. Because of this lack of success, a change in approach became noticeable around 1976. Financial cutbacks were biting deeper, even under a

Labour government. Most planners working on these plans were forced to accept reality and changed their aims to facilitate development more. This was in line with current Department of the Environment advice to local authorities. It also recognised, though reluctantly, the decline of the corporate planning movement. Corporate planning - the adoption of a common view by all local authority departments - had been encouraged by central government in the sixties. But there had been no legislation to establish it. So it lacked legitimacy. Resistance by individual local authority departments, concerned to maintain their own independence, inevitably meant that the necessary support was missing.

The feasibility of such local plans was not high. Firstly such plans adopted a comprehensive approach, which generally requires well-integrated and expensive programmes to implement. Secondly it became recognised during the 1970s that there are deficiencies with an area-based approach. The problems of such areas cannot be solved within the areas. Detailed studies both by the Community Development Projects and the Inner Areas Studies showed this. The problem areas in the inner cities often rely for some of their employment on multi-national companies who are not willing to be subject to local pressures. These areas also have little attractiveness to the private sector development industry. So many of the messages in local plans for such areas are either unwelcome or unnecessary to the private sector. Such areas also have difficulties of gaining access to employment, as it increasingly decentralises from metropolitan areas. Some Metropolitan Counties have used this as one of the justifications for massive public transportation projects. Also such areas are typically council housing areas, suffering the problems of residential mobility common to this housing sector. Solutions to this problem are also not to be found within such areas only.

The problem-investigation approach tended to overlook the development control function. The plans instead depended upon obtaining commitment from usually reluctant funding bodies. Yet development control was a function much easier to implement.

The re-orientation of such plans towards facilitating development which took place in the mid-1970s led to ad hoc, opportunistic decisions being made on smaller sites. The emphasis was on small changes, 'limited objectives planning', 'getting something done'. The emphasis was on easy implementation, not on profound analysis.

This change led to the discovery of physical planning problems which had previously been neglected. Here are some of the types of problem which were discovered.

(i) The need for a land use context for designating Housing Action Areas and General Improvement Areas.

(ii) The removal of the blighting effect of road and other proposals which were now not going ahead because of the cuts in public expenditure.

(iii) The use of large areas of vacant land, much owned by local authorities, which were no longer required due to the cutbacks, and of other vacant sites ignored by the private sector.

(iv) The promotion of job-creating activities within such areas.

(v) The provision of a planning framework for spending specifically-targetted central government grants such as money under the 1978 Inner Areas Act, to improve and use derelict sites and increase confidence in the inner city, as well as to bid for more of such resources.

This change led to the use of development control as the main implementation method. The problems above were all suitable for treatment by the development control function. Many local plans which had formerly been aimed at investigating problems comprehensively were modified to address these problems. Others were abandoned. This new type of post-1976 plan was legitimate since it used development control powers and funding under Parliamentary legislation. It was feasible because it was incremental and small-scale. It had support because it was required by development agencies - usually in the public sector. It also helped to reinforce the professional well-being of the professional planners concerned.

THEORETICAL POINTS

(i) There are three questions to ask about a Local Plan if we wish to predict its technical effectiveness
(a) Has it got legitimacy? (i.e. is there legislation which backs it up?)
(b) Is it feasible? (i.e. are there the resources to back it up?)
(c) Has it got support? (i.e. is the plan required by development interests?)

(ii) There were two types of Local Plan in use in the 1970s. The type which facilitated development scored well on all three of these criteria. The type which investigated problems comprehensively did not, and tended to be modified or abandoned.

(iii) Although it is tempting to lay blame at the door of the private development industry, the public sector development agencies act in just the same way to planning. It is only plans which facilitate development which can assure their continued support.

NOTES

[1] The material for this chapter comes from R. Farnell, Case Studies in Local Planning, Gower, Aldershot, 1983.

5 Rural settlement policy in Warwickshire

Recent moves by central government to reduce public expenditure have several serious implications for rural areas. Falling school rolls, combined with rationalisation of rural education, are leading to the closure of many village schools. The 1985 Transport Act, bringing privatisation of bus companies, will, it has been argued, bring a reduction in the number of unprofitable rural routes. And many rural post offices will continue to close: [1].

The Warwickshire rural settlement policy indicates 'key' villages - where growth in population and services is allowed - and 'non-key' settlements, where such development is not allowed. In an era of cutbacks in rural services, the policy offers a basis for informed decisions on where to cut. 'Non-key' villages are obviously more at risk than 'key' villages.

THE ROLE OF COUNTY COUNCILLORS

In relation to making cuts in services, local councillors cannot escape the consequent unpopularity. Cuts in schools and social services are decisions made directly by them. And the terms of the 1985 Transport Act state that local authorities will be the bodies responsible for issuing licenses to local private bus operators. Granting a license to an operator who wants to operate a profitable route but who does not want to operate an unprofitable one can thus also lead to unpopularity.

In relation to rates, the trends are pushing local councillors in the direction of worrying more about rises in rates than about loss of services. More and more local services have to come from rates income, as the proportion of local authority income derived from central government continues to fall. Rates reform will if implemented take pressure off industrial ratepayers and put more pressure on domestic ratepayers, thus adding to the worries of councillors about putting up the rates.

The result of these two preoccupations is that local councillors are trying to distance themselves from cutbacks. Urban riots have provided one opportunity for the local authorities concerned to argue that they need more, not less, central government money. Other problems have led some local authorities to argue that they are in a state of financial crisis. And some evidence exists that the process of withdrawal from commitments is already occurring among hard-pressed central government departments.

THE KEY SETTLEMENT POLICY

Warwickshire has operated a key settlement policy since 1966, when 33 key settlements were designated. The policy was revised in 1975 when the number of key settlements was cut to 17. But in 1982 a major change came about in the policy. It was made more flexible, and, more importantly, the power to select key settlements was given to the Districts. We must therefore ask ourselves why such a major change took place.

In order to answer this question we must look at the problems that the policy was trying to alleviate. Between 1961 and 1981 there was a need to contain population pressures. Warwickshire was a large net gainer of migrants. The key settlement policy helped to channel development pressures to the right places, and helped maintain blanket restrictions on development in large parts of the County. After 1981 development pressures eased considerably. The County became a small net loser of migrants. Accessibility has now replaced development pressures as the main planning problem. The key settlement policy helps to concentrate limited resources in the places where those resources will be most effective.

There are a number of factors causing problems of rural accessibility in Warwickshire. Firstly there has been a fall in employment in traditional industries and in agriculture. There has been a rise in white collar jobs in the small towns, but a larger growth in the workforce has meant that the unemployment rate doubled between 1971 and 1981. So the first problem concerns accessibility to employment. Secondly 17 village schools closed between 1974 and 1984 - all in non-key settlements. Many village children must now travel to school by bus. Thirdly 56 villages lost at least one shop between 1978 and 1983, and 14 lost a post office. So shopping now involves longer journeys in some cases. Fourthly the Midland Red Bus Company has reduced its mileage - from 7.1 to 5.9 million passenger miles between 1976 and 1984. Despite this it still requires local authority subsidies, so that privatisation of its services leaves many rural routes in jeopardy.

The advice of County Councillors to planners is ambiguous. On the one hand they are worried about the prospect of villages dying. On the other hand they do not want to open the floodgates to housing developers.

The 1982 change in Warwickshire's policy on rural settlements was started in 1979. It began due to evidence that development pressure was easing, and that some sites in key villages were completely developed. Also there was some criticism that the key settlement policy had been ineffective.

WAS THE POLICY INEFFECTIVE?

17 villages have been key settlements since 1966. Another 17 villages have been chosen - non-key villages - as a control group.

In terms of population change, the 1966-1982 policy was generally effective. Generally there was growth in key settlements and a static or slightly declining population in non-key settlements.

Would this change have come about without the policy? To answer this question we must look at refusal rates of planning applications (that is number of refusals divided by numbers of all applications) weighted by number of houses. Refusal rates over the period were much higher in non-key settlements. So the Districts were supporting the County's policy.

Also planning inspectors were supporting the policy at appeals. 22 per cent of appeals were allowed in key settlements. 12 per cent of appeals were allowed in non-key settlements.

Also mention of the policy in minister's decision letters gradually increased over the period.

So generally the policy was effective.

WHY WAS THE POLICY CHANGED?

There are two aspects of the change. The policy became more flexible, and power to select key villages was given to Districts. The greater flexibility was probably due to the fact that the Secretary of State is now removing lists of key settlements from some Structure Plans. The selection of key villages by Districts fits in with other preoccupations of county councillors. If cuts in services are to be made, it will be easier to escape unpopularity if such cuts are seen to be dictated by a key settlement policy drawn up by some other body.

THEORETICAL POINTS

Most Districts have a relatively small rural electorate. Economies in rural services are not such an issue as cuts in urban services. Thus the new power of Districts to select key settlements has led to reduction of accountability of decision making on the provision of rural services.

NOTES

[1] J.A.A. Sillince, 'Why did the Warwickshire key settlement policy change in 1982? : an assessment of the political implications of cuts in rural services', Geographical Journal, Vol.152, No.2, July 1986.

6 Planning in Spain

Under the 1956 Planning Act Spanish local authorities had powers to control densities, land use, service provision, plot ratios, and design matters. There was to be a hierarchical structure of plans - a national plan, city plans, and local plans: [1].

From the beginning the structure had its problems. The national plan was begun in 1959 and reached its draft stage in 1975. Of the provincial plans only 3 had been approved by 1975. Also there were problems of metropolitan government. For example there were 23 local authorities in the metropolis of Barcelona alone. A planning board had been established for this area since 1953 but it had proved ineffective in influencing decisions by individual local authorities.

Planning law in Spain is based upon a fundamental legal principle which has been part of the undoing of good planning ever since. There are a set of abstract rules by which certain categories of land are fixed or defined. These include 'urban land', 'reserve land', 'rural land', and others. These categories give landowners rights, without specifying duties such as the provision of services. The influence of right-wing political thinking is thus very apparent. Also, as with British planning law, the conditions under which compensation is payable are very strictly limited.

AN EXAMPLE : PLANNING IN BARCELONA

There are several problems of planning in Barcelona. The local authorities there have been seriously under-financed, and thus understaffed. Also local authorities are very small and numerous. There are 300 local authorities in Barcelona Province alone. They are not very competent to deal with experienced development companies. Also Barcelona has been subject to considerable development pressures, due to large-scale immigration, mainly from Andalucia.

The 1956 Planning Act was precise but had an escape clause. It allowed plans to be changed in special circumstances. This has resulted in much bad planning. The modification of plans is a general phenomenon. Developers approach a local authority with housing or other development proposals.

The local authority has little cash to build roads, sewers, and so on. The new population will therefore be a good source of local taxes. The developer indicates that the plan is asking for too much open space, too low density, and so on. The local authority usually gives in and the plan is modified.

THE PROBLEM OF UNDERFINANCED LOCAL AUTHORITIES

Local authorities have powers to levy only very low local taxes. This forces them to accept, for example, extremely high densities. In parts of Barcelona densities can reach 1,500 persons per acre. (Compare this with the 25 persons per acre in a typical British suburban estate of semi-detached houses.) This means no land is made available for clinics and schools.

THE PROBLEM OF IMMIGRATION

In the Cataluna Region in which Barcelona is located, the population grew from 4 million to 6 million between 1960 and 1980. 40 per cent of the region is immigrant. 600,000 immigrants in the region live in shanty towns, usually with no infrastructure provided, although this problem is starting to be tackled now.

THE CONTROL OF POLLUTION

Planning law in Spain was toughened up in 1972. But the law has not been enforced. This is most noticeable with regard to the control of pollution. For example, there is a Rio Tinto explosives factory located in the middle of a complex of five oil refineries in Tarragona, near Barcelona. New housing downwind from this area has recently been constructed.

THE PROBLEM OF LAND SPECULATION

Employment is still very centralised in Barcelona. Residential areas are sometimes redeveloped for industry. Local authorities do not have the money to control land speculation which is partly to blame for the high urban densities.

THE IMPORTANCE OF INSTITUTIONS

Government under Franco was highly centralised. Franco chose all the town mayors. Centralisation helped to contain the threat of regionalism and dissent; (Cataluna fought against Franco in the Civil War.)

Now local and regional government is democratically elected. Regional devolution, though a slow process, is a hopeful sign. Also advocacy planning has begun. Residents' groups are provided with professionals to advise them about housing improvement schemes. So the move to a more fragmented and competitive political system bodes well for planning in Spain, as the reverse process bodes badly for planning in Britain. This is not the conventional wisdom because it is generally believed that strong central control and planning are synonymous.

THEORETICAL POINTS

Some current trends in British planning include more central control, greater emphasis on economic matters, and a desire to save public money. The question therefore arises as to whether local authorities will attempt to evade their legal duties, to try to get the private sector to take more of the burden for providing services, and to evaluate private development schemes in financial rather than social or environmental terms.

It is useful to look at Spain because while the environment there demonstrates little evidence of controls, an elaborate system of planning law has existed since before Spain's period of rapid economic development. There may therefore be lessons to draw about the ineffectiveness of planning law when the social and political will does not exist. Another warning comes in the form of the debilitating effect on the environment when economic goals are all-important.

NOTES

[1] This chapter is based on J.A.A. Sillince, 'Town planning and local authorities in Spain : some implications for Britain in the 1980s', <u>Planning Outlook</u>, Vol.25, No.3, 1982, pp.110-16.

7 Housing policy in Hungary

Several questions are raised by this case study: [1]. One is to what extent is housing a social rather than a historical problem - is the main problem allocation and access - or is it one of shortages? Another question is about the nature of the similarities and differences between capitalist and socialist urbanisation processes. Is there a uniquely socialist approach to urban and regional planning?

In order to understand the Hungarian housing problem we must first look at both the official and the unofficial view. The official view is that shortages are the problem, due to the situation prior to 1949, due to war damage, to rapid post war urbanisation, and to large scale post war internal migration. This leads to official policy. People are encouraged to pay for their own housing rather than relying on an over-stretched state. Migration from the villages (where housing is relatively plentiful) is discouraged.

The unofficial view sees housing as a social problem. Free housing is a right but little new state housing is available. The allocation mechanism used is to give such accommodation to 'key-workers' - bureaucrats, teachers, doctors - who receive the cheapest best, and newest state flats. Older, less-well equipped flats go to lower-status people. The majority of people have to pay for their own housing. So the better-off people get the best and newest housing, which is also cheapest housing, since it is subsidised most.

This problem comes about because housing is seen in Hungary as a kind of wage-supplement. All types of housing - either rented from the state or purchased with a mortgage - are massively subsidised. Rents and mortgages are on average 6-9 per cent of wages (compared with 20-30 per cent in Britain). Wages, however, are relatively low - £90 per month is the average, although most women work also, and prices are generally a third of Britain's.

It has been suggested that the Hungarian housing system should move more in the direction of the market. Higher prices and rents would reflect more the higher construction costs of the newer and better housing, and would thus be fairer, it has been argued. Whether because of these criticisms or for other reasons, government policy has changed since 1970. There has been a big expansion in the availability of mortgage credits. And it is easier now for small private builders to operate. But this merely reflects the official view of the problem as stated above. There were, admittedly, rent rises in 1972 and 1983-5 but these only led to a catching up with inflation, not to a more market-oriented system.

Between 1945 and 1960 housing provision was connected with large scale industrialisation, especially involving heavy industry in the North and in Budapest, near the coalfields and the gas and oil pipelines. 400,000 left agriculture and migrated or commuted to urban areas to work in industry. The large towns and Budapest suffered increasing overcrowding.

In the late fifties there was much criticism that not enough resources were going into housing investment. There was a big expansion in house-building. By the end of the sixties eleven new factories for making industrialised housing (usually in high-rise form) had been created. These now employ large numbers of unskilled workers. They enjoy a privileged political position because housing is such a high priority. Their workers earn higher wage increases than others in different industries. But they are inefficient and find it difficult to develop new products. But such is their entrenched position now that a TV debate on the high costs of construction and the ever-present housing shortages, which began in the early eighties, was mysteriously and abruptly stopped. The government obviously decided that reform of the industry was not possible.

Besides expanding the resources given to housing compared to other sectors, the government since 1960 has developed other policies designed to contain the problem of shortages. One aspect of this is that while industrialisation has proceeded rapidly, urbanisation has been relatively slow, if one compares post-war rates of addition to the urban population with rates in the nineteenth century. This has meant that urban housing shortages have been exaggerated, and that commuting has become increasingly necessary for many workers.

A process which has helped the government in this respect has been the more extensive and equal development of underdeveloped and rural parts of the country. After 1960 there was a big change in industrial investment towards a regionally more equal distribution. Some measures were taken to contain the expansion of Budapest. In 1951 there was a strict control on migration to Budapest. Unfortunately this led to the rapid growth of a poorly-serviced outer ring outside the controlled area. In 1961 there was a control on Budapest workplaces hiring new workers, but this was not strictly enforced, partly due to political lobbying by workplaces, partly due to fears about the effects on industrial growth if control were strictly enforced. In 1960 growth poles began to be developed to take the weight off Budapest. Expanding Budapest industries were tempted away by generous government grants. Housing spending was, for a time, switched marginally away from Budapest towards the other towns.

By far the most benign influence in the regional equalisation process (with its beneficial effects or reducing housing shortages in the big towns) has been the labour-intensive nature of Hungarian industry. Labour is the scarcest resource in industry, and consequently industry is more prepared to relocate to where labour is in surplus than in capitalist countries. 40 per cent of the workforce still works in agriculture, which continues to shed labour to industry. This has led to fast growth in small towns and even some villages. It also helped the process of regional convergence until the late 1970s, when the difficulty of obtaining foreign capital for new projects led to retrenchment in the areas of existing industry - the richer regions - so that regional divergence took place back (by 1980) to the 1960 level.

Since 1975 housing policy has specifically favoured rural areas. The plan to 1990 tried to discourage housing investment in large urban areas. But this plan is now at odds with the policy of retrenchment in industrial investment.

Despite the creditable drive by the government to reduce housing shortages, the problem of inequality of access remains. During the 1960s the value of almost-free government housing was eight times the average annual income (the British figure is about 2-3 times). But this almost-free housing goes to the better-off groups. This happens even more in Budapest where there are proportionately more state flats and more higher-status people: (in Hungary 75 per cent own their own house, while the Budapest figure is 35 per cent). Also the problem is continuing into the mortgage sector - surprisingly, mortgages are cheaper for higher status people.

THEORETICAL POINTS

(i) Hungary, like Britain, experiences policy conflicts with respect to housing. Its aims, often contradictions, include overcrowding in the towns, increasing fertility (rates are higher in the villages), using housing as a means of indirect income redistribution, encouraging key workers, encouraging migration of key workers to high priority areas, discouraging general migration to the urban areas, and reducing the money burden created by state housing finance.

(ii) Hungary, like Britain, experiences lobbying from powerful industrial interests whose aims sometimes conflict with the government's stated housing objectives.

(iii) Hungary, like Britain, experiences only limited success in controlling the flow of migration and the rate of growth of settlements. Shortages of housing in both countries serve to discourage inter-regional migration. Also government policies in both countries are prone to rapid changes when the international economic situation worsens.

(iv) Unlike Britain, labour is the scarcest industrial factor in Hungary. This has meant that industry has until recently been prepared to seek out spare labour in the underdeveloped and rural areas.

NOTES

[1] This chapter uses material from J.A.A. Sillince, 'The housing market of the Budapest urban region 1949-1983', Urban Studies, Vol.22, 1985, pp.141-9, and from J.A.A. Sillince, 'Housing as social problem versus housing as historical problem : the case of Hungary', Environment and Planning C : Government and Policy, Vol.3, 1985, pp.299-318.

8 Nuclear power in Britain

The future of nuclear power in Britain depends to a great extent on future public attitudes. How can such attitudes be predicted? Can we as planners find lessons from looking at what has happened in other dangerous technologies and in other countries?: [1].

If we look at the rest of Western Europe, opposition to nuclear power can be crudely indicated by the growth of Ecology Parties. The membership of these parties is socially and economically very specific. Two types of member predominate. There is the young, well-educated person employed in the non-productive sector, including students and government employees. And there are older members of conservation groups. Numerically, such memberships are very small. However, these parties can exert a much larger influence than their size suggests because they publicise local environmental hazards, with the effect of increasing public fears, and with the effect of reducing the 'acceptability' of a nuclear accident.

In the rest of Western Europe there was early development of commercial large scale nuclear energy and this, coupled with a lack of public participation, led to a rapid growth in opposition. America is a more difficult case and seems less comparable with Britain. Initially in America there were low safety standards. They have an open judicial and governmental system ensuring wide publicity of investigations into mistakes and accidents. And they have the Three Mile Island accident, which led to a rapid rate of cancellations of orders for new nuclear power plants.

Despite the narrow political base of Ecology Parties in Western

Europe, most have been formed during the last 10 years, with anti-growth policies in a period of falling employment. Their potential membership if the economic situation improved is therefore difficult to know.

The British Ecology Party is just about the least successful of the European Ecology Parties. In the national election of June 1983 all its 118 candidates lost their deposits. The narrow political base is revealed by the fact that there were only three types of area represented - well-to-do areas in cities, well-to-do rural towns, and agricultural areas. Only nine candidates contested poor city areas.

The size of Ecology parties' support is small. The exception is Centrum in Sweden (20 per cent of the 1981 vote) which is however, the only one to be pro-nuclear (after a 1980 referendum established that 60 per cent of voters were in favour of nuclear energy). The ambiguity of these figures however is revealed by the fact that while divided, the Swedish electorate does feel strongly on the issue. In 1976 the Social Democrats there fell from government after 44 years in power. The winner was on an anti-nuclear power platform. Similar divisions exist in Switzerland and Austria. In the latter country public protests have led to the closure of the only nuclear power station.

Britain obviously needs proportional representation for its Ecology Party to have an electoral chance. Therefore most of its efforts go into public inquiries together with Friends of the Earth, the Political Ecology Research Group, and the Council for the Preservation of Rural England. The weakness of the British Ecology Party is that the other parties can easily steal its clothes. The Labour and Alliance parties both opposed nuclear power in the May 1983 General Election. Both their leaders gave major speeches on the environment prior to that election. And the government in 1983 produced legislation limiting lead in petrol and decided to safeguard West Sedgemoor as a wetland habitat.

Britain, though an early researcher, was a late commercial starter. Apart from the 1979 Torness AGR there have been no other nuclear power station starts since 1970. The Fast Breeder Reactor is still some way into the future. Britain's largest anti-nuclear power demonstrations recently have been in 1978 - 10,000 people and 1979 (at Torness) - 4,000 people. Compare this with 100,000 at a site in France in 1977, and 80,000 at a site in W Germany in 1977. And compare it with the 250,000 who demonstrated in Hyde Park against nuclear weapons. So in Britain things are relatively passive. But with more nuclear plants planned opposition will undoubtedly grow, perhaps to West European levels.

Away from the national stage, it can credibly be argued that Ecology Parties enjoy even more influence than in national politics. For example, the West German Green Party, with only 5 per cent of the vote, were able to stop a government plan for a large nuclear waste dump in Lower Saxony by alerting local residents to the dangers of leaks into local water supplies.

If we look at similar technologies, what can they tell us about future reactions to nuclear power? For example, the fear of radiation can decline, since x-rays gained public acceptance after initial distrust. And the fear of catastrophe affecting large numbers can be reduced if the responsible agency is trusted and if there are undoubted benefits. The storage of nerve gas in the USA provides an example here. Such storage has not incurred one accident since the start of storage in 1942, so that the agency responsible - the US Army, is trusted. And local residents benefit economically from the Army bases. This said, it is interesting that the Bhopal accident in India, which killed 2,500 and injured a quarter of a million, led to a public re-examination of similar chemical plants in America. The effect of world-wide news is therefore considerable.

The strategy of the Central Electricity Generating Board has been to attempt to divide local opposition. For example, there was a plan for a 'nuclear island' of nine nuclear plants at Oxford Ness on the Suffolk Heritage Coast. When the debate about the nearby Sizewell B plant began residents were told that the 'nuclear island' idea would be dropped if Sizewell B was successful.

The influence of location on acceptability of nuclear power is considerable. Nearness to London probably scores high against acceptability, what with the capital's large population and media. It seems likely that the anti-Cruise demonstrations would not have got so much publicity in a remoter location. Other locational factors are probably important too - high unemployment, low average social class, an older population, a high proportion in dangerous occupations all probably make a location less liable to be the subject of local controversy.

How much can we believe about policies of the major political parties? Both Labour and the Alliance opposed nuclear power in 1983. Can we believe them? Looking at France, policy change does seem possible. President Mitterand was initially very pro-nuclear, but with declining political support, a declining oil price, and high unemployment in the coalfields he has substantially cut back on the nuclear programme.

THEORETICAL POINTS

The public mistakenly believes planes are more dangerous than cars, because of the imageability of TV crashes and the newsworthy nature of such events. They perhaps associate nuclear energy accidents with atomic explosions, an equally irrational attitude. So how much should decision makers listen to the public?

On the other hand, nuclear energy experts make mistakes, and decision-making committees (because of the lack of individual accountability) take risks that one decision-maker might avoid. Also the nuclear power industry is a powerful lobbyist, with promises of future export orders. Also how much can we be sure that present government commitment to nuclear energy is motivated by a desire for the safest and cheapest energy, rather than by a wish to reduce the political power of the National Union of Mineworkers?

NOTES

[1] The material for this chapter has been taken from J.A.A. Sillince, 'Will the British public accept nuclear energy?', _International Journal for Energy Research_, Vol.8, 1984, pp.351-60.

PART II
STRATEGIES AND ARGUMENTS

9 Three methods of evaluating planning

Every year something like an eighth of the country's gross national product is invested in land and buildings - a not inconsiderable sum. The responsibility for guiding this investment from the point of view of its environmental impact rests upon the town and country planning system. Increasingly such decisions controlling development are being set within a wider framework of plans at the regional, sub-regional, and district levels. The effect of this wider setting is to bring into the debate (about development versus the environment) another dimension - that of conflict with other elements of the plan. Such conflict is usually referred to in terms of conflict with goals or objectives, or in terms of making worse existing or future problems. The goals and problems are often defined widely and span physical, social, and economic matters. One dimension of complexity, therefore, in the evaluation of planning is that we in fact must evaluate two very different things: we must evaluate plans, and we must evaluate decisions: [1].

Implicit in the idea of evaluation is that we can - or should try to - distinguish good plans and decisions from bad ones: [2]. But how can we tell good plans and decisions from bad ones?

This is a problem to which no definitive solution can be offered. One attempt at a solution is by evaluating the results after the event, with the wisdom of hindsight. We will use this method occasionally (for example, in considering high rise housing). However, as we will show later in this chapter, such attempts are enormously risky and do not offer a satisfactory method of evaluation. Another attempt at a solution is to consider the results from the decision maker's viewpoint.

This is only feasible if the viewpoint is reasonably short term so that consequences are easily predictable. This begs the question of how the decision is made - which brings in the third approach to the problem - evaluating the process by which the decision is made.

All three evaluation methods - evaluating results after the events, evaluating results at decision time, and evaluating the decision process - are used by planners and politicians as and when it suits them. Planners usually combine the last two methods and it is to this combination that the major part of what follows is devoted. The investigation of this combined evaluation approach will hopefully be critical, but wherever possible constructive criticisms will be offered as guides to best practice. A study of a District planning office found that planning practitioners found no help or guidance for day to day planning work from planning theory textbooks: [3]. Obviously there is therefore a need for such textbooks to be constructive: [4]. We will outline an evaluation method which in best practice is probably used in an implicit way. We attempt to make the method explicit.

Another aim of what follows is to undermine the view of planning as a technical discipline. While many aspects of planning are becoming more and more technical the essential, defining character of planning decisions and of plans is political. Judgements of value and arguments about values - these are the essential ingredients. So the setting out of a method of evaluation will lay most stress upon the importance of argument and values. At each stage the reader may be left with questions rather than answers. This is because planning as an activity cannot avoid these questions. So the view that planners answer questions which have been supplied from elsewhere is, we feel, misguided. Much of government and politics is a process of discovering which questions are most important: [5]. Planning is a part of this process: [6].

But first we must outline in more detail the three methods of evaluating plans and planning decisions, describe their difficulties and come to some conclusion on a suggested approach for the investigation which follows.

METHOD ONE: EVALUATING THE RESULTS OF DECISIONS AND PLANS AFTERWARDS

The chief difficulties are the following:

(i) The planning process: [7] takes place over a long period of time, leading to difficulty in explaining the 'process' as a simple unit: [8]. Even if one wants to explain particular outcomes, the explanatory forces invoked almost always involve characteristics of this long and shifting process. Two sorts of difficulty arise:

(a) As the process proceeds over time, it can involve a large number of decision points. For example, a development control officer may decide that an application for a factory in an inner city area is environmentally unsound. The policy team may however consider that the area's residential zoning should be changed anyway, and so it uses the application as a justification for the change. The application is eventually turned down, but the change of policy (industrial zoning) leads to the applicant submitting a much larger application.

The contents of each of these outputs might be called 'policy'. But we do not want to study inconclusive or tentative outputs. Nor do we want to study decisions which are 'rubber-stamping' earlier outputs. But how do we find the 'significant' decision?: [9].

(b) The idea of evaluating results afterwards demands that our values be determined at some beginning point. Such values, however, are likely to change as the process unfolds: [10]. Considering the above example, we may initially think that no large industrial application is likely to be forthcoming in the inner city area since greenfield sites are more attractive. This means that such an industrial zoning would just lead to inner city blight. The subsequent larger application then changes our view of the situation.

(ii) Any given policy proposal, or 'output', or 'outcome' is in itself complex. It may have many different aspects. This multiplicity may make the planning policy or decision extremely difficult to place in any single category: [11]. Thus a decision to allow a new business park near to the National Exhibition Centre between Birmingham and Coventry may be advantageous to the region but disadvantageous to Birmingham's inner city area, in economic terms. It may encourage incursions into the Green Belt. Thus not only are environmental considerations pitted against economic ones, but even consideration of economic benefits depends upon one's view of how regional economic recovery should be achieved.

Another example of this problem arises when we try to construct zonal indices of accessibility for alternative plans. The score for one zone will heavily depend upon whether or not adjoining zones are developed. It thus proves difficult in practice to give a score to a zone independently of what happens elsewhere: [12].

Also evaluation of alternative land use arrangements is impossible to completely disentangle from an evaluation of alternative transportation systems, since the viability of one depends largely on the viability of the other.

In many cases policies overlap or conflict with one another, so that the attempt to determine the effects of a particular town and country planning policy is undermined by complexity. Which planning policy caused the effect? Perhaps no policy caused it - the effect may be the result of forces outside the control of planning. To overlook this fact can cause considerable errors. For example, the number of rural acres which the 1947 Town and Country Planning Act saved from urban sprawl has been estimated: [13]. The calculation overlooked the fact that the war and government decisions to encourage agriculture after 1940 meant that there were other factors discouraging urban sprawl. Agricultural land prices rose, farming became more profitable, especially on the good land near the lowland towns, and farmers became more reluctant to fragment their operations.

This complexity can be further illustrated by a study of the effects of alleged restrictive housing land policies: [14]. This study found that the proportion of house prices in the area studied which was due to land prices rose alarmingly between the mid-fifties and the mid-sixties. The study did not take account of the rise in the amount of mortgage money available, nor of the inflationary effects of the British system of flexible mortgage rates: [15].

(iii) In any decision or plan there are usually a large number of participants. This gives rise to two types of difficulty:

(a) Subjective. The view of the situation as seen by each participant may vary. Residents of Birmingham's inner city areas may say that a new greenfield business park will bring in workers from outside the region rather than solving inner city unemployment. Others may argue that such a development will have important multiplier effects - service jobs for inner city residents for example.

(b) Objective. How does the evaluator assess the relative importance of the views of inner city residents as compared with suburban residents in the case of the new business park near Birmingham?

(iv) Decisions and plans are formed by a process which is not simply additive: [16]. If we are attempting to understand how the quality of an environment has changed - say from rural to urban, or from ordered to disordered, or from an area which has a high level of community environmental awareness to one with a low level, we might be able to select significant decision points. But some decisions may have more crucial effects than others on character, or predictability, of an environment, or on morale of the inhabitants, and earlier decisions may increase the effect of later decisions in a multiplicative way: [17]. Moreover, the problems of retrospective understanding are compounded by the ambiguity of records, the partiality of memories, and the desire by participants to impose order and coherence on past events: [18].

For all these reasons, and because of organisational influences investigated below, planners generally carry out few systematic analysis of past policies.

METHOD TWO: EVALUATING THE LIKELY RESULTS OF DECISIONS AND PLANS AT THE TIME

Because of the enormous difficulties of Method One, planners are forced to consider the less ambitious evaluation of results at the time they are making a decision or formulating a plan. Of course, the second and third problems of Method One still apply here. The second problem, in particular, raises questions about what we mean by 'results'. Here are some possible answers: their very variety means that defining what we mean by results is an extra dimension of difficulty.

> "1. Because the decision will ultimately favour long-term political or ideological objectives. (But will it? And are we clear, and agreed, about our objectives?)...
> 2. For reasons of efficiency. (But efficiency for what? For saving lives? For saving costs? For speeding up something? Why is that better?)
> 3. Because later on we (or the recipients of the decision) approve of the outcome. (But why do we approve? And was the outcome really caused by the decision? Could it be that we

approve of the short term results, but may change our minds when we see the subsequent outcomes?)
4. Because the decision is satisfying to committee member X (he will find it easier to explain, to carry out; 'we got what we wanted' from it).
5. Because the decision satisfies some of the personal needs and hopes of committee member X ('it will give my section more influence'; 'now they will have to give me that promotion'; 'my wife will be pleased if we can move'; 'that's one in the eye for old so-and-so').
6. Because it will help the committee, or its parent organisation, to survive/give it more power ('now they'll have to increase our budget' - organisational politics).
7. Because it preserves the committee's unity, reflects the 'real' balance of views, of power. (Committee chairmen, in particular, hate to see anyone rocking the boat, but the price of consensus may be a decision they will come to regret.)
8. Because it can readily be defined against attack; no-one could blame the committee for it. (The search for safety, a low profile, and buck-passing.)
9. Because it gives the appearancc of prompt action while, in fact, doing very little; (the PR cosmetic job).
10. Because it seems to meet most aspects of the problem, at least in the short run, (the problem solving approach).
11. Because it redresses some perceived imbalance within the committee ('it's time those fellows stopped having it all their own way') without doing lasting damage.
12. Because the decision is morally right. (But are we agreed as to what is morally right here, and can we afford it?)
13. Because it either challenges or restores the status quo (moves in the power game; the struggle for stability).
14. Because it is 'adaptive' to changed conditions. (But is adaptation always a virtue? Who will decide what is adaptive? And to what ought we to adapt? Is appeasement adaptive?)": [19].

As suggested above, the ability to evaluate policy intelligently depends on how short-term it is. This raises the question of how the policy is made and implemented.

METHOD THREE: EVALUATING DECISIONS AND PLANS ACCORDING TO THE PROCESS BY WHICH THEY ARE MADE

Again we avoid the most difficult problems of Method One, but we are faced with a multitude of conflicting definitions of process. Here are some of them.

(i) Judicial procedure.

The Statutes and Circulars provide procedures for the making of planning decisions and plans. However, they are usually vague and allow wide discretion:

> "The judicial procedure, then, provides safeguards against the simpler forms of corruption, and the subtler administrative vices. In matters closely affecting individual choice of

action, it tends to be more strictly predictable than administrative action, because judges are reluctant to recognise the relevance of exceptional features without authority. And in private and criminal law, it is of supreme importance that the individual should know in advance what legal consequences his acts will have. Modern administration deals, however, with some matters, like town planning, where the special features of particular cases may well be more important than any they have in common; general rules can provide only the broadest guidance. Administrative action in these cases affect private interests in unforeseeable ways; but if the policies are to be at all rationally implemented, predictability must yield to flexibility.
In these matters, the problem is to devise procedures that will elicit all the relevant facts, give interested parties the opportunity to state their claims, and ensure that the responsible official is without personal interest in the outcome. Broadly speaking, these are the criteria known in English law as 'the rules of natural justice'.": [20].

What is the importance of natural justice in the current planning system? To answer this question we must consider the current operation of planning procedures as they affect public participation. And we must also consider the merits or otherwise of public participation itself.

(a) Criticisms of public participation: [21]. These are:

1. Public participation bypasses the traditional rôle of the local councillor as the locally elected representative of public opinion: [22]. Some of the fiercest opposition to the introduction of public participation came from councillors.

2. Public participation raises expectations of citizens to unrealistically high levels and is doomed to creating cynicism. This criticism, however, can be reduced by sensitive handling of the questions put to residents to make sure that they understand the local authority's resource limitations.

3. Public participation increases the time between the identification of a problem, or an application for planning permission, and when something is finally done about it.

4. Often ordinary people do not understand the complex issues involved. If the public reacts 'irrationally' to an issue should the planner overlook such a reaction? For example, most people consider airplane travel as riskier than car travel because of the 'imageability' and media coverage of air crashes. It is argued by some that such distorted perceptions alter people's reactions to nuclear energy. Should such perceptions be treated as 'irrational' and overlooked?: [23].

(b) Arguments in favour of participation: [24]: These are:

1. The scope of central and local government is always expanding. Local councillors cannot cope with the workload of modern local government. This usually leads to greater discretion being given to

local officials, including planners. Public participation is merely one method of scrutinising the actions of local officials. But could not this be an argument, rather, for more full-time and better-trained local councillors?

2. The local democratic system does not work. Local elections express popular dissatisfaction with the parties in Westminster rather than with local political parties. A study of Kensington and Chelsea concluded that councillors were insulated from local opinion - they only listened to what they wanted to listen to: [25]. But is this not an argument in favour of reforming local government (for example, the rating system) rather than introducing pulbic participation?

3. Party politics are often irrelevant to local issues and spontaneous reactions by local people are often more appropriate: [26]. But if local government were reformed would not this argument be weakened?

4. In planning, consensus policies are not possible. Someone will always be adversely affected. Public participation fits naturally into this view of planning, with the planner playing the role of umpire rather than of expert.

5. Protest must be ventilated. Public participation plays the role of safety valve.

6. Public participation gives decision makers more information. For example the only nuclear power station to be completed in Austria had to be closed down after public protest. A cheaper approach might have been to bring in public participation before the project had started.

7. We tend to start the decision-making process with an open mind and with several alternatives. Later on we narrow down the alternatives and our mind becomes closed to new information. Therefore we are more prepared to listen to all the conflicting views early in the process. Indeed, this has become one of the definitive properties of public participation, that it should take place before decisions and commitments are made.

8. Procedural justice must be seen to be done. Government must be _perceived_ to be open to public pressure. Decisions must not be generally suspected to be taken in secret. Decision-makers must be identifiable and thus accountable: [27].

(c) Some current procedures with regard to public participation: [28].

(1) _Public participation prior to submitting a Structure Plan to the Department of the Environment_. The local authority must ensure adequate publicity and give the public at least six weeks to make their views known. If the minister is not satisfied this has been done or that (when submitted to him) the structure plan does not take account of these views he can modify the structure plan himself.

Before submitting the structure plan to the minister the local authority holds a public examination of the structure plan in the local area. A Department of the Environment inspector presides. The issues are selected by the local authority on the basis of previous comments by the public.

If the local authority is thinking, for example, of putting a new roadline through its area, the value of affected properties will fall. This is what is known as planning blight. If the local authority published two alternatives there would be twice as many properties whose values will fall - twice as much planning blight. Because of this the law states that local authorities should only publish realistic alternatives. However the local authority is itself the judge of what is a realistic alternative - and so it is both judge and jury in its own case.

Also it is very difficult for the Department of the Environment to be sure that publicity and participation procedures have been adequate. The local authority may claim that a lack of objectors is a sign of general acceptance of the plan. But it could of course mean a lack of publicity.

Another problem is that the general strategic policy (i.e. the structure plan) must be approved first, and the local, detailed plan (i.e. local plans) prepared afterwards. Structure plans do not show realistic maps. They only show diagrams. Their aim is to communicate concepts, not fixed proposals. Ordinary people relate easier to fixed proposals, preferring to judge local and detailed proposals from the viewpoint of their property. Unfortunately by the time these detailed proposals (local plans) have been made, and people have reacted to them, the major determinant of these specific proposals (i.e. the structure plan) would have been approved.

However, such a situation is necessary because the present system successfully screens out objectors whose only interest is the safeguarding of their own property. For example, under the pre-1968 planning system, there were 20,000 objectors to the Greater London Development Plan, the great majority of which were solely concerned with the effect of the plan on the objector's property.

(2) The Examination in Public of the Structure Plan. Unlike public inquiries and appeals, examinations in public do not involve barristers and legal procedures but instead are played out in the form of a seminar directed by a DOE inspector. Lay people may find this difficult to participate in. Also such seminars are inevitably conducted between professionals in a dry, technical manner. Conflicts are avoided and discussion is low-key. Such proceedings do not invite intelligent participation by non-specialists.

The greatest problem however is the ability of the host local authority to select objectors from the list of those who have previously offered comments. There is always the possibility that a structure plan's harshest critics may in this way be ignored.

(3) Regional and Subregional Planning. Increasingly structure plans are based on regional plans. These plans are not subject to any statutory public participation, nor are they the product of an easily accountable body. Yet once they are approved by the minister they provide the policy foundations for structure plans. The question

arises therefore whether the growth of regional planning without public participation undermines the use of public participation in structure planning and renders it less effective and useful.

(4) Local Plans. The minister has no dealings with local plans as he has with structure plans. The law merely requires the local authority to carry out public participation to the best of its ability and then, when the draft local plan is complete, to hold a local plans inquiry.

There are two emergency powers over local plans which the minister retains. Firstly in the last resort if he feels it necessary he can direct that a local plan should not have effect. However it is unlikely that this power would ever be used unless over some source of political controversy. The other power is that the minister's inspector chairs the local plans inquiry. However, the local authority can reject his advice. So the local authority producing the local plan is virtually judge and jury in its own cause.

There is one qualification needed here. The county council (the structure plan authority) has the power to say whether or not a local plan is in conformity with the structure plan. If the local plan conforms then the county provides a certificate which allows the local plan to take effect. Certification is needed before a local plan can take legal effect.

Because this could be a source of needless conflict, or at least uncertainty, between counties (structure plan authorities) and districts (local plan authorities) the law requires that counties prepare what is called a development plan scheme. This is a document which sets out the allocation of responsibility for preparing local plans and the timing of them. It is prepared by counties after consultation with districts. Yet counties have the final decision on what goes in them. Counties can more or less circumscribe what goes into local plans and what areas the local plans are for. Districts can 'go slow' on producing local plans. Indeed they can refuse to produce them since there is no mandatory duty to prepare them. But counties can decide to prepare these local plans themselves as indeed they do on certain topics (e.g. minerals, key settlement, and green belt subject plans).

So any question about the importance of natural justice in plan making must receive only a qualified confirmatory answer: [29]. Local authorities have considerable discretion, and the matter is further complicated by the inevitability of district-county conflicts. Moreover the move towards public participation in the early seventies was in some ways an efficiency exercise by central government. Instead of all plans needing to be sent to the Department of the Environment (with the consequent delays) local authorities were required to use public participation as the external check.

Thus statutory procedures provide a very imperfect means of evaluating plans and planning decisions. To find other types of procedural evaluation we will now turn to processes which are not recognised by the statutes but which are nevertheless of great importance. Consider the following remaining types of procedural evaluation:

(ii) A decision or plan is good because a majority of the committee voted for it. Voting ensures group involvement and collective commitment, a sense of fair play, and the sharing of responsibility for whatever may happen subsequently. But these are all advantages for the committee members rather than for the decision. Committee decisions are sometimes riskier than individual decisions, because one isolated individual can be held accountable while a committee cannot: [30].

(iii) A decision or plan is good because the correct methods were used. Because of the complexity of plans and planning decisions this type of evaluation is inevitably of major importance. Briefly, this type of evaluation refers to the use of the 'rational-comprehensive' strategy, involving a central decision-maker carrying out a comprehensive set of tasks in a 'rational' chronological order.

(iv) A decision or plan is good because it is in line with existing policy. However this rule would allow us to justify all sorts of decisions by arguing their 'consistency' with a 'policy'. We might even reinterpret the policy in order to allow our decisions to fit in. This may, however, be the way many organisations work, since they favour consistent, self-perpetuating policies because these save thinking time and create an impression of stability.

(v) A decision or plan is good because it is easily implemented, or can be readily enforced, or fits in with existing standard operating procedures. But such a rule favours conservative decisions and plans, or ones which fit in with existing bureaucratic boundaries and preoccupations. And to demonstrate ease of implementation we must necessarily want to see if implementation took place. We would then be using Method One, with all its difficulties.

(vi) A decision or plan is good because it keeps all options open until we have more detailed information: [31]. But waiting may mean that we wait too long - that problems are not tackled.

(vii) A decision or plan is good because it accords with precedent, with the law, or with the terms of reference, and therefore requires no change in principle. Long term plans which assume existing trends will continue are essentially using this evaluation method, but can be criticised for 'steering by looking in the rear-view mirror'. Usually, however, precedent and the law offer no firm guidance for most planning decisions. Close study, for example, of appeal decisions would offer very imperfect guidance about the outcome of the next appeal elsewhere, since the nature of the application and the problems of the area are so different.

CONCLUSION

We have considered three ways of evaluating plans and planning decisions. The first method is to carry out the evaluation afterwards. This has severe problems, since it is very difficult to disentangle decisions and plans from the pattern of institutional and political forces in which they are embedded, because values change, and because earlier decisions can have a qualitative as well as quantitative effect on the effectiveness of later decisions: [32]. The second method is to evaluate the results of a decision or a plan at the time it is made. Here the difficulties, though still present, are much reduced, apart from the presence of a variety of conflicting definitions of what we mean by 'results'. This type of evaluation method is often referred to as 'utilitarian', since it is concerned solely with consequences. It is, we will argue later, together with the third method (evaluation of decision - or planning - process) the dominant method of evaluation in planning as it is currently practiced. This method of evaluation is nearly always an implicit one. Much is unstated, and more importantly, unquestioned. It shall not be our intention in what follows to provide an alternative method. We shall merely attempt to make explicit and formalise some of the main ideas embedded in the method, as well as demonstrating that there exist many questions and difficulties in the use of the method. In best practice some of these questions and difficulties are often dealt with. We hope that by raising them and presenting the method in a formalised and explicit way that not only will practitioners find their onerous task more understandable but that what follows will serve as a practical guide.

In suggesting that the following evaluation method is the one used in practice, it should be added that outside of this evaluation process regarding substantive questions there is another one which relates to the planning organisation's goals, and involving procedural or structural questions. Often planners have to pay more attention to procedural matters than to substantive ones. Thus the true situation is of a set of constraints which are created by simultaneously seeking to satisfy a large number of criteria. Some are substantive, to do with the content of policy and its impacts. Some are procedural, resulting from government objectives such as efficiency and integrity. And some are structural, to do with survival or growth of the planning organisation: [33].

The third method of evaluation, we have said, is that of evaluating the decision - or planning - process. It was suggested above that legal procedures to ensure natural justice offer a poor standard by which to judge decisions and plans chiefly because so much is left to the discretion of the local authority. Another definition of a good process was the 'rational-comprehensive' strategy. The remaining definitions fell in with accepted bureaucratic custom or administrative convenience and can be subsumed within a strategy of decision that has come to be known as 'disjointed-incrementalist': [34]. It is to these two strategies that we now turn.

NOTES

[1] An early criticism of treating plans and policies as decisions writ large or as chains of decision-outputs is T. Lowi, 'Decision making vs Policy making : toward an antidote for technocracy', Public Administration Review, Vol.30, May/June 1970, pp. 314-25.

[2] The attempt to do so cannot be said to be 'scientific' or empirical, since it involves analysis of value and of philosophy. The difference between these two approaches to planning theory is an important one to bear in mind : see N. Taylor, 'A critique of materialist critiques of procedural

planning theory', Environment and Planning B, Vol.11, 1984, p.103-26.

[3] J. Underwood, Planners in Search of a Role, Centre for Advanced Urban Studies, Bristol University, 1976.

[4] There is a division between theorists who take this view and those who take a more 'critical' approach : see M. Hebbert 'Four approaches to the planning theory syllabus', in P. Healey, M. Hebbert, and S. Hopkins (eds), The content of a planning theory course, Dept of Town Planning Working Paper No.25, Oxford Polytechnic, 1976, pp.160-8.

[5] For this reason it would seem that there is no distinction between planning theory as explanation of how planning objectives are achieved and planning theory as social philosophy. Planning's objectives include the exploration and manipulation of values. For an argument that such a distinction exists see N. Taylor, 'Planning theory and the philosophy of planning', Urban Studies, Vol.17, p.159-72.

[6] (The) 'assertion - that politics can be avoided, and that we are better off without them - is the most truly political of all political ideologies, and the most frightening, for it transfers power to those who assert it, while simultaneously concealing the fact that this has occurred'. E.J. Reade, 'Some educational consequences of the incorporation of the planning profession into the state bureaucracy', paper for the Annual Conference of the Sociologists in Polytechnicas Section of the British Sociological Association, Oxford, April 1977.

[7] Such results have often been disaggregated into 'outcomes' and 'outputs' : see A. Ramney 'The Study of Policy Content' in A. Ramney (ed.) Political Science and Public Policy, Markheim, Chicago, 1968, p.8-9.

[8] One example is the 'strategic warning' function of plans. For example, plans warn of urban decay, of urban riots, of loss of agricultural land, of energy shortages, etc. Such warnings may or may not be heeded. If we evaluate them as simple forecasts, they may not be correct because the warning was heeded. If the forecast turns out to be correct, we may be tempted to say that the warning was not heeded. But our ability to put forward evidence (on heeding of warnings) may be poor, compared with our expectation of a firm relationship (or none) between these aspects.

[9] The 'significant' decision may be a 'non-decision', i.e. the suppression of choice at some critical moment. See P. Bachrach and M.S. Barat, 'Decisions and non-decisions', American Political Science Review, Vol.57, 1963, pp.632-42; G. Debnam, 'Non-decisions and power', American Political Science Review, Vol.69, 1975, pp.889-907; R. Wolfinger, 'Non-decisions and the study of politics', American Political Science Review, Vol. 65, 1971, pp.1063-80. These decision points are qualitatively different from one another in many cases - some are 'policy' decisions, some are 'implementation' decisions. It is not always possible in retrospect, for example, to disentangle whether failure is due to policy or implementation : D. Dery, 'Evaluation and problem redefinition', Journal of Public Policy, Vol.2, No.1, pp.23-30.

[10] Also, our choice of an evaluation point betrays our attitudes towards policy-making. For example, a preference for an evaluation point before the beginning of the policy formulation

process suggests a preference for the rule of law, or for non-incremental policies, or for the attitude-changing aspects of indicative plans.

[11] H.B Milward and H.G. Rainey, 'Don't blame the bureaucracy', Journal of Public Policy, Vol.3, No.2, pp.149-68.

[12] N. Lichfield, P. Kettle and M. Whitbread, Evaluation in the Planning Process, Pergamon, Oxford, 1977.

[13] L. Allison, Environmental Planning : A Political and Philosophical Analysis, G. Allen and Unwin, London, 1975.

[14] P. Hall, R. Thomas, H. Gracey, and R. Drewett, The Containment of Urban England, PEP, London, 1973.

[15] J.B Ramsey and D.K. Shepard, 'Mortgages, interest rates, and changes in the housing stock', Bankers Magazine, 1973, pp.18-21.

[16] G.D. Greenberg, J.A. Miller, L.B. Mohr, B.C. Vladeck, 'Developing public policy : perspectives from empirical research', American Political Science Review, Vol.71, 1977, pp. 1532-43.

[17] G.D. Greenberg et al., op.cit., pp.1532-43.

[18] J.P. Cornford, 'The illusion of decision', British Journal of Political Science, Vol.4, 1974, pp.231-44 at p.235. See also R. Gregory, The Price of Amenity, MacMillan, London, 1971, p.XII.

[19] A.N. Oppenheim, Decision-making : a review, D 203, VII, Part 4, Open University, 1979.

[20] S.I. Benn and R.S. Peters, Social Principles and the Democratic State, G. Allen and Unwin, London, 1977 at p.131.

[21] See also D. Lock, 'Structure plans : a review of public participation methods and current ideas', paper to Town and Country Planning Association Conference, Shepperton, 25-27 April, 1965.

[22] For analysis of similar arguments in national politics see R.J. Williams and J.R. Greenaway, 'The referendum in British politics : a dissenting voice', Parliamentary Affairs, Vol.31, 1978, p.250-60.

[23] D. Parfit, 'The Further Future : The Identity Problem', pp.175-76 in D. MacLean and P.G. Brown (eds), Energy and the Future, Rowman and Littlefield, Totowa, New Jersey, 1983; D.A.J. Richards, 'Contractarian Theory, Intergenerational Justice, and Energy Policy', pp.139-42 in D.MacLean and P.G. Brown op.cit; D. MacLean, 'A Moral Requirement of Energy Policies', pp.181-84 in D. MacLean and P.G. Brown op.cit; D. Thompson, 'Philosophy and Policy', Philosophy and Public Policy, Vol.14, No.2, Spring 1985, pp.205-18 at pp.215-17.

[24] See also C. Pateman, Participation and Democratic Theory, Cambridge UP 1970. J.R. Lucas, Democracy and Participation, Penguin Books, 1976.

[25] J. Dearlove, The Politics of Policy in Local Government, Cambridge University Press, London, 1973.

[26] A. Aldous, Battle for the Environment, p.268, Fontana, Glasgow, 1972.

[27] A. Aldous, op.cit., p.267.

[28] For a fuller investigation of this subject see P. McAnslan, Land, Law, and Planning, Weidenfeld and Nicholson, 1975.

[29] Public inquiries have not been dealt with here. But see R. Kemp, 'Planning, legitimation, and the development of nuclear energy : a critical theoretic analysis of the Windscale inquiry', International Journal of Urban and Regional Research, Vol.4, 1980, p.350-71.

[30] R.C. Raack, 'When plans fail : small group behaviour and decision-making', Journal of Conflict Resolution, Vol.14, No.1, 1970, pp.3-19.

[31] J.K. Friend and W.N. Jessop, Local Government and Strategic Choice, Tavistock, London, 1969.

[32] However, for a call for this type of study of after-the-event effects see E.J. Reade, 'The Theory of Town and Country Planning', pp.43-58 in P. Healey, G. McDougall, M.J. Thomas, Planning Theory : Prospects for the 1980s, Pergamon, Oxford, 1981.

[33] A. Dunsire, Implementation in a Bureaucracy : the Execution Process, Vol.1, Martin Robertson, 1978, at p.231.

[34] A further definition of process which has not been developed is put forward in D. McRae Jr., 'Scientific communication, ethical argument, and public policy, American Political Science Review, 1971, Vol.65, p.38-50.

10 The rational-comprehensive strategy

The following is a brief definition of the rational-comprehensive strategy. It implies a fixed sequence of tasks by a central-decision maker.

(i) Define issues or goals completely.

(ii) Analyse the issues or goals disaggregating into clusters of sub-problems or objectives.

(iii) Generate a complete array of alternative solutions.

(iv) Evaluate the alternatives and choose the preferred one.

(v) Implement the preferred alternative, while continuously reviewing the situation.

It is generally agreed that this strategy is an ideal and is unworkable in practice. It is also generally agreed that despite this planners should try to get as near as is practically possible to achieving this ideal strategy. In doing so they have derived considerable benefits. Planning has been perceived to be rational by some significant and powerful groups in society. These groups are those who reject the role of government as merely helping to make market forces more perfect. They therefore can be described in party political terms as being on the left and centre of the political spectrum. Conservatives, especially those towards the extreme political right, have not regarded highly the need for rational planning, since their perception of its essential tasks has been so limited that rational coordination of those tasks has not seemed to be necessary. We will see later that in fact planning cannot be rational in the sense implied by using the rational-comprehensive strategy. But this does not affect the perception of planning by outsiders. It does not matter to politicians that the rational comprehensive strategy is an unworkable ideal. They need a set of concepts to justify their policies, and concepts, such as 'coordinated', 'premature', 'planning procedures', 'rationally planned' have powerful connotations of rationality.

There is another way in which politicians of all political persuasions have used the ideal of rationality and comprehensiveness. Increasingly, it has been argued, the ideal of rationality and comprehensiveness has gained force as a political symbol, able to sway mass audiences in a politician's favour. This has increased the public standing of planning as an intellectual discipline (while simultaneously various factors - the growth of environmental conflicts, planning blunders, and greater availability of environmental information - have made planners' activities more readily questioned).

These encouraging reactions by politicians to planners' claims of rationality and comprehensiveness have had the unfortunate effect of making the rational-comprehensive strategy become more deeply ingrained in planners' thinking. It has encouraged them to pursue the strategy in the unprofitable arenas of public controversy and participation, and of bureaucratic infighting. And it has rendered plans and planning much less open to questioning and criticism.

A study of Haringey District Planning Department brings out many of the problems encountered in practice by those imbued with the rational-comprehensive approach. The study found that in general planners thought their main task was to provide comprehensive policy advice and supporting evidence as part of an annual policy process. Their view was therefore to see all urban problems as their domain, in a comprehensive and strategic vision. But in practice their influence was restricted to providing technical and procedural advice to other departments of the local authority. This was partly because there was no developed authority-wide approach to policy - merely a series of uncoordinated, ad hoc decisions recommended by separate departments. In trying to work against this departmental bias the planners attempted to enlarge the role allotted them by those in other departments. They used their land use responsibility to gain entry to meetings with officers in other departments where they tried to move away from their statutory role in land use planning, instead concentrating on inadequate service delivery, poor spatial distributions, and gaps in decision making. This was resented by members of other departments: [1]. Moreover, planners suffered from a lack of legitimation. They were the only local government profession which did not have a definable client group. Planners tried to develop notions of clients but their confusion led to difficulties in defining issues. While they had strong orientations to the disadvantaged, such orientations were not supported in the Planning legislation. Their confusion over issues arose therefore from not knowing which groups should be given priority: [2].

The planners were thus seeking to apply the rational-comprehensive strategy. They sought to define issues widely, yet found their brief was so wide that they had little tangible evidence of how to establish priorities between issues. And their claims to discuss policies operated by other departments gave rise to resentment and conflict. This practical example of some of the difficulties of the rational-comprehensive strategy can now be formalised and extended.

THE DISADVANTAGES OF THE RATIONAL-COMPREHENSIVE STRATEGY

(i) The rational-comprehensive strategy is unable to deal with man's limited problem-solving capabilities. In public planning and policy making, even the form of problems is difficult to understand. Issues change as attention shifts between different values and different facts. Some form of method of simplification is inevitably required: [3].

(ii) The rational-comprehensive strategy is unable to deal with inadequacy of information or to costliness of analysis. Moreover it fails to specify how alternatives are discovered and what procedures govern the decision to stop searching for alternatives.

(iii) The side-effects of action may be unpredictable. They may also be invisible when they do occur. They may occur long afterwards, so that it is impossible to know whether or not our policy caused them. Similar problems attend any evaluation of alternatives which differ more than marginally from one another and these difficulties are increased the further into the future we are planning for.

(iv) The rational-comprehensive strategy overlooks the closeness of fact and value in decision making. For example, if we wished to understand the characteristics associated with general improvement areas where improvement grant take-up was highest, we might find that such areas were occupied by low-middle income groups - i.e. not the poorest groups. However, these 'facts' call for further value judgements - is our aim to conserve the housing stock or to house the poor?

(v) The rational-comprehensive strategy tries to separate consideration of means and consideration of ends. Once goals have been specified at the initial stage (without considering resources to implement those ends) they are not redesigned or altered in any way. In practice however, one usually simultaneously contemplates ends and the means to carry out those ends.

(vi) The rational-comprehensive strategy does not take account of the fact that decisions and policies are made in complex, vaguely-defined environments. In real situations one is continually discovering new things that are relevant, and continually altering one's values.

(vii) The rational-comprehensive strategy does not take account of how inter-locked problems are approached in practice. It demands that, besides the analytical and information difficulties mentioned earlier, another layer of difficulty - the inter-connection of problems - be faced head on. Yet in reality one usually only has an evolving pattern of reconciliations and temporary agreements about what these inter-connections mean.

The rational-comprehensive strategy, besides advocating a chronological sequence of tasks (see above) also brings with it an associated value system which comprises four themes:

(i) The decision-maker should take account of 'inter-related decision areas' - that is the inter-connectedness of different issues, problems, and decisions. This commends the policy maker to have a wide acquaintance of physical, social, and economic matters. It also commends him to be unconstrained by existing institutional arrangements, such as boundaries between departments in local government. We shall call this theme 'comprehensiveness' (an admittedly narrow definition).

(ii) That plans should be long term and that the long-term overall outline should influence what is decided to be done in the short-term.

(iii) That large-scale public projects with long lead-times are required to deal with the goals and problems identified in long-term plans.

(iv) That the implications of plans be considered from what happens in a large area towards what happens in smaller parts of that large area. Small area plans should be influenced by large area plans and not the other way around.

Having considered in outline the main features of the rational-comprehensive strategy to planning, its advantages and disadvantages, and some of its related values, we shall now consider an alternative strategy - that of disjointed incrementation.

NOTES

[1] J. Underwood, Town Planners in Search of a Role, Centre for Advanced Urban Studies, Bristol University, 1976.

[2] J. Underwood, op.cit.

[3] D. Braybrook and C. Lindblom, A Strategy of Decision : Policy Evaluation as a Social Process, Free Press, New York, 1963.

11 The disjointed-incrementalist strategy

The strategy of disjointed-incrementalism was suggested in the early sixties as both a description of how decisions are usually made and a prescription for how they should be made. The outlines of this strategy will be discussed first, and then the special case of planning, which has aims seemingly incompatible with those of the strategy, will be considered. Here is an outline of the strategy: [1]:

(i) CHOICE IS MADE ONLY AT THE MARGIN

Rather than making choices across a wide range of alternatives, the decision-maker considers alternatives which are very similar to each other.

(a) Organisations often compare alternatives, all of which are similar to the status quo: [2].

(b) This means that the policy maker does not need to understand future social states which are very different from those existing now.

(c) Also he does not need to understand abstract concepts. He need not ask himself if the free operation of the land market is precious, and if so, whether it is more precious than good design. He only need ask himself if, in a particular situation, some kind of development control intervention into the land market will improve an environment.

(d) Disjointed incrementalism advocates trade-offs. Thus politicians may talk about the need for improving an environment. The disjointed-incrementalist asks 'how much improvement?' and 'what is to be traded-off (efficiency in the land market? public expenditure?) to gain such an improvement?'

(e) Choice among policies is made by ranking in order of preference the increments by which social states differ.

(f) Conflicts take the form of questions about the analyst's or evaluator's trading ratios at the margin between pairs of values.

(g) The resolution of a conflict over two values is not expressed as a principle. It is best expressed by stating how much of one value is worth sacrificing to achieve an increment of another.

(ii) THERE ARE ONLY A SMALL NUMBER OF ALTERNATIVES

This restriction is not necessarily irrational. Many extreme alternatives are politically irrelevant anyway. Also alternatives which are very different from one another are more difficult to rationally evaluate and choose.

(iii) A SMALL NUMBER OF CONSEQUENCES IS CALCULATED

For example road building could have indirect effects on the cohesion of family groups, through its indirect effect on population mobility. But these consequences are difficult to estimate and are therefore not considered.

(a) However, the strategy does not mean that long run effects are necessarily neglected in favour of short run effects. Some long run effects are relatively easy to evaluate. For example the need for schooling for the population cohort born this year can be estimated with certainty for the next 16 years.

(b) What is excluded is often without discussion. Experienced professionals often share an agreed consensus about what consequences to include.

(iv) GOALS ARE ADJUSTED TO WHAT IS FEASIBLE

While the conventional view of policy making is that means are adjusted to ends, the strategy recommends precisely the reverse procedure. Ends are adjusted to suit means.

(a) The policy maker chooses as relevant only those objectives worth considering bearing in mind the means available.

(b) He automatically includes ideas of costs in his thoughts about alternatives.

(c) He thinks about means and ends simultaneously.

(v) INFORMATION IS VALUE-LADEN

Data are not objectively given facts, but carry their own value judgements with them and are subject to the disjointed-incrementalist's manipulation.

(a) Evaluation is not rigidly bound to treat problems in their original form. It transforms problems in the course of exploring data. For example the disjointed incrementalist engaged in a slum clearance process might begin with defining the problem as one of demolishing poor housing and replacing it with good housing. In the course of the process however, he might discover that many in private rented accommodation have to find even worse and more overcrowded accommodation elsewhere.

(b) This leads policy makers to express values as themes of concern rather than as rigid prescriptive rules, since fluid themes invite flexible responses.

(vi) PROBLEMS ARE NOT SOLVED. THEY ARE ONLY ALLEVIATED.

Organisations and policy makers do not solve a problem and then disband. They take it for granted that their problems will rarely be 'solved' but only alleviated.

(vii) SYMPTOMS RATHER THAN CAUSES ARE THE TRUE SUBJECT TO BE REMEDIED

Policy makers prefer to identify problems and dissatisfactions rather than aiming at vague, idealistic goals. Dissatisfactions and problems can be identified more easily than can abstract goals.

(viii) THERE ARE MANY DECISION MAKERS

Decisions about policies take place at a very large number of points in society: [3]. This makes disjointed incrementalism more realistic than the rational-comprehensive strategy because disjointed-incrementalism is a social process. The advantage of many different participants is that many different points of view are represented.

CRITICISMS OF DISJOINTED-INCREMENTALISM

Since the early sixties there have been many criticisms made of disjointed incrementalism: [4]. The most serious of these suggest that in some cases the strategy is not appropriate. Others allege that in some cases the end results of using the process are poor: yet the evidence on this is very inconclusive - some have indeed argued that evaluation of end results is impossible, since (among other reasons) there are many possible reasons why policies and plans 'fail' besides the process by which they were formulated.

(i) Many decisions are not incremental.

Decisions by governments to sponsor long term research and development into military and industrial hardware often commits then to non-incremental policies of support: [5]. After a certain length of time the compelling argument becomes one of continuation of the policy in order to justify the enormous sunk cost. When these developments come up against environmental arguments - such as in the case of the nuclear energy programme - some fear that the momentum has become too great for a rational weighing of evidence to take place.

Similarly many government projects fall into the policy areas where foreign relations and domestic economic policy meet, so that decisions about the advantages of development become pre-empted by higher level considerations. It may be that construction firms' ideas on new methods of town building have in the past been given greater weight because of the promise of later major export breakthroughs.

In such cases one can argue that decisions are essentially 'political'. Yet any such strict demarcation of responsibilities of planners and public administrators on the one hand, and politicians on the other, is dangerous. Planners can anaesthetise the implications of nuclear power by categorising and naming emotionally-disturbing aspects of it, or by using analyses in which such aspects can have no telling place. And new methods of town building have in the past flowed partly out of the visions and theories of planners and architects. Wherever there are such non-incremental pressures, then, professional integrity should dictate that planners should emphasise the dangers as well as the advantages, and that they should make a choice either for or against: [6].

The evidence suggests that there is now greater awareness of the dangers of non-incremental planning policies. Surely this awareness has increased due to the unpopularity of some high rise and urban motorway projects, and due to increased media interest and wider public knowledge of such problems. Also public arguments have shown how complex are the nature of man-environment relationships: the meaning of a 'safe' environment, the meaning of 'community', the needs of families with small children, and so on. Also planners are more experienced in the ways that environmental fashions can be manipulated by politicians for their own ends. For example, early concepts of high rise assumed plenty of space between tall blocks, so that overall densities were only moderate - and government advice in the late fifties reflected this idea. Yet by the sixties high rise had become a method of obtaining high densities (sometimes extremely high densities).

This increasing suspicion of non-incremental policies may also have come about due to the increasing area of concern of planning. We argue later that this trend favours a disjointed-incremental approach to planning. A commentator on British planning in 1960 suggested that the (then) relatively separate strands of physical planning and social planning led to a dangerously poor evaluation of the social effects of physical plans.

> '... town planning has tried to hedge as between physical planning and social planning, has developed something of an ideological basis for doing this, and has thus never fully

faced up to its responsibility for catalysing social goals and fully analysing what physical environmental improvements most realistically faciliated these social goals.': [7].

That this separation of physical and social planning has now partly ended can be shown by comparing two similar paragraphs in planning statutes - one in 1962 and one in 1968:

'Town and Country Planning Act 1962, Section 4.
(3) Subject to the provisions of any regulations made under this Act for regulating the form and content of development plans, any such plan shall include such maps and such descriptive matter as may be necessary to illustrate the proposals in question with such degree of particularity as may be appropriate to different parts of the area; and any such plan may in particular -
(a) define the sites of proposed roads, public and other buildings and works, airfields, parks, pleasure grounds, nature reserves and other open spaces, or allocate areas of land for use for agricultural, residential, industrial or other purposes of any class specified in the plan;
(b) designate, as land subject to compulsory acquisition by a Minister, local authority, or statutory undertakers, any land allocated by the plan for the purposes of any of their functions (including any land which that Minister or authority or those undertakers are or could be authorised to acquire compulsorily under any enactment other than this act);
(c) designate as land subject to compulsory acquisition by the appropriate local authority -
(i) any land comprised in an area defined by the plan as an area of comprehensive development (including any land therein which is allocated by the plan for any such purpose as is mentioned in paragraph (b) of this subsection) or any land contiguous or adjacent to any such area;
(ii) any other land which, in the opinion of the local planning authority, ought to be subject to compulsory acquisition for the purpose of securing its use in the manner proposed by the plan.'

'Town and Country Planning Act 1968, Section 1.
(3) Without prejudice to the generality of the foregoing provisions of this section, the matters to be examined and kept under review thereunder shall include the following, that is to say -
(a) the principal physical and economic characteristics of the area of the authority (including the principal purposes for which the land is used) and, so far as they may be expected to affect that area, of any neighbouring areas;
(b) the size, composition and distribution of the population of that area (whether resident or not);
(c) without prejudice to para (a) above, the communications, transport system, and traffic of that area, of any neighbouring areas;
(d) any considerations not mentioned in any of the foregoing paragraphs which may be expected to affect any matters so mentioned;
(e) such other matters as may be prescribed or as the Minister may in a particular case direct;
(f) any changes already projected in any of the matters

mentioned in any of the foregoing paragraphs and the effect which those changes are likely to have on the development of that area or the planning of such development.'

There is a very definite change of tone between the physical planning orientation of the 1962 Act and the orientation to physical, social, and economic planning in the 1968 Act. Local planning authorities are, however, still limited by their institutional context, and further discussion of the difficulties (yet necessity) of maintaining and developing this comprehensive approach in the face of departmentalism in local and central government will come later.

(ii) Many incremental decisions have non-incremental implications.

There are two ways in which this problem occurs.

(a) Many situations occur in planning where a seemingly unimportant and minor decision has major and irreversible consequences. We can exclude here development control decisions which create precedent, or which create blight, since these are largely foreseeable. A better example is the following. A new road will encourage more people to own cars, which will in turn generate greater demand for more cars. Should not, the argument against disjointed-incrementalism goes, planning attempt to take these effects (comprehensively) into account? The answer is most definitely, no, for the following reasons. Let such decisions be taken. Let such effects accumulate. And let knowledge of such effects become gradually known. If the tide of opinion becomes more 'anti-car' or more 'pro-public transport' then these considerations will be included in later disjointed-incremental decisions. Moreover it is impossible to speculate about such effects before they occur. Railways in the nineteenth century were accused of all sorts of things, from spreading diseases to increasing crime. Yet no one takes these accusations seriously today: [8]. And such arguments are usually invertible. A motorway into a poor region might make it easier for people to leave, but it might also attract new employment.

(b) Some planning decisions produce not only an incremental quantitative change in an area (some extra houses in a semi-rural area) but also produce a major qualitative change (eventually the area becomes 'urban'). Should not we attempt to be rational-comprehensive in defining these quality-thresholds? To do so as a rational-comprehensive exercise, it is argued here, would be a mammoth undertaking. Rather, the important thing is to be sensitive about when one gets near such quality thresholds. For example, does the proposed superstore in a Georgian street bring in discordant horizontal elements in a street comprised of a zig-zag of verticals of varying heights? Will the fact that we grant permission for controlled dumping of low-level nuclear waste create a thin-end-of-the-wedge argument in favour of later dumping of more radioactive waste? Such judgements require enormous skill and professional experience.

But there are philosophical questions to be answered here as well. Sometimes elements - such as a line of pylons - which were thought to be ruinous of a landscape - are found to be not noticed by people. Such intrusions are ignored or screened out. Do we therefore become more tolerant of these intrusions? The same question arises when we consider environmental risks - how much ought we to learn to tolerate and accept them? Should planners granting permission to an environmentally hazardous factory accept responsibility for a lower local tolerance of additional environmental hazards? These questions are not definitively answerable, nor do the planning procedures take them into account. Decisions, nearly always made incrementally, in an isolated way, overlook them.

How are quality-thresholds used in practice? They are certainly important elements in planning decisions. A planning inspector at an appeal into refusal to allow an advertisement hoarding in an area will undoubtedly visit the site to decide for himself whether the area is urban or rural. If it is urban are there any special reasons (picturesque townscape, residential use, distraction of motorists) why it should be refused? Such categorisations of areas into quality-classes are important value-judgements that planners learn to make: [9].

(iii) The disjointed-incrementalist strategy ignores our expectation (or ideal) of accountable government.

However this is based on an ideal rather than reality. Take the example of the recent discovery of major structural problems in concrete buildings. Should there have been more 'centralisation'? The flimsy evidence available suggests that the government regulatory agency 'responsible' for chemical and other tests on concrete was too much under the control of successive ministers who had a vested interest in a rapid programme of building works which used concrete.

Is there a case for retrospective appraisals of individuals by the planning profession? The answer must be negative, for the following reasons. Firstly plans and planning decisions are nearly always the fruits of team work and committees. Secondly no other profession carries out similar appraisals, since peer-group appraisal is a much more acceptable method which moreover keeps skeletons well and truly hidden away. It would, however, be a constructive step to take, and a self-protective one, for the planning profession to set up working groups to monitor major issues about which there was major concern, or which might turn into major issues later. Nuclear power suggests itself as a topical example.

(iv) Disjointed-incrementalism leads to systematic distortions in the production of public goods.

Since a central feature of disjointed-incrementalism is that there are many power-centres, or groups which influence decisions, such as planners, councillors, pressure groups, developers, some strong groups will have a much greater influence than others: [10]. For example, on the issue of high rise and industrialised housing, the construction industry may have had too powerful a voice, so that too much was produced, compared with more conventional methods which provided lower profits. Another example is the strong and effective government lobby for road-building, which may have in the past provided roads where public money would have been better spent on public transport.

(v) Disjointed-incrementalism under-values the effect of externalities.

Usually when decisions are taken the consequences of alternatives are appraised in the decision-maker's terms. Advantages and disadvantages to the decision-maker are paramount and advantages and disadvantages to other groups or individuals (externalities) are overlooked: [11]. The plurality of interests represented in the disjointed-incrementalist strategy ensures that most, at least, of these externalities are brought up for consideration. However the influence of powerful groups, such as government or industry, may in some cases outweigh such considerations.

Thus, for example, some have argued that the drive in the sixties and early seventies to modernise city centres, reduce city centre traffic congestion, and attract City capital to such projects were factors which outweighed the interests of local residents and small businesses. Many of the 'external costs' were therefore borne by less powerful groups.

In the case of nuclear power the external costs are largely borne by future generations, who are represented in arguments, but who understandably do not have a powerful voice in a disjointed-incrementalist process.

(vi) Disjointed-incrementalism under-represents minority interests.

While the majority have a rising standard of living, it is easy for decisions made within the disjointed-incrementalist strategy to be preoccupied by the problems generated by affluence. Yet for some groups and increasingly for some geographical areas of the country the problems will be defined very differently. Unfortunately minority interests are often those which are ineffective in putting their case, and so there is a double handicap.

(vii) Disjointed-incremenalism leads to immobility of resources.

Because only small deviations from the status quo are envisaged, change is very slow: [13]. Moreover there is a time lag between when a group has sufficient numbers to have an effect on policy, and its having significant influence. Every device is used by status quo interests to ensure that the time lag will be as long as possible: [14].

We have now considered two simplified models of how the planning process should work. The criticisms of the rational-comprehensive strategy are mainly about its impossibility, and raise serious questions about the disfunctional effects of attempting and failing to achieve the strategy. Inevitably one would have to make all sorts of compromises - limiting the number of alternatives for example, and if there were one central decision maker this would lead to some form of personal and arbitrary bias. The disjointed-incrementalist strategy on the other hand, is criticised for being too conservative and accepting of existing biases and sources of irrationality. But at least it has the advantage that the operational disadvantages are clearly knowable. And it emphasises that since decisions are tentative, mistakes can later be corrected: [15].

But these are only a priori, theoretical evaluations of the two strategies. They are both simplified models. To what extent does the real world and the planning environment allow us to have confidence in them as guides to planning decisions? We attempt to answer this question in the next chapter, by attempting to see the extent to which organisations, politicians and culture influence the appropriateness and effectiveness of each strategy.

NOTES

[1] For a fuller analysis of the strategy see D. Braybrooke and C. Lindblom, A Strategy of Decision : Policy Evaluation as a Social Process, Free Press, New York, 1963.

[2] In a detailed study of Kensington and Chelsea Borough, this behaviour was called 'policy maintenance' : see J. Dearlove, The Politics of Policy in Local Government, Cambridge University Press, London, 1973.

[3] This aspect of political processes has been labelled 'pluralism'. For arguments for and against see E.C. Banfield, Political Influence, Glencoe, 1961, pp.330-40; B. Barry, Political Argument, Routledge and Kegan Paul, 1965, p.272-4; D. Hardy, 'Constraints to power sharing', Built Environment, May 1974, pp.260-62; N. Beckman, 'The planner as a bureaucrat', American Institute of Planners Journal, 1979, pp.323-27.

[4] A. Schick, 'Systems politics and systems budgetting', Public Administration Review, Vol.29, March-April 1969, pp.137-151.

[5] R.P. Schulman, 'Non-incremental policy making - some notes towards an alternative paradigm', American Political Science Review, 1975, Vol.69, pp.1354-70.

[6] Arguments in favour of non-incremental policies often tend to stress the fact that a completely new situation is envisaged. This in fact is one of the difficulties of evaluating such arguments : whereas they may not result in the particular policy advocated, (and therefore 'fail') they do, claim their proponents, cause a sea change of opinion. Strategic warnings (housing crisis, agricultural land shortage, energy shortages, ecological doom) are of this kind, where evaluation is almost impossible, and where, since people do not wish to believe the worst, the odds are weighed heavily against credibility. For this reason they often function less merely to warn others than to further particular interests - for example, getting one's own organisation's budget increased. The primary weakness of strategic warnings is not that they can be invalidated - their horizon is usually vague - but that they can be charged with the unpopular qualities of pessimism, lack of confidence in the future, alarmism, and that such qualities can be related, through the simplification and distortion processes of political argument, to a fear of crises, poor leadership, and inability to govern.

[7] D.L. Foley, 'British town planning - one ideology or three?', British Journal of Sociology, Vol.1, 1960, pp.211-31 at p.228.

[8] L. Allison, Environmental Planning : a Political and Philosophical Analysis, G. Allen and Unwin, 1975, p.125.

[9] A similar problem is when increasing access to a remote area gradually reduces or changes its qualities. Thus the value of an area can be changed when everybody has access to it, (though

this deterioration may occur incrementally) : see F. Hirsch, Social Limits to Growth, Routledge and Kegan Paul, London, 1977.

[10] S. Chan, 'The intelligence of stupidity : understanding failures in strategic warning', American Political Science Review, Vol. 73, 1979, pp.177-79: Chan's point is that 'competing power centres' do not in fact have competing viewpoints - their view is homogeneous, partly because there is only one consumer - government - of their ideas, and partly because the organisational goals of autonomy and rivalry conflict.

[11] This immobility of resources has been called the 'colonisation of the future', whereby 'today's powerful interests organised in established institutions, prolong the prevailing situation into the future' : A. Sandberg, The Limits to Democratic Planning, Liberforlag, Stockholm, 1977.

[12] For a precursor to D. Braybrooke and C. Lindblom which generalises the question of choice of strategy up to the level of political philosophy see K.R. Popper, The Poverty of Historicism, Routledge, 1976, pp.83-104. See also D.A. Schon, Beyond the Stable State, Penguin, 1971, Ch.7.

[13] The tendency is accentuated because multiple viewpoints are not expressed - instead bargains are struck to conceal differences and these viewpoints also take account of government's prior commitments : S. Chan op.cit. p.178.

[14] The criticism is least true for planning, where consideration of externalities is important : E.J. Read, 'The Theory of Town and Country Planning', pp.43-58, in P. Healey, G. McDougall, M.J. Thomas, Planning Theory : Prospects for the 1980s, Pergamon, London, 1982; R.E. Klosterman, 'Arguments for and against planning', Town Planning Review, Vol.56, No.1, 1985, pp.5-20. The criticism reinforces the need to define the role of planning as one of comprehensiveness, albeit in a disjointed-incrementalist political and organisational environment.

[15] This is the conventional view. But, for detailed evidence that the rational comprehensive approach may have similar effects see R. Darke, 'The Dialectics of Policy Making : Form and Content', pp.194-210 in P. Healey, G. McDougall, M.J. Thomas, Planning Theory : Prospects for the 1980s, Pergamon, London, 1982, p.203.

12 Institutional and cultural determinants of choice of planning strategy

In order to investigate the extent to which the rational-comprehensive strategy and disjointed-incrementalist strategy influence decision-making it is necessary to look at the institutions and culture of the decision-maker. In order to do this we shall look at three different perspectives on the problem. The first of these considers how government organisations work, and how they interact with politicians. The second of these considers pressures within those organisations themselves that bring about a need for a rational-comprehensive strategy to decisions. And lastly we shall look at the wider political culture and its influence upon the choice of strategy.

HOW GOVERNMENT ORGANISATIONS WORK IN PRACTICE

This perspective has developed out of the study of organisations in general, and the attempt to find explanations for the way they behave. Here are some generalisations.

(i) Organisations are badly suited to changing conditions.

Organisations use 'standard operating procedures', which are standardised methods for dealing with routine situations. These standard operating procedures and the conformity they induce: [1] make it much simpler for the organisations to operate, since for any problem a standard operating procedure can be used. However, many problems are new and non-routine, so that the prevalent use of standard operating procedures means that many organisational responses are badly adapted to the current problem with which they try to deal.

Thus standard operating procedures break down in non-standard situations.

Policies are usually a cluster of standard operating procedures. They are rarely tailored to the specific problem. Rather, a policy is usually the most appropriate collection of standard operating procedures in the organisation's repertoire. Since repertoires are developed by organisations with limited objectives, the repertoires of standard operating procedures are usually themselves limited in scope.

(ii) Organisations usually consider only a limited number of alternatives.

The cost of generating further alternatives is too high. Also the organisation is interested in controlling rather than presenting alternatives to politicians: [2]. One method which organisations use to control the range and choice of alternatives is to present a preferred alternative framed by two extremes which are unlikely to be chosen.

Organisations are good at presenting alternatives which reflect their existing goals. So a planning department which has developed an expertise in the acquisition and compensation procedures and design problems of slum clearance programmes will tend to have a bias towards presenting this type of solution rather than presenting a rehabilitation alternative to politicians.

For example, between 1954 and 1964 Liverpool obstinately refused to consider housing improvement, and continued its massive slum clearance and new house building policy. During that period 24,000 new houses were built, but 33,000 extra houses slipped into the 'substandard' category. With 10 per cent of the unfit houses in the country, the city took up less than a quarter of one per cent of the country's improvement grants: [3].

Organisations are bad at presenting alternatives which require coordination with other organisations. For example, Structure Plans sometimes avoid housing policies involving public housing provision because this involves the uncertainties of coordinating the housing policies of several different Districts.

(iii) Organisations are not very flexible and plan only for the short term: [4].

For example, organisational budgets are changed only gradually, both with respect to the organisation as a whole, and to divisions within it. Organisations could divide the budget in new ways according to changing priorities. But usually they avoid doing this. So policies which require drastic budgetary changes are unlikely to be implemented. Therefore organisations tend to have stable policies and priorities. Consequently standard operating procedures are updated only infrequently.

A policy, once embarked upon, is not dropped when costs outweigh benefits, or when it becomes inappropriate. Organisational momentum takes it beyond this point. For example, despite the fact that central government housing policy switched in 1969 from slum clearance and new house-building to housing rehabilitation, several local authorities were still pursuing vigorous slum-clearance policies until the early 1970s.

(iv) Long-range planning tends to become institutionalised and then overlooked.

Most organisations have long range planning units. But available standard procedures, and the pressures of day to day decision-making, usually are treated as more relevant data than long term predictions or scenarios. In government, new long-term units are set up when crises occur, but their influence declines after the crisis has passed and new crises in different policy areas arise.

(v) Organisations frame their objectives in terms of minimum standards.

When a conflict between two objectives arises, organisations often neglect one and select the other rather than trading-off one against the other: [5].

Also the complexity of relationships between different organisations, and the conflicts which exist between them, mean that long term and comprehensive vision is often lost. An example of this is provided by the Community Land Scheme, which operated in the late seventies. It aimed at encouraging local authorities to take a long term and comprehensive approach to land development through a gradual process of increasing public land ownership. Local authorities were put in the position of having to deal with private landowners and developers in a totally new way. Yet most found this difficult. The interaction between the public and private sectors was supposed to have been clarified by local authorities issuing Land Policy Statements. Yet most were confused about how such statements were to be written, due partly to ignorance of the private sector's intentions, and partly to uncertainty about future government funding. Also they had conflicting objectives. Development of greenfield sites was administratively easier and more profitable for the local authority, yet many recognised that urban sites with poor access, layout or inappropriate use offered the greatest planning benefit.

Another example is that there is strong evidence to suggest that housing improvement grants are not reaching those (generally the poorest) in the worst housing. There are two objectives being pursued by local authorities in housing improvement. One is to improve the housing of the poor (i.e. to encourage those who would not otherwise improve to do so) and the other is to maximise the local housing stock in good condition. But these objectives conflict, since if local authorities concentrated on the poorest localities, the grant-take-up would probably be low. So local authorities usually choose to maximise the local stock of good housing.

(vi) Organisations develop a sense of 'territory', or area of perceived responsibility, which they jealously guard and which they strive to enlarge.

In most cases it is this sense of 'territory' which planners' claims to comprehensiveness offends. It was also this sense of territory which central government encouragement of corporate planning in local government attempted to break down. Most departments saw it as a threat, so that corporate planning (policy-making across departmental boundaries) did not generally succeed. In other local authorities both Treasurers and Planning Departments attempted to assume the mantle - striving to enlarge their area of responsibility.

In central government there are inter-departmental committees which try to get departments to talk to each other on issues of mutual interest without encroaching on departmental 'territory': [6]. Also the objective of enlarging 'territory' and departmental budget is much more prominent, restrained in most cases by Treasury policies.

(vii) New organisations especially created by politicians in order to increase the number of options open to them or to promote favoured policies face great problems of effectiveness and are resisted by existing organisations.

If faced with organisations which are deliberately limiting the number of options presented, politicians often find it tempting to create new organisations tailored to their needs. However, these organisations have only a small chance of success.

An example is provided by the Land Commission, set up in 1967. The then Labour government considered that local authorities, particularly the shire counties, were restricting the supply of housing land. Local authorities, through the granting or refusing of planning permission for housing land, had the power to limit housing development within their borders. Often the city authorities were trying to lower residential densities by redevelopment and slum clearance, and by moving people to 'overspill' areas in neighbouring rural authorities. Many rural authorities, however, wanted to conserve their rural environment, or feared that overspill would be unpopular or lead to a great increase in expensive services, or to a shift in political power at local elections. The Labour government wanted to help maintain the impetus of the slum clearance programme. The Land Commission was set up in order to buy up land where it was needed and make it available for housing. It had compulsory purchase powers, but it could proceed much faster if it had the agreement of the local authority concerned. Few local authorities chose to cooperate, so that by 1970, three years after its inception, the incoming Conservative government was able to justify its abolition on the grounds of ineffectiveness.

(viii) Organisations have imperfect theories of how policy is made and implemented.

It is possible, from the behaviour of individuals within an organisation, to see that their operating methods and concepts of what they are trying to achieve fit into a shared theory. Such a theory is usually imperfect in its understanding of policy formulation and implementation. It usually assumes the following:

(a) policy is formulated in a policy-centre, and implemented at a lower level in the command structure of the organisation;

(b) little attention is given to the choice of issues while much attention is given to how to tackle (given) issues: the organisation sees its role as answering questions which are supplied from elsewhere;

(c) issues are treated as stable over time;

(d) testing of policy finishes when a new policy has been agreed;

(e) the responsibility for policy change is given only to the policy-centre.

This theory derives from what can be called the 'rationalist tradition' of policy making and is imperfect since it devalues the contribution that those implementing the policy can make to making new policies, and it ignores the creative way that implementers reinterpret policy: [7]. Within planning authorities, for example, the first people to know when a policy is inappropriate are often those in development control. Instead of this knowledge being used to create new policies however, usually development control officers try to make up for such deficiencies in their bargaining with applicants. Thus the theory is imperfect in that it fails to account for the real nature of policy implementation.

Also the theory overlooks the true way in which issues arise. While it says that issues are given from outside the organisation, in reality the members of the organisation are continually applying value judgements which include ideas about problems and priorities. Those in policy making positions usually phrase these decisions as if they were rational and objective answers to pre-existing questions addressed from outside. Those in implementation positions continually have to make choices which reveal that they too have priorities which change with each new situation. Indeed the distinction between policy makers and implementers is not a real one, since all within the organisation are, in their individual tasks, reinterpreting past policies. This reinterpretation is only partially successful since it is done within the framework of a repertoire of standard operating procedures: [8].

The theory becomes increasingly unrealistic when it is applied to more than one organisation. For example, in local government there is one, higher-level, organisation (for example, the County planning authority) and a lower-level authority (the District planning authority). The theory states that the County formulates policy (the Structure Plan) and the District implements policy through its own, lower level policies which must conform in some way with the Structure Plan. The theory overlooks the fact that often Districts' plans, though 'in conformity with' the Structure Plan, are often used for purposes which undermine it, that Districts develop their own distinctive view of strategic issues, and that they often take advantage of the lack of local knowledge by the County.

For example, consider the relationship of the Greater London Council with the London boroughs:

> 'The fervour with which the suburbs would resist attempts to implement a continuous and concerted redistributive housing strategy may be gauged from the obstacles which County Hall interventionists encountered in trying to effect their modest

policies. Even the nominations policy, which entailed the very minimum trespass upon local territory and maintained the symbolism of borough autonomy, was notoriously difficult to operate. That the GLC lacks the power that it needs to carry out its purposes is to some critics self-evident, for it seems to them to be axiomatic that if the GLC had more power it would be more effective. This is a misunderstanding, While it is true that the GLC lacks statutory powers that would enable it to enforce policies rather than negotiate them, the notion of County Hall violating the normal diplomatic procedures and acting unilaterally on land-use issues is far-fetched. It overlooks the necessity for the GLC actually to bargain, negotiate and manipulate the diplomatic network if only in order to attain many of its secondary objectives.
Greater formal powers perhaps along the lines of the 1962 memorandum, might have been granted to the GLC and still could be. Yet formal power is not the crux of the issue of metropolitan effectiveness. The resource deficiencies of the GLC are not statutory but arise from a lack of information on local housing and land-use situations, combined with a lack of appreciation of local political conditions.': [9].

PRESSURE TOWARDS ADOPTION OF THE RATIONAL-COMPREHENSIVE VALUE SYSTEM

The above discussion of the operation of central and local government organisations suggests that those organisations resist pressures put upon them to change. Consequently there exist thresholds of organisational resistance which politicians wishing to promote change must overcome. Also there exist certain discontinuities in social and individual behaviour which bring about large changes in attitudes and fashions, which demand large changes in policies. Also when there is a major change in government policy (usually at an election) there is a preparedness by politicians to risk a major policy change. Usually, however, politicians prefer to hedge their bets, and it is often local government officers and civil servants who attempt to engineer the political commitment they think is necessary to a large-scale project. All these are examples of how concepts of government action can be made grander, less tentative, and more large-scale and ambitious: [10]. They may not involve use of or reference to the rational-comprehensive strategy as such, but their sheer size (or degree of policy change) means that firstly they are likely to be large-scale, and secondly that the discipline and caution of disjointed-incrementalism have been avoided. We shall now consider each of these pressures to adoption of the rational-comprehensive value system in turn.

(i) The existence of known organisational apathy.

When existing organisations are known to be apathetic to a government policy, it is tempting to create a new organisation to carry out the policy itself. Examples include the ill-fated Land Commission and the ineffective Civil Service Department responsible for implementing Civil Service reform in the sixties.

(ii) The existence of a vast monetary requirement before a plan will work.

Possible examples include large scale urban redevelopment and urban mass transit systems.

(iii) The existence of a crisis: [11].

Examples include the creation of Ministers without portfolio for the north-east region (Lord Hailsham), for water supply (Mr Howell), for Merseyside (Mr Heseltine). However it is doubtful that large scale, long term, comprehensive planning lasted much beyond the crises (regional unemployment, a dry summer, urban riots) concerned. Indeed all three appointments may have been merely temporary, cosmetic actions.

A more certain example is the sterling crisis and government cutbacks of 1966 which generated further worries about government expenditure and which together with the Housing Condition Survey of 1967 led to a fundamental reappraisal of national housing policy.

Another possible contender with planning implications is the coal dispute of 1972 and the miners' strike of 1974 which brought the Conservative government down and which probably provided extra reason for the 1979 Conservative government's commitment to a rapid scaling up of the nuclear power programme, in order to reduce the political power of the miners.

(iv) The existence of environmental disturbances.

When incremental intervention will begin predictable reactions of an adverse nature in the wider environment, a more rational-comprehensive approach is sometimes argued to be justified. For example, incremental land-buying by the state tends to force up the price of other land which eventually is also needed: [12]. New Town Corporations' land acquisition strategies fall into this category. Also comprehensive redevelopment and town expansion schemes are similar examples.

(v) The engineering of large-scale political commitment by officials.

The strategies whereby officials persuade politicians to commit themselves have been termed 'commitment generating strategies': [13]. They are as follows:

(a) Espousal when an official gains a politician's personal attachment to an action. An example might be where a planner explains his proposals to the planning committee chairman prior to the committee (i.e. prior to criticisms of the proposal) and gains his personal support. For the chairman to go back on this support in committee would involve a loss of face in front of the planner.

(b) Activation of Obligation. Many opportunities exist for officials to remind politicians that their commitment is a lasting one because an obligation exists. Thus politicians can be manoeuvred into positions where statutory requirements, or the moral obligation to act fairly, commit them to policies which the official favours.

(c) Expiry of Opportunity. Usually this is in the form of the passing of a deadline which represents the passing of low cost opportunities to gain information or knowledge of interests. For example, in the mid-sixties a scheme for the pedestrianisation of a shopping street in Coventry was put forward. Many shopkeepers in the street objected saying they feared loss of customers. In the end the Town Clerk set a deadline - the 1 October 1969 as the date for pedestrianisation. Everybody - the bus company, servicemen, shopkeepers, had to abide by this date and prepare themselves for it. The deadline helped to 'close' the debate.

(d) Promises. Officials can remind politicians of promises they have made, in order to arrive at schemes they prefer. Also they can make half-promises themselves. This practice is widespread in development control. The planner reaches an unspoken agreement with the applicant that planning permission will be forthcoming if the applicant makes certain changes to his application. The committee is often put in the position of not wishing to break this promise.

(e) The public or semi-public declaration. Politicians not only make promises they can be held to, but they put forward opinions, and arguments. These, say, in minutes of meetings, can become 'shackles' binding a politician to some past argument. White Papers similarly commit politicians. Another example is Anthony Jay's preference (when minister) for Stansted as the third London airport, (stated publicly), and Edward Heath's preference for Maplin: [14].

(f) The Investment of Effort. Officials can gently manoeuvre political commitment down a particular path, until the argument against turning back is one of not wasting effort (time, money, political reputation) already expended. The larger the scale of the project, the more room there is for this type of argument.

(g) Multiple Clearance. The trick is to pass the proposal through a series of unimportant, uncritical committees, and friendly individuals, until sufficient support has been conjured up that the proposal sails through the formal decision procedure since enough friends and supporters have already been made.

(h) The Limited Study. One method of getting politicians to commit themselves completely to a scheme is to carry out a 'limited study' where the terms of reference are heavily circumscribed in favour of the plan one wants adopted. Politicians are often prepared to accept a scheme which is 'good enough'. Once the losers from the scheme attack it, it is too late, since the politicians do not want to lose face by backing down. One of the most well-known examples was the Roskill Commission Inquiry on the Third London Airport. It was asked to consider only sites within the South East Region, and to assume that an airport was needed.

(i) Direct Action. It is possible to bring about action in the environment so as to tilt the decision in one's favour. The obvious planning example of this is the engineering of planning blight. For example, Bedford District Council wished to develop an outer Western Bypass in the mid seventies, against the wishes of the strategic highways authority, Bedfordshire County Council. The bypass was proposed by the District to pass through a working class owner-occupier area. The District, having produced blight by announcing its roadline, bought up the properties, then demolished them. The County's main practical argument against the roadline had been the fact that a certain number of houses were affected. By 'direct action' the District skilfully sidestepped this argument: [15].

(j) The Hidden Link. This occurs where the commitment to one action more or less leads to commitment to another action. The most obvious planning example is the statutory requirement (now relaxed in certain circumstances, for example, inner city areas) that structure plans should be approved before local plans are approved, and that local plans should 'conform to' the structure plan. The layman finds he relates most to the more concrete local plan. He objects to the local plan. He finds that the substance of his objection was dealt with at the already completed structure plan examination in public. His objection is therefore over-ruled.

These 'commitment generating strategies' enable officials to push through policies without the discipline of the disjointed-incrementalist process. They also favour the single-decision maker, and thus can be included within pressures which increase the adoption of the rational-comprehensive value system: [16].

CULTURAL FACTORS WHICH INFLUENCE CHOICE OF STRATEGY: [17].

The belief in either strategy involves belief in a value system. Belief in the rational-comprehensive strategy is a belief in order, rationality, consensus, comprehensiveness, and central control over events. Belief in disjointed-incrementalism is a belief that events are usually unpredictable and sometimes irrational, that conflict exists, that one should take a partisan view, and that there are many power centres. We would suggest that in pursuing their aims planners often take a partisan view (for example, their attempts to assume the mantle of corporate planning in the seventies), while in deciding on planning matters they usually are comprehensive (for example, in seeing two issues as connected despite the fact that they are the 'territory' of two different departments). It is this kind of limited comprehensiveness, combined with disjointed-incrementalism, that is the dominant mode of planning today. The rational-comprehensive strategy, however, retains a deeply-ingrained place as an ideal and often influences planners' behaviour. Besides these professional beliefs, how do more widely-held values influence the choice of strategy? There are several dimensions along which choice of strategy is influenced.

(i) The public image of society.

Is society a collection of individuals, largely uncoordinated or in conflict, who hold no common beliefs and duties strongly enough to form a recognisable group? If we think this, we can describe our image of society as atomistic. Or is the dominant quality of society one of structure - shared beliefs, a common past, a common future, duties and rights. If we think this, we can describe our image of society as structuralist. Someone holding an atomistic image of society will tend to favour disjointed-incrementalism, while someone holding a structuralist image of society will tend toward favouring the rational-comprehensive strategy.

It would seem that these images are relevant to the kinds of manipulation of public opinion carried out by politicians. At particular times (a period of national crisis, or the beginning of a new era) politicians appeal to the commonly-held values (patriotism, or responsibility) using stereotypes: [18] of national character or metaphors of family-unity. At other times (for example, in mid-term when government politicians wish to stress the lack of importance of government so as to limit their responsibility for broken promises) they will appeal to atomistic images (individual initiative counts more than government actions etc.).

Such elasticity of images enables politicians sometimes to justify greater centralisation of power (in crises, in periods of reconstruction), while at other times to avoid personal or governmental responsibility for events. It also enables them sometimes to justify long term thinking (for example, the argument that drastic means are required to redress the nation's long term industrial decline). Generally, however, political survival usually dictates that priorities shift as new problems or crises arise, that promises are made as vague as possible, and that responsibility for failure is avoided while credit for achievement is claimed wherever this is credible: [19].

(ii) The size of the area of concern.

The wider the area of concern of a plan, the more will it come to be processed by means of a disjointed-incrementalist strategy. The smaller the area of concern of a plan, the more narrow and technical that it becomes, the more will it be processed by means of a rational-comprehensive strategy. When the area of concern is wide, the consequences and alternatives are more uncertain, the means of assessment are unpredictable, and the interests involved are more disparate and uncontrollable. When the area of concern is small, it becomes easier to stipulate (though complete success is usually still unattainable) that objectives and alternatives be considered in a complete manner, and that objectives be formulated prior to considering alternatives.

(iii) Expanding or contracting government resources.

When plans are accompanied by expanding budgets, it is easier to predict the likelihood of future implementation, and it is easier to pay off unsatisfied or losing interests. In such situations plans are more likely to be processed by means of a rational-comprehensive strategy: [20]. Where budgets are contracting, each government or local government department looks to its own interests, neglecting more comprehensive concerns, and reduces its planning horizon to thinking in the short term. Consider the following description of reactions by some departments in central government to contracting resources:

> The planning systems developed in the mid-1970s depended crucially on some degree of certainty about medium term resource constraints - on the volume figures in the public expenditure white paper. As these become meaningless with the imposition of unrealistic cash limits so the whole purpose of the exercise is undermined. By the beginning of 1980 there

were signs that this was in fact happening. The March 1980 public expenditure figures were less detailed than previously and focussed on the year ahead. The personal social service planning statements had been discontinued. The health service planning system was to be "simplified" and was not in practice working at the local level in many instances. The last HIPs (Housing Investment Programmes) returns by (local) authorities had been so severely cut as to produce a near standstill in public housing in 1980. A further effect of tight financial constraints may well be to reduce inter-agency cooperation. Where resources are contracting a department's natural desire is to unload its difficult and expensive cases onto another agency and to avoid taking on any extra commitments.': [21].

(iv) The relative degree of autonomy of the planning authority from government politicians.

Where autonomy is great, as in the New Town Corporations, there is a tendency for plans to be processed by means of the rational-comprehensive strategy. In the case of the early development of the new towns in the fifties and sixties, the aims and objectives were already stated in broad terms, and the resource constraints were known. Very little meddling by central government took place, apart from raising population targets (and hence available resources). And the Corporations were insulated from local political interests since they were non-elected bodies. The regional gas, water and electricity boards enjoy a similar planning environment, except for government intervention to fix prices and rates. Often their decisions have major planning implications, and Local and Structure plans have to adapt themselves to decisions made by the Boards.

(v) The low political salience of an issue.

It has been suggested that planners have most influence when the political salience of an issue is low: [22] so that the issue is treated with the rational-comprehensive methods of planners rather than being called into the political limelight and being subjected to the disjointed-incremental process. Low political salience results from lack of political conflict on an issue by powerful interests.

(vi) The degree of non-local development interests: [23].

The more that development interests are non-local, the more that reasoned arguments and coordinated policy (the rational-comprehensive strategy) have to be prepared to guide or confront them. Where, however, development interests are local (for example, big local landowners who take a lead in pressing for or denying development) then local political pressures on the planning process will mean that disjointed-incrementalism will tend to be used.

Consideration of these six dimensions suggests that the planning environment is subject to much variation over time: [24]. Periods of crisis, national reconstruction, and expansion give rise to new, ambitious planning legislation backed by expanding budgets. These developments are phrased and interpreted in rational-comprehensive terms. But when such periods have passed (1950, 1966, the late seventies) the planning environment changes and becomes more disjointed-incremental. Often this leads to definitions of the planning task which are more exacting and ambitious than the developing planning environment allows.

HOW ARE PLANS FORMULATED IN THE CURRENT PLANNING SYSTEM?

Because of administrative, political, and resource constraints, even Structure Plans are formulated and implemented in a disjointed-incrementalist way. Consider the case study of the 1976 Bedfordshire Structure Plan: [25].

The 'plan is substantially predetermined by existing constraints' (marginal-dependent choice) 'or because so much is beyond the control of the planning authority' (ends are adjusted to suit means) 'or because decision makers have excluded those issues which do not fall within their ideological predilections' (a restricted range of policy alternatives are considered). 'Party political debate over structure plans tends to centre upon relatively small-scale localised issues or upon those which are perennially in dispute between the parties' (a restricted number of consequences is considered for any given policy). 'Consensus over policy-making is achieved through recognition that local planners have little control over the plan's implementation, acceptance of the continuous revision of the plan in the light of changing circumstances', (data treated creatively, analysis and evaluation done serially) 'and expression of policies in terms likely to prove acceptable to the majority of the population' (analysis and evaluation are socially fragmented).

Moreover, Local Plans are formulated against the continual background of development pressures:

> 'However, plan preparation does not take place in a development vacuum. There are continuing market pressures for land release: and housebuilders will not hold back development proposals in the hope of a particular plan being completed. The result is a conflict between developers swayed by a variety of non-planning considerations and local planning authorities seeking to maximise the ability of local plans to help in making the right decisions.
> 'But planning theory is tempered by practical realities. In the area covered by a local plan a considerable number of dwelling may already be "committed" (i.e. under construction or with unimplemented planning permission). Consequently, the freedom of local plans to take locational and quantitative decisions on new housebuilding may be considerably diminished. Local planning authorities also recognise the futility of calling for a total embargo on fresh planning permissions. Minor residential development (i.e. infilling or conversions) and small-scale development within built-up areas is characteristically granted planning permission independently of the process of local plan preparation ... a prematurity objection is valid only if it can be clearly demonstrated which of the plan's policies or proposals would be prejudiced by the proposed development.': [26].

Also the formulation of Local Plans is often beset by resource and institutional difficulties. A participant-observation study in

Harringey Borough, for example, found that the formulation process was a process by which planners explored, and eventually had to accept, these constraints. Means and ends were continually being reshaped in the light of new information, a process suggestive more of disjointed-incrementalism than of the rational-comprehensive strategy: [27].

CONCLUSION

Consideration of how organisations work and interact with politicians, and of the processing of plans in the current planning system, tends to suggest that the dominant process by which decisions and plans are made is by use of the disjointed-incrementalist strategy. Standard operating procedures tend to be limited in scope, the number of alternatives considered is usually limited, organisations only make incremental changes, they overlook long-term considerations, and they comprise individuals who use their discretion to produce multiple perspectives on how policy is implemented. Moreover organisations develop partisan perspectives, and develop strategies to promote these perspectives in competition with other organisations whose concerns overlap their own.

Moreover, the increasing sophistication of planners in social and economic matters means that the area of concern of plans is increasing, a further influence towards disjointed-incrementalism. And concern for the state of the economy and restraining the growth in public expenditure are further, perhaps temporary, influences in the same direction.

The situations which encourage a rational comprehensive strategy are thus isolated and temporary ones - when a policy requires a vast monetary contribution from government to be effective, when there is a crisis, when there are adverse and easily predicted side effects of incrementalism, and when political commitment is engineered either by officials or by industrial pressure groups. These situations seem to wax and wane with government commitment to intervention and with the build up of social problems. However their importance is greater than would appear since firstly planning is often defined (through legislation and topical argument) at such moments of optimism or crisis, and since secondly in such situations are initiated many long term and large scale projects.

In general then, with these notable exceptions, we can treat disjointed-incrementalism as the dominant process by which plans and planning decisions are made.

Therefore in our subsequent discussion of arguments and values in planning, we must continually keep in mind that such arguments and values are expressed within a disjointed-incrementalist setting.

NOTES

[1] P.M. Blau, Bureaucracy in Modern Society, Chicago, 1956, p.53-57.

[2] For arguments that politicians need to be more closely involved

in plan-formulation, see T.M. Ridley and J.O. Tressider, 'Replies to comments on "the London Study and Beyond", Regional Studies, 1970, Vol.4, No.1, pp.81-83, and A.T. Blowers 'Transport Planning : a new direction?', Town and County Planning Summer School, Report of Proceedings, Nottingham, 1976, pp.16-20.

[3] F. Gladstone, The Politics of Planning, Temple Smith, 1976 p.92.

[4] A. Blowers, The Limits of Power, Pergamon, 1978, p.138; also 'Strategic issues are rarely susceptible to specific decisions but develop gradually as constraints are recognised and the feasibility of different alternatives is tested. They need to be tackled in depth by informal processes...', p.139.

[5] S.H. Linder, 'Decision rules and regulatory reform', Journal of Public Policy, Vol.2, No.4, pp.379-94.

[6] For an example of different central government departments playing conflicting planning roles see P. Self, Administrative Theories and Politics, G. Allen and Unwin, London, 1977, p.104.

[7] M.T. Pountney and P.W. Kingsbury, 'Aspects of development control, Part 2 : The applicant's view', Town Planning Review, Vol.54, No.3, 1983, p.285-303.

[8] V.A. Thompson, Modern Organisation, New York, 1961.

[9] K. Young and J. Kramer, Strategy and Conflict in Metropolitan Housing, Heinemann - CES, 1978, pp.222-3.

[10] See D. Collingridge, The Social Control of Technology, Frances Pinter, London, 1981. Collingridge argues that if a project involves any of : wide dissemination, great expense, long lead times, or development of infrastructure, it will be difficult to alter or control, and even after detrimental side effects have been noticed, almost impossible to change. He suggests that, in a competitive market, decision makers tend to hedge their bets by making decisions which seem least prone to error. He argues that the social and technological system then adapts to the decision and reinforces the need for the technology. As it becomes more and more established, with increasing numbers of subsystems dependent on it, it becomes more difficult to control and more sensitive to errors in forecasting. This reinforces a tendency to growth and expansion, which ultimately tends to expensive collapse. Two of his examples are energy and leaded petrol.

[11] G.E. Edwards and O. Sharkansky, The Policy Predicament, Freeman, 1961, Chapter 9.

[12] The need for comprehensive control is often argued as a means of preventing the bad effects of speculation, although often such speculation is itself sparked off by public intervention. For example, the land rights nationalisation powers in the Town and Country Planning Act 1947 resulted at least partly from loopholes in the compensation and betterment provisions of the previous Act of 1932 and the speculation which it produced.

[13] P.H. Levin, Government and the Planning Process, G. Allen and Unwin, 1976, Ch.3.

[14] D. McKie, A Sadly Mismanaged Affair, Croom Helm, 1973, p.243.

[15] A. Blowers, 1978, op.cit. at p.85.

[16] For a partial defence of commitment generating strategies see P.H. Levin op.cit. Ch.12.

[17] See also A. Faludi, Planning Theory, Urban and Regional Planning Series, Vol.7, Pergamon, 1973, Chapters 7, 8, and 9.

[18] P. West, 'The family, the welfare state, and community care : political rhetoric and public attitudes', Journal of Social Policy, Vol.13, No.4, pp.417-46.

[19] M. Laver, 'How to be sophisticated, lie, cheat, bluff, and win at politics', Political Studies, Vol.XXVI, No.4, 1978, pp.462-73.

[20] Schulman has noted:

> 'The correspondence between social movements and non-incremental policies is striking and politically significant. Both require an extensive mobilisation of public resources and support for their start-up. Both must then maintain this mobilisation above a critical level or they will rapidly disintegrate. Both, in effect, require the presence of expansive goals as the primary means of protecting themselves from erosions of support':

P.R. Schulman, 'Non-incremental policy making : notes towards an alternative paradigm', American Political Science Review, 1975, Vol.69, pp.1354-70 at p.1366.

[21] H. Glennerster, 'From containment to conflict? Social planning in the Seventies', Journal of Social Policy, Vol.10, No.1, pp. 31-51 at p.50-51.

[22] A. Blowers, 'Much Ado About Nothing - A Case Study of Planning and Power', p.140-60, in P. Healey, G. McDougall, M.J. Thomas, Planning Theory : Prospects for the 1980s, Pergamon, London, 1982.

[23] P. Healey, '"Rational Method" as a mode of policy formation and implementation in land use policy', Environment and Planning B, Vol.10, 1983, pp.19-39.

[24] Hopefully these (and perhaps others) are a start at answering one of Self's criticisms of disjointed-incrementalism:

> '...it does not say how far polycentricity should be pushed and in fact fragmentation of decision making soon becomes rather absurd; nor in what circumstances some of the gains of polycentricity might be worth sacrificing for some integrated planning';

Administrative Theories and Politics, G. Allen and Unwin, 1977, p.41.

[25] A. Blowers, 1978, op.cit., p.138; for a similar process on the Yorkshire Structure Plan see R. Darke, 'The Dialectics of Decision-Making : Form and Content', p.194-210 in P. Healey, G. McDougall, M.J. Thomas, Planning Theory : Prospects for the 1980s, Pergamon, London, 1982, p.202.

[26] J. Wilson, 'The prematurity objection', Estates Gazette, 1982, Vol.261, pp.123-24, 127 at p.133; for another discussion of the lack of coincidence of the process of plan-making and of planning see F. Medhurst, 'The Planning Perspective', in D. Jones, (ed.) Communications and Energy in Changing Urban Environments, Butterworth, London, p.24.

[27] J. Underwood, Town Planners in Search of a Role, Centre for Advanced Urban Studies, Bristol University, 1976.

13 The public presentation of planning arguments

Often the rational-comprehensive planning process is used as a shield behind which a plan is made to seem automatically the best solution to a problem. The fact that the recommended process has been followed, it seems, acts as a powerful disincentive to the layman to question or criticise. As plans are often presented currently, the things that often stand out are the stages of the rational-comprehensive planning process. For example, public opinion surveys and census material are used to justify a definition of issues, sometimes in a one-dimensional way, as if public opinion and demographic data were unambiguous about what the issues are. The planning document can therefore bypass the question of conflicting definition of issues. Yet it may be that issues exist which have not been raised by public participation exercises or census analysis. This would be true for issues about the future, or about technically complex matters, or about matters under-valued by local or national media. Similarly even a number of alternatives cannot be said to be exhaustive, and some justification should be made (though this is rare) for the exclusion of alternatives. Similarly the present state of evaluation methods cannot give rise to complete confidence that the selected alternative is the best one. A certain degree of extra justification, plus some reservations and uncertainties, would therefore seem appropriate here too. The fact that reservations and assumptions are not mentioned and that justification and argument are kept to a minimum is probably due to a number of factors. Firstly planning departments for various reasons have problems of influencing other local authority departments. So any arguments presented in the plan are an invitation to these other departments to criticise. Secondly the rational-comprehensive planning process is taught as an ideal in planning schools. Yet such an ideal is not realised in practice, and it would make more sense to prepare for this by learning how to argue a plan: [1], rather than expecting a plan which followed the comprehensive approach to be accepted. Thirdly there is an imperfect knowledge of what public participation means. Usually it is assumed that if opinion surveys are properly carried out and if these influence the definition of issues then public participation has been completed. But what about public reaction to the plan? Can plans be read and understood by the layman? What stands out to a layman is often that which is inviting him to participate - the explicitly-stated assumption, the inserted question, the presence of conflict - all these are assessable by the intelligent layman. Unfortunately plans usually avoid conflict (sometimes omitting conflictual issues for political reasons) and are expressed as an agreed consensus, an open and shut case.

So one can understand why argument plays such a small place in planning documents (although arguments cannot be avoided in appeals and public inquiries). And among the reasons, there is the unwillingness to be criticised. Arguments are an invitation to be criticised. They bring the message, wherever we see them, that there always exists another point of view.

To demonstrate these criticisms of the practice of plan-making we shall analyse the West Midlands County Structure Plan, 1980. We shall attempt to show that the Structure Plan, on the surface, follows the classical comprehensive planning process. It begins with an analysis of issues and opportunities, then narrows these areas down to a section of key-issues, and then sets up three alternatives which are then evaluated in terms of the key-issues, to decide which is best. It will be suggested here that

(i) there is no automatic or natural transition from the 'issues and opportunities' identified, to the 'key-issues'. Many assumptions or omissions of evidence are made in order to make that transition;

(ii) throughout the analysis of 'issues and opportunities' and 'key-issues' there is a strong implicit commitment to inner urban area renewal: yet this should have been one of the alternatives about which the document kept an open mind;

(iii) there are three alternatives given in the third section of the Plan, yet by this time it has been made clear that one of them - that for inner urban area renewal - is to be chosen. Thus the impartial planning process has not been followed.

(iv) What happened is that a political commitment was first expressed for inner area renewal, and then the Structure Plan, with its pretence at open-minded investigation of alternatives, was used as a respectable cover for this political commitment.

THE CASE STUDY : WEST MIDLANDS STRUCTURE PLAN, 1980.

The Structure Plan begins with a discursive section outlining what it describes as 'issues and opportunities'.

WMMC, 1980, West Midland County Structure Plan, October 1980, as submitted to DOE : Issues and Opportunities.

2.1 The Reports of Survey published in October 1978 highlighted the variety of inter-related problems facing the West Midlands County. It is to these problems that the Structure Plan strategy must address itself, recognising that the policies and proposals put forward do not, in themselves, provide complete solutions. In practice, the Plan will provide the broad land use policy framework within which the decisions of individuals and organisations, both in the public and private sectors, are to be made. It is through these subsequent activities that the problems will ultimately be solved.

2.2 The Structure Plan provides the starting point for the co-ordination of action. Its major role is to set down clearly a common direction or "strategy" for other policies to follow, in order to reinforce the impact of subsequent decisions.

2.3 The selection of a strategy for the County is no simple task since it involves fundamental areas of choice. The key issues and opportunities for solving problems and promoting new growth, are set out in the following pages.

The effect of population losses

2.4 For many years, the West Midlands County attracted people because of its ready supply of well paid jobs. At the same time, there has been a consistent movement of people from the older urban areas to the suburbs and into the adjoining counties. Between 1971 and 1978, for example, 130,000 more people moved out of the County than moved in.

2.5 Whilst population loss of this magnitude by migration may not be a significant problem in itself, it is the type of people choosing to move out which gives rise to concern. In particular, the loss of professional and managerial people from the County which already has a low proportion of such persons (Fig.2), coupled with the fact that they are often in the younger (25 to 40) age group, means that the population of the County is becoming older and socially imbalanced.

2.6 If homes are relatively easy to obtain in the shire counties and fewer jobs are available in the West Midlands, it is possible that even more people will move out of the County. While there may be positive advantages in fewer people living in the West Midlands, there is a danger that, as in the past, the people who are able to move out will be the younger, more affluent and more able. The result would then be that social and environmental problems now affecting the older urban areas would spread much wider to include many inter-war local authority housing areas.

2.7 In the longer term, the loss of younger and more skilled people would reduce the advantages of the West Midlands for employers. Industry would then begin to adjust to the changing distribution of its workforce by moving out of the County. It is essential in social and economic terms that the loss of population be kept within reasonable bounds by improving the West Midlands as a place in which to live and by providing a wide range of housing.

The quality of the existing housing stock

2.8 Although new houses will be built during the next 15 years, they will represent only a limited addition to the existing housing stock. If significant progress is to be made in making the West Midlands more attractive, the quality of the existing housing areas must be raised. Greater encouragement must be given to people improving their own houses; the local authorities must continue and if possible expand their existing programme of modernisation and improvement; new methods must be examined and where appropriate introduced. At the same time, an increase in the rate at which houses are replaced must be achieved; this does not imply a return to sweeping redevelopment.

2.9 There are major difficulties in implementing these policies but, if they do not succeed, more and more houses will prove to be unacceptable. The result would be a continuing deterioration of existing housing with more people living in poor conditions. In turn, this would increase the demand for houses in the suburbs and adjoining counties leaving others standing empty particularly in the older and inter-war local authority estates. In the longer term, therefore, there would be a need to clear more houses.

2.10 There are opportunities for improvements, however, in spite of government financial restrictions. Building societies are beginning to show interest in this field, while local authorities are experimenting with approaches such as 'homesteading' which enable people to buy old houses for a nominal sum after agreeing to improve them. There is also potential for the wider application of the 'envelope scheme' approach adopted in Birmingham where external house repairs are undertaken on a block by block basis.

2.11 As a result of past policies, the overall condition of housing in the West Midlands is not as bad as in many other areas. It is therefore realistic to talk of regeneration, particularly in the Black Country where local communities have exceptionally strong roots and demand for housing is often still high.

The need for new housing

2.12 Even accepting that some population movement will continue out of the County, approximately 100,000 new homes will be required by 1991. These must be built in those areas where the needs occur; it would be unrealistic to assume that the needs of Coventry could be met in Wolverhampton or vice versa. At the same time, there must be a wide range of housing opportunities if movement to the shire counties is to be reduced.

2.13 This Plan therefore provides an opportunity to provide new homes, to encourage housing for sale in the older urban areas, and at the same time to protect the environment to a greater extent than the previous Plans.

The needs of industry and employment

2.14 Manufacturing industry has been the basis of the prosperity of the West Midlands. Although the prospects for this sector are uncertain, the existing industries of the County still have potential for providing both economic growth and employment. It has been the relative decline of the traditional metal based manufacturing industries in terms of output, investment, productivity and employment that has been responsible for the higher levels of unemployment that currently exist. The need to reverse this decline and to provide alternative employment opportunities is a major issue that the Structure Plan must face.

2.15 The County depends upon many thousands of individual firms, of varying sizes, involved in many different processes. These firms are closely interlinked by an established network of purchasing and supply which is both a major opportunity, but also a major source of uncertainty because of the dependence of many firms upon a few large industries, particularly the motor industry. Planning and other local authority policies must, therefore, take full account of the needs of industry and should be designed to give it a high priority. At the same time, the development and broadening of the economic base of the County must be pursued through encouraging the development of new industries and by taking advantage of the potential growth in distribution, warehousing and offices.

2.16 The West Midlands has traditionally been economically successful as reflected in the development and adaptation of industry and the growth of commerce to serve its needs. One of the most important factors in this success has been the human resources of the area, in particular the enterprising spirit and manufacturing skills of the population. These resources have been fostered by the County's universities, polytechnics and further education colleges.

2.17 The reputation of the workforce of the County, as one which is fully accustomed to modern industrial processes, provides one of the greatest opportunities and advantages for the future. This reputation must be preserved by seeking to ensure that the area continues to be associated with a prosperous and efficient industrial economy.

Potential for growth

2.18 The potential for growth provided by new major industrial development is likely to be very limited in the next few years. While this reinforces the need to encourage existing firms, it does not mean that new firms should be ignored. There is a shortage of prime industrial sites in the West Midlands; many of the existing sites will be difficult and expensive to develop. Action must be taken to identify and make ready sites which would attract new industries.

2.19 The success of the National Exhibition Centre has demonstrated the advantages of the West Midlands, particularly its location at the centre of a complex network of road, rail, air and telecommunications links. The National Exhibition Centre itself will continue to act as a stimulus for growth in industry, commerce and tourism.

2.20 Birmingham city centre, and to a lesser degree Coventry and Wolverhampton, have also shown that they can attract new investment and employment. Following a period of over-provision, the demand for offices in central Birmingham is now increasing and the economic potential for growth in office employment must be realised.

2.21 The mining of coal in Coventry will continue to create new employment and it is hoped that the long-term nature of reserves may encourage the development of associated industries.

The need for transport

2.22 A significant increase in highway capacity in the last ten years, coupled with a significant decrease in economic activity, has kept the rate of provision of road space just ahead of increasing demand. However, it is now clear that the resources previously assumed to be available will not be provided so that a balance will have to be maintained between future demands for road space and its supply. This is a particularly critical issue in relation to Birmingham city centre where existing road capacity is limited but where potential service sector employment growth could substantially increase demand.

2.23 Before carrying out major improvements to the urban road system, it is sensible to ensure that the best use is made of existing transport infrastructure. One of the few areas in which some additional transport capacity is available for journeys to work is in travelling outwards from the urban centres to the suburbs. The development of more suburban employment centres, however, rather than generating outward commuting might simply encourage more inward commuting from the shire counties and thereby generating a greater population loss from the West Midlands County.

2.24 Although recent increases in fuel costs have not so far had a dramatic effect on journeys to work, further significant increases resulting from either long term fuel shortages or conscious government policies to conserve oil, could result in people living closer to their place of work and/or making more use of public transport. Either trend would increase the attractiveness of the West Midlands, assuming that jobs were available.

2.25 One of the effects of past migration from the West Midlands is that there are now substantial flows of commuters into the County from the surrounding shire counties. Much of this commuting is by car, but it does not usually cause problems until it enters the Metropolitan County where roads are already congested.

Improving the environment

2.26 The image of parts of the West Midlands is one of an inter-mix of older housing and industry, with low standards of open-space, creating a generally poor environment. While over much of the County this is not a true picture, there are many areas where these claims can be substantiated, particularly in the Black Country and inner Birmingham, and this is a negative factor working against the attraction of new enterprise.

2.27 It has been emphasised that the County is no longer in a situation where the major problem to be faced is how to accommodate high levels of growth. In this situation, there is now the possibility of focusing attention on how areas can be regenerated and improved. The provision of central government resources for the 'Inner Areas' clearly supports this approach and considerable opportunities also exist to improve local environment through housing and industrial improvement areas, derelict land reclamation, the maintenance and improvement of canals, and the development of land for recreation.

Protecting the environment

2.28 If the West Midlands is to become more attractive and if resources are to be concentrated on the existing urban area, it is essential that building is not allowed to spread without limits. In particular, the wedges of open land which extend into the built-up area must be protected and enhanced to provide opportunities for recreation.

2.29 The Green Belt outside the main urban area is used for agriculture, the protection of which must be a high priority. The area between Solihull and Coventry is particularly sensitive and will be retained as open land.

The areas in greatest need

2.30 The impact of many of the key issues is concentrated on certain parts of the County, particularly the Black Country, inner Birmingham and inner Coventry. Some, but by no means all, of the areas concerned are already recognised under the Inner Urban Areas Act. Efforts must be concentrated on regenerating and improving these areas which may mean that opportunities elsewhere will have to be restricted.

2.31 The problems of the older urban areas are, however, not so severe in the West Midlands that regeneration is impossible. There are excellent opportunities to attract private housing and small industries. These opportunities must be carefully balanced against the risk that using all possible land for building will create such as a poor environment that the movement of people out of the older urban areas continues. The quality of life will be more important than the number of new buildings, and factors such as shopping, education and open space must be given emphasis.

The best use of resources

2.32 Limited economic growth, particularly when combined with stronger controls on public spending, will severely restrict investment. It is essential that the local authorities develop a new role, acting in partnership with private investors, to ensure that the best use is made of existing resources.

2.33 It is also essential at the present time to ensure that energy and fuel resources are managed efficiently. Given the lead by central government, local authorities will need policies which minimise the social and economic impact of high energy prices or actual shortages of fuel. Moreover, failure to manage the energy problem nationally could undermine many basic assumptions, not only in respect of transport, but also employment, housing and the environment.

These can be summarised into 13 issues and opportunities:

(i) The out migration of young managers and skilled workers.

(ii) The poor housing and environment, and a need to clear some housing; (this is linked to industrial decline).

(iii) A lack of housing; (this is linked to industrial decline).

(iv) The decline in metal-based and car industries.

(v) The narrow economic base.

(vi) The large potentialities of existing labour skills and educational institutions.

(vii) Good modern communications and centrality in the national communications network - evidenced by the success of the National Exhibition Centre.

(viii) The growth potential of Birmingham centre.

(ix) The growth potential of the South Warwickshire coalfield.

(x) The need for more roads in Birmingham centre.

(xi) Substantial in-commuting from outside the County by young managers and skilled workers.

(xii) The potential for improvement of the urban fabric with a strong underlying preoccupation with the renewal of inner urban areas.

(xiii) The need to protect the Green Belt.

A LACK OF ANALYSIS OR ARGUMENT

The presentation of issues and opportunities in the 1980 West Midlands Structure Plan gives the strong impression of a lack of analysis. The following are some reasons for this.

(i) The presentation quoted above in full confuses reasons for industrial decline with out migration. Stopping out migration will not halt industrial decline. And halting industrial decline will not stop out migration since out migration is often to pleasant commuter environments. The quoted passage thus gives a strong impression of a poor background in supporting surveys of preferences and behaviour.

(ii) The quoted passage does not come to terms with the fact that some of the changes are usual ones in metropolitan areas - a decanting of white collar groups and some employment to areas beyond the green belt and a consequent increase in cross-green belt commuting. There is no sense of comparative knowledge of what has been tried and made to work in other similar metropolitan areas.

(iii) Paragraphs 2.26 and 2.27 mention the improvement of poor environments. No attempt is made to assess the cost of this compared with allowing the drift of people to continue away from such environments. This strengthens the impression that a choice of alternatives has been made <u>prior</u> to the <u>first</u> section of the Structure Plan.

(iv) Paragraph 2.29 asserts the need to protect the Green Belt without any justification whatever. The implication might be that this was something everybody agrees about and that justification is therefore not necessary. But subsequent events, particularly the County's later plan to develop a high-technology business park near to the National Exhibition Centre, within the Green Belt, undermine this hypothesis.

(v) Paragraph 2.31 has an inherent contradiction. The implication of simultaneously attracting new private housing, and small industries, and of improving the environment of inner areas is not explored.

(vi) Paragraph 2.6 makes explicit the assumption that net out migration is partly due to a lack of housing within the County. But no evidence is used to support this hypothesis.

(vii) Paragraph 2.26 suggests that the poor environment of the County is a disincentive to investment. This is not supported by the evidence, and is rather undermined by the drying up of footloose industries since the 1960s. Industry has been increasingly loyal to the home region.

Thus while we would expect an objective approach to be impartial in its presentation of issues, the above signals strongly a political commitment to inner area renewal. This does not therefore follow the classical planning process. Yet the Structure Plan tries to appear that it does so - it proceeds through the various stages of the rational-comprehensive planning process as if the classical method is being followed. Thus the appearance of the rational-comprehensive planning process is being used to make the conclusions of each section seem reasonable, and to make the transition from one section to the next to seem smooth and uncontrived.

AN UNSUBSTANTIATED JUMP FROM ISSUES AND OPPORTUNITIES TO KEY ISSUES

The transition from the first to the second section of the Structure Plan is, however, very contrived.

The 13 issues and opportunities identified above are reformulated in five key issues or principal objectives.

WMCC, 1980, West Midlands Structure Plan, October 1980, as submitted to DOE : The Strategy : Principal Objectives.

> 3.1 Following from the identification of the issues and opportunities facing the County, a number of objectives were defined as a basis for the development of the Structure Plan Strategy. These principal objectives may be summarised as:
>
> (i) Regeneration of the older urban areas to improve the overall quality of life.
>
> (ii) Encouragement of economic prosperity and development of employment opportunities throughout the County.
>
> (iii) Improvement of housing conditions.
>
> (iv) Conservation and the best use of resources in terms of energy, land and money.
>
> (v) Protection and enhancement of open land and the built-up area.
>
> 3.2 It is the overall aim of the Plan that all action leading to the fulfilment of these objectives should be complementary. However, in developing the Plan, it was recognised there could be different approaches to the resolution of issues. Three alternative strategies were devised, therefore, in order to set out the relative merits of different patterns of land use. These were set out in "Strategic Choices" which, accompanied by the Reports of Survey, formed the basis of the public participation carried out between October and December 1978.
>
> 3.3 It was not intended that any one of the approaches should necessarily be chosen as a preferred strategy but that the effects of each on different areas and groups of people should be examined to produce a strategy giving maximum assistance to those areas and people in greatest need. Indeed, the strategies included many common elements since the possibilities for major changes in land use are limited.

The first key issues or principal objectives do not follow smoothly from the 13 issues and opportunities identified in the first section of the Structure Plan. Several questions about the transition arise from this.

(i) The 13 issues include lack of housing and the need to clear some housing. If met by key issue 3, this would use up more open land (undermining key issue 5) since new densities would inevitably be much lower than existing densities.

(ii) If individual housing consumers are the best judge, moving out to the outer ring outside the West Midlands conurbation green belt is the surest way to improve quality of life. Thus the intention to regenerate inner areas requires a lot more supporting argument.

(iii) If communications are a principal feature of the West Midlands' economic advantages, and the NEC a specific example of this, why should the regeneration of the inner areas of the conburbation be a natural consequence when the lack of roads in inner Birmingham is actually mentioned specifically as a problem?

(iv) The 'best use of resources' (see key issue 4) has several meanings. The most obvious one is financial. If this were the chosen meaning, then a strong case could be made for abandoning the outworm infrastructure of urban centres and allowing new growth in rural areas near to metropolitan areas. The fact that this is not even argued through is another indication that the audience is a council strongly committed to inner urban area renewal.

A RITUALISTIC USE OF ALTERNATIVES

The 'key issues' section is followed by one which presents three alternatives. Three very different alternatives are evaluated. One is a 'trend-planning' solution which allows growth where the market wants it, in the peripheral areas of the region. The second is a concentration of all possible resources on the inner urban areas. The third is a concentration of housing investment in inner areas and industrial investment in the suburbs.

Yet by this time we have already developed the strong suspicion that the investigation is spurious since the decision on inner area renewal had already been made at the start of the exercise. Subsequent reading of the Structure Plan proposals merely confirms this suspicion. Lo and behold, the inner urban area renewal alternative is the one 'finally' chosen.

One must ask the question of such a plan - why have the planners abused the rational-comprehensive planning process in such a way? The impartial search for the best alternative is what most people hold the rational-comprehensive planning process to signify. Yet when the best alternative is known from the start it would seem wiser to make this known and argue, all the way through the document, why this has been chosen.

A yet more important question is whether the semblance of impartiality in the rational-comprehensive process is a dangerous delusion. No one knows all the answers. So it is better to start from the position that all parts of a plan need to be argued, not only within sections, but from one section to the next, as we saw above.

The strong impression given, therefore, by analysis of the West Midlands Structure Plan 1980 is that, while the real planning process followed was definitely not the rational-comprehensive strategy, the presentation of the plan for the public was carefully dressed up to make it appear as if the rational-comprehensive strategy had been followed. One alternative to this approach is for plans to be much more open about advocating particular political principles, values, or assumptions. This necessitates inclusion of the other conflicting values that exist. This suggests the notion of dialogue as a form of objectivity: [2], a notion long accepted in natural science.

NOTES

[1] H.A. Goldstein, 'Planning as argumentation', Environment and Planning B, Vol.11, 1984, pp.297-312.

[2] M. Hesse, Revolutions and Reconstructions in the Philosophy of Science, Harvester Press, New York, 1980; J. Habermas, 'Rationalism Divided into Two', pp.195-224 in A. Giddens, (ed.), Positivism and Sociology, Heinemann, London, 1974; R. Darke, 'Rationality, Planning and the State, pp.15-26 at p.26 in M. Breheny and A. Hooper (eds), Rationality in Planning : Critical Essays on the Role of Rationality in Urban and Regional Planning, Pion, London, 1985; A. Wildavsky, Speaking Truth to Power, Little Brown and Co., Boston, 1980, (published in UK as A. Wildavsky, The Art and Craft of Policy Analysis, London, Macmillan, 1980); J. Forester, 'The policy analysis - critical theory affair : Wildavsky and Habermas as bedfellows?', Journal of Public Policy, Vol.2, No.2, 1984, pp.145-64.

14 The logic of arguments in planning

We have now suggested that the disjointed-incrementalist strategy fits the reality of the planning process more closely than does the rational-comprehensive strategy. In a sense disjointed-incrementalism is just as much an ideal type as is the rational-comprehensive strategy. But we have put forward some arguments why disjointed-incrementalism is nearer to the real planning environment, and we shall accept this simple model, or abstraction, from here on.

Also we have put forward reasons why plans should be presented as arguments. In the planning environment the planner is only one of many decision-makers. His peculiar role is his commitment to coordination and comprehensiveness (paradoxically in a planning environment which is disjointed-incrementalist). He should therefore relinquish any public claims to omniscience, and instead try to present and analyse the arguments from all points of view. We do not argue that this will magically produce a best answer. Rather, it would allow the planner to be both comprehensive and open about the non-rational, disjointed-incrementalist nature of the planning environment.

This then raises the question of <u>how</u> arguments (by various parties) are to be analysed. In order to answer this question we must do two things. Firstly we must attempt to understand the logic and underlying assumptions of arguments and how these interact in a dynamic setting with several participants: [1]. Secondly, we will have to develop an approach based upon a weaving together of utilitarianism and disjointed-incrementalism, of how in best practice planning decisions are actually evaluated. We will offer many reasons why this approach, which we consider is the best one available, and the one which is used in best practice has serious flaws.

But we start with the logic of arguments: [2] as used in planning practice. We shall deal with this topic: [3] by investigating a number of types of logical fallacy.

FALLACY ONE : MAKING A STATEMENT IN WHICH 'ALL' IS IMPLIED BUT 'SOME' IS TRUE.

Imagine you come across the argument : 'If freedom to object to planning proposals is lost, then tyrany reigns.'

The fallacy lies in the omission of the word 'all' in front of 'freedom'. The statement : 'A condition in which (all) freedom to object to planning proposals is lost is one in which tyrany reigns' is only true if 'all' is the missing word.

Imagine there is the argument : 'If public transport declines, the transport system becomes unworkable.'

The fallacy lies in the omission of the word 'critically' after 'declines'. If public transport declines by a small amount, the effect may not be noticeable.

FALLACY TWO : PROOF BY SELECTED INSTANCES.

Say you are deciding whether or not to give planning permission to an application to extract minerals in a scenic area. The question arises of re-instatement of the area after minerals have been extracted. Someone knows of another case where a company extracted minerals and then left the area without properly re-instating the area.

To argue that because of what happened with the other company means that it is highly likely it will happen with your present applicant is to use proof by selected instances. It is better to seek wider experience, and to find instances of situations where re-instatement conditions have been met. Then you can ask : does my knowledge of the applicant suggest he is the type to reinstate or not? Use of only one example in an argument is nearly always misleading.

FALLACY THREE : EXTENSION OF AN OPPONENT'S PROPOSITION BY CONTRADICTIONS OR BY MISREPRESENTATIONS OF IT.

Say you are representing a District planning authority at an appeal into your refusal of planning permission for a proposed housing development in a village in your area. Your refusal has contradicted the County's key settlement policy since the village is in the County Structure Plan as a key settlement where housing development is allowed. The County Council are therefore represented at the appeal as objectors to your decision. And of course the appellants, the housing developers, are also represented at the appeal.

Suppose the County's barrister puts to you the proposition, which he says he sympathises with, that Districts have the advantage that they have greater knowledge about the local circumstances of their area. On the other hand Counties cannot hope to acquire this knowledge for all the Districts under their jurisdiction. You probably agree. This all sounds harmless enough. Then the County's barrister goes on, saying that the kinds of development pressures in the rural parts of your District are often unpredictable. A farmer wants to build a bungalow for his retirement and hand the farm to his son. A remote hotel wishes to provide separate modern accommodation for staff. And so on. Therefore, he continues, it should be these developments that dictate the pattern of change rather than planned developments in particular villages. You find this sensible enough and agree.

Now the barrister takes a different tack. But also, he says, the agencies which provide infrastructure and services - schools, bus services, electricity, sewers - want to know in advance whether an area is going to lose population or gain in population. So they do want a plan. And there is a recognised demand, by commuters and pensioners, for new village houses.

The barrister has thus invited us into a position of saying - all developments are for local needs, so Districts should have the control. Then he has shown that villages do expand, and that infrastructure needs to be concentrated where it is needed most. He can now show that our position is parochial. It does not meet all needs, all pressures. Therefore some overall responsibility for reconciling all these pressures is needed. He then suggests that it is the County which fulfils this very necessary role.

This trick is best dealt with by giving only qualified agreement to the development of the other person's argument.

FALLACY FOUR : DIVERSION TO ANOTHER QUESTION, TO A SIDE ISSUE, OR BY IRRELEVANT OBJECTION.

Suppose you are a County planner at a liaison group meeting discussing a neighbouring County's Structure Plan. Your line of questioning is about some of the assumptions underlying the population projections. You think the Structure Plan under-estimates out-migration of young people, especially fertile women, so that the population projections for 20 years ahead are too high. One of the planners from the neighbouring County begins by saying that forecasting is only an art and not a science, and then goes on quite correctly to look at the land use implications if the forecasts are wrong. His position is that the land use strategy of the Structure Plan is flexible enough to adapt to higher or lower than planned population levels.

This is clearly a diversion. The point is that Structure Plan population forecasts are used for many purposes outside the Structure Plan itself. For example, bids by the County for more grant from central government partly depend on present and future population levels. So even if the Structure Plan is robust enough to adapt to different future levels of population, this is no reason for not being careful about assumptions made in forecasting population.

FALLACY FIVE : THE ARGUMENT THAT WE SHOULD NOT MAKE EFFORTS AGAINST X WHICH IS ADMITTEDLY EVIL BECAUSE THERE IS A WORSE EVIL Y AGAINST WHICH OUR EFFORTS SHOULD BE DIRECTED.

It is frequently argued that large areas of our inner cities should be free of planning controls (in the manner of enterprise zones). While this argument admits that the creation of eyesores and environmental nuisances in our inner cities is an evil, an even worse evil is the stiffling of the spirit of enterprise as small businesses in our inner cities struggle to expand.

What should be done is carry out experiments to see how big each evil is, and also whether planning controls do actually stiffle enterprise. After all the above may merely be a political argument to weaken planning controls in areas where people have no political voice on the quality of environment (the inner cities) while retaining planning controls for the middle class (in the suburbs and the country side).

FALLACY SIX : THE ARGUMENT THAT WE SHOULD NOT BE OVERWHELMED BY FEAR OF RISK A BECAUSE OF THE EXISTENCE OF RISK B, C, ETC: [4].

Consider the following:

> 'Even though we need nuclear power, some people think it too risky to use. "Carelessness costs lives" is a saying that is certainly true of nuclear energy. Should we do without it, then, even though we need it, in order to avoid any risk of carelessness causing deaths?
> 'If nuclear energy were the only form of risk there was, this might be a sensible thing to do. But of course it is not the only form of risk we have to consider. There are risks everywhere.
> 'At home you risk falling over and hurting yourself. There are serious risks in crossing the road on the way to school. At school there are risks of catching an illness from someone, risks of being injured playing games.
> 'There are risks in driving a car, risks in flying an aircraft, risks in eating butter, risks in keeping a dog. There are, as we have seen, very serious risks in digging coal and burning coal, oil or gas as fuel.': [5].

This is a method of undermining the seriousness with which we treat risk: [6]. Besides the fact that the various risks have not been compared quantitatively, and that we may reject some (e.g. eating butter) as individuals, there is the more fundamental point that the argument encourages us to accept a riskier way of life.

FALLACY SEVEN : THE RECOMMENDATION OF A POSITION BECAUSE IT IS THE MEAN BETWEEN TWO EXTREMES.

For example, although to many people the Sizewell Inquiry was about the threat of nuclear power and its associated risks, a clever argument which attempted to show nuclear power as a moderate risk was put forward:

'First, the Inquiry must consider the problem of acid rain. This is not simple, but at least there is no doubt that coal fired power stations are a major source of what is eventually deposited, often hundreds of miles from source, as sulphuric and nitric acid. I personally think that the seriousness of the acid rain problem may sometimes be exaggerated, but nevertheless I believe that there will soon be so much international pressure that we will be forced to extract sulphur dioxide and oxides of nitrogent from flue gases, a costly process, and one which must be considered in comparing the economic costs of different forms of power stations. Coal will clearly become less attractive, and many new problems will have to be faced.

'Secondly, there is growing concern about the rise of carbon dioxide in the atmosphere. Much has recently been written about this, but we are still completely uncertain about its importance. However, we are increasingly coming to realise that the carbon dioxide could have quite drastic global effects, possibly melting polar ice and raising ocean levels so that many of our major cities, including London, are flooded. There may also be changes in climate causing droughts in many of the world's most important food producing areas. On the other hand, none of these things may happen. But it would be foolish not to be prepared ... we should seriously make plans to stop using coal (which for a given amount of energy, liberates much more carbon dioxide than does oil or natural gas) without totally disrupting the world's economy.

'At present the only alternatives we know we could use is nuclear power. This is why I believe that we should, purely as an insurance policy, immediately build the PWR and also a commercial fast breeder reactor, so that we have the experience and knowhow...': [8].

To what extent does this represent a fallacy? The fallacy arises when the argument is accepted at face value, without much more evidence than that given above. The three alternatives then become no nuclear energy, some nuclear energy, and a large-scale programme of nuclear energy. Immediately the no-nuclear option becomes relegated to a peripheral status. Yet there is no logical reason why a medium between extremes has any greater merit. Such merit must be established with much more evidence (which may, or may not, exist).

FALLACY EIGHT : PROOF BY INCONSEQUENT ARGUMENT.

Consider the following:

'London was subjected to intensive gravel working without adequate restoration in the days before the GLC was set up and a legacy of this is the existence of over 3,000 acres of derelict land.': [9].

The implication is that the arrival of the GLC has provided better control of mineral workings. The publication referred to fails to say how much damage was done before the 1947 Town and Country Planning Act or subsequent legislation nor why planners acting for the GLC rather than local boroughs should have had greater motivation or powers to control gravel workings. There are steps in the argument which have thus been omitted. In its present form the premise (the existence of the GLC) does not lead to the desired conclusion (greater control over gravel workings).

FALLACY NINE : THE NATURALISTIC FALLACY.

This occurs whenever one tries to define ethical characteristics in non-ethical terms or to deduce ethical propositions from non-ethical ones: [10]. Those who commit this fallacy do so because they specifically assume, wrongly, that ethics is no more than an empirical science: [11].

Consider the following argument, which is a precis of one made by the Rasmussen Committee: [12].

> '(i) All major nuclear reactor accidents are technological and industrial catastrophes, each of which could result in a total of approximately 5,000 additional cancer deaths.
> (ii) All technological and industrial catastrophes, each of which could result in a total of approximately 5,000 additional deaths, are accidents which could cause less than a 1.66 per cent increase in the 300,000 cancer deaths per year.
> (iii) All accidents which cause less than a 1.66 per cent increase in the 300,000 cancer deaths per year are insignificant risks which ought to be taken, in return for economic benefits.
> (iv) All major reactor accidents are insignificant risks which ought to be taken, in exchange for economic benefits.'

The interesting premise, from the point of view of the naturalistic fallacy, is (iii). Here moral acceptability is defined in terms of statistical significance. Consider the following statement from the Rasmussen Committee:

> 'Since US burial of its radioactive wastes within one mile outside the established territorial waters of Great Britain would cause less than a 1.66 per cent increase in cancer deaths per year, this risk ought to be taken.'

So because large short term economic benefits would result for the US from the burial of nuclear wastes, and the risks (especially to the British) are 'statistically insignificant', premise (iii) would suggest that the action would be morally desirable. However, say if we demand that the US bear responsibility for its own nuclear waste, that it should not subject other nationals to any risk, however small, and that those who bear the benefits of any technology should also take the risks.

If premise (iii) is accepted, then we say that as individuals, human beings have no rights to life. Instead only statistically significant numbers of human lives have a moral significance. But if human lives are only important when considered as groups, then we deny the principle of individual rights. Thus the naturalist fallacy can lead to some unpleasant conclusions.

FALLACY TEN : BEGGING THE QUESTION

Or assuming what is to be proved.

Many arguments concerning high-technology industry involve this source of misunderstanding. Generally, politicians think favourably of the benefits both in terms of the local economy and in prestige of attracting newer types of industry. Planners and others may point out the difficulties of defining what a high technology company is. For example, a firm may make a high-technology product but may require a warehouse. What economic spin off comes from this? Or a high-tech firm sells its factory to another company, which is definitely not high-tech. Thus in many ways high technology industrial sites can prove difficult to manage or control. In many arguments with politicians, however, planners may come up against the idealised notion of what the politician *believes* 'high-tech' to be. The question is thus begged by the politician's definition. Clearly one could prove a large number of propositions by a similar method.

FALLACY ELEVEN : PUTTING FORWARD A TAUTOLOGY (SUCH AS THAT TOO MUCH OF THE THING ATTACKED IS BAD) AS IF IT WERE A FACTUAL STATEMENT.

Let us suppose that A and B are arguing about the merits of different kinds of plan. A is a supporter of physically-based plans, while B supports the more modern type of socio-economic based plan. At some stage in the argument A says 'You will admit that too much attention in a plan to social and economic matters is a bad thing'. B feels at something of a disadvantage. He is asked to admit a proposition that seems damaging to his case, and yet realises that it is a purely verbal proposition, since it says nothing factual at all. The meaning of 'too much' is 'a quality so great that it is a bad thing'. It is indeed a tautology. That is, it is a verbal statement of the form 'X is X'. While a tautology cannot reasonably be denied, it also cannot be said to prove anything. This trick can be dealt with by pointing out that the statement is necessarily true from its verbal form.

FALLACY TWELVE : THE USE OF A SPECULATIVE ARGUMENT.

By speculative thinking, man has created pure mathematics. But speculative argument has not helped him to advance his understanding of the natural or social sciences. While speculative thinking is by no means completely absent from discussions of practical matters, it is mainly in those questions of a semi-philosophical nature where speculative argument is at its most dangerous: [13].

Consider the statement:

> 'Green belts act both as a lung to help the city to breathe, and as a corset to prevent it from sprawling.'

Both analogies (lung, corset) are misleading. Thanks to clean air legislation the air in cities is not heavily polluted now. Moreover, the cleanliness of city air is unaffected by the use to which the Green Belt is put (so long as present controls are obeyed). So the lung analogy is clearly misleading. Also in practice cities spready beyond their green belts - something that people obviously cannot do with corsets! So the corset analogy is wrong too.

FALLACY THIRTEEN : THE USE OF A CONTRAST WHICH IGNORES A CONTINUOUS SERIES OF POSSIBILITIES BETWEEN THE TWO EXTREMES PRESENTED.

Within the planning world we find properties which show continuous variation. Yet we find this property obscured by the use of words implying sharp distinctions. 'Long term' and 'short term', 'optimistic' and 'pessimistic', 'radical' and 'conservative' can all be used to describe extreme kinds of plan. But many possibilities exist between these extremes.

An argument, therefore, which begins in some such way as follows: 'We must distinguish between whether a plan is short or long term, and a long term plan is one which has a horizon of more than ten years...' is an over-simplification. Some aspects of the plan may be extremely long term. Many aspects may have an unclear completion date. Some aspects may be for immediate implementation. And furthermore the timescale may not be the relevant dimension to choose, to explain something about the plan.

This kind of over-simplifying argument is best dealt with by refusing to accept either alternative, but pointing to the fact of the continuity which the person using the argument has ignored. Since this may appear over-subtle to an opponent using the argument, it may be strengthened by pointing out that the argument is the same as that of saying 'Is this paper black or white?' when it is, in fact, a shade of grey.

FALLACY FOURTEEN : THE 'CATCH-22' TRICK.

Often people who have been caught by this trick accuse their opponents of having changed the rules, or 'moving the goalposts'. A good example is when developers are told their application is premature pending (a) a plan for the area or (b) comprehensive development of the area. In (a), 'moving the goalposts' is the same as promising a date for a plan, and then postponing the plan. This can go on indefinitely. In (b), however 'comprehensive' the developer tries to make his proposal, the local authority can always expand their definition of 'comprehensive development'.

FALLACY FIFTEEN : ILLEGITIMATE USE OF OR DEMAND FOR DEFINITION.

Anyone defining 'local needs' as needs arising from expansion of rural employment activities is defining his terms badly.

But also the device of badgering one's opponent to define his terms may sometimes be a piece of crooked argumentation, since it may be an invitation to him to over-simplify his case unjustly compared to the complexity of the facts under discussion. The best way out of such a corner is to refuse to make an inevitably brief formal definition, but to use some other method of making your meaning clear.

For example, if we were asked to define 'local needs' in a Structure Plan, we could make an appropriately vague answer 'elements of need which are generated at the local level and which could not be predicted at the time of preparing the plan'. Giving a catalogue of all instances of local needs might be disastrous since we might miss something out. But the easiest answer, by far, and one which avoids any chance of omissions, is to give an example - say - 'an example of local needs is where a farmer wants to build himself a bungalow on his land and hand his farm on to his son'.

FALLACY SIXTEEN : THE USE OF QUESTIONS DRAWING OUT DAMAGING ADMISSIONS.

One device that depends upon suggestion is when the answer is dictated by the question. Most simply this happens when the question suggests its own answer. Suppose you are at an examination in public, representing a County Council's Structure Plan. The County Council has a transportation policy which encourages public transport and discourages new road and multi-storey car park building. The barrister representing the District in which is situated the main county town is pressing for more car parks to be built there. He argues that the town's prosperity depends on car-owners being able to drive in and park easily.

He asks 'Surely you accept that we must keep this town prosperous?' Obviously the answer is dictated by the question. You cannot deny that you wish the town to prosper. But you can point out that congestion in the town may be just as much a deterent to prosperity as the discouragement of unlimited use of the private car.

FALLACY SEVENTEEN : CREATING A SMOKESCREEN TO BLUR AN ISSUE ON WHICH ONE'S ARGUMENTS ARE WEAK.

In criminal cases juries are more heavily influenced by evidence which, while not very conclusive in establishing innocence or guilt, at least has the advantage of not being contradicted by other evidence, than evidence which, while conclusive in establishing guilt or innocence, has been questioned or contradicted in some way.

Similarly planning arguments which are clear and understandable have more force than ones about which there are connections of an obscure nature, or where the logic, assumptions, or relevance have been questioned: [14]. It is therefore a great advantage to be able to lay a smokescreen around one's opponents' strongest arguments.

Such a device was employed by the appellants at the Fullers Earth public inquiry at Aspley Heath, Bedfordshire, in November 1976. The appellants' application for permission to mine Fullers Earth had been refused by Bedfordshire County Council and the matter had gone to a public inquiry. Although a matter very relevant to the local residents was noise, the appellants succeeded in making the aspect of noise one which was obscure and inconclusive:

> 'The debate on standards, corrections, and measurement of noise was esoteric and inconclusive. The local interests argued that average measurements failed to account for individual variations

> in susceptibility to noise levels. Residents in the area were liable to be sensitive to any new noise intrusion. The consultant for the local interests made the somewhat gratuitous observation that "There is no doubt, therefore, that the only way to reduce the possibility of noise nuisance from the proposed workings to zero is to refuse them"': [15].

Thus the appellants were able to undermine any sensible attempts to define an acceptable noise level, and thus were able to show the residents as being against a rise in noise levels of any kind whatsoever.

FALLACY EIGHTEEN : CIRCULAR ARGUMENTS.

The general form of the argument in a circle is 'If A then B, if B then C, if C then A'. The most frequent circular arguments in social and policy science arise from poorly constructed social surveys which give the results that the survey designer wants. The process then reduces to the circular form : The survey results are determined by the (poorly constructed) hypothesis; the hypotheses are validated by the survey results.

Circular arguments often come into play when attempting to understand an obscure human behaviour such as migration or choice of shopping centre. It is sometimes argued, for example, that migration is relatively unusual because the stronger motive (to stay in the same place) overcomes the impulse to migrate. If we further ask how we know that the impulse to stay in the same place was stronger the reply is that it must be because that is the behaviour that actually took place.

> 'Perhaps the most obvious example is the forecasts made by urban planners of traffic demands which, by extending the network of roads for the benefit of the private motorist, helps to prove the forecasts right.': [16]

In arguing the importance of logical arguments in this chapter we are not making a claim that planners should use arguments which are more logical than other professionals or the lay public. But by stating, in the previous chapter, that arguments should not be suppressed in plans, we are saying that since arguments should play an important role in the presentation of plans (and the justification of decisions) those arguments would be better the fewer the number of logical fallacies contained in them: [17].

It might be thought that logical argument could be raised to the status of ultimate evaluation method, so that the plan with the most perfectly and logically argued reasoning would be accorded the highest evaluation. Unfortunately this cannot begin to be the case: [18]. A plan may be perfectly argued but may address the wrong issues, or may accord too much weight to a consideration which is in fact valueless: [19]. Logical argument, or at least the avoidance of logical errors, is merely one among many reasons why a plan has merit: [20].

NOTES

[1] G. Cronkite, Persuasion : Speech and Behavioural Change, Bobbs Merrill, New York, 1969; H. London, P.J. Meldman, and A. Van.C. Lanckton, 'The jury method : how the persuader persuades', Public Opinion Quarterly, Vol.34, pp.171-83; B. Danet, "The language of persuasion in bureaucracy : 'modern' and 'traditional' appeals to the Israel customs authorities", American Sociological Review, Vol.36, October 1971, pp.847-59.

[2] J.H. Johnson, 'The logic of speculative discourse : guidelines for decision-makers', Environment and Planning B, Vol.9, 1982, pp.15-32.

[3] R.J. Fogelin, Understanding Arguments : an Introduction to Informal Logic, Harcourt, Brace and Jovanovich Inc., New York, 1978; R.H. Thouless, Straight and Crooked Thinking, Pan, 1968; W.L. Brembeck and W.S. Howell, Persuasion : a Means of Social Control, New York, Prentice Hall Inc., 1953. Many of the fallacies are taken from Thouless.

[4] For criticisms of the use of 'what is normal' in moral justification see K.S. Shrader-Frechett, Nuclear Power and Public Policy, Reidel, Dordrecht, 1980, pp.143-51.

[5] The Electricity Council, The Need for Nuclear Energy, 1980, pp.15-16.

[6] The public however makes its own mind up about risk. Unfortunately this often is a rather bigotted mind. For example, a public inquiry on the siting of a nuclear power station recently heard evidence that the responsible government agency had instituted safety precautions for each of the twenty different ways in which radioactivity could trickle into the underlying rocks. The audience was not reassured, because the fact that safety measures were being taken was less interesting to it than the fact that there were twenty things that could go wrong : B.L. Cohen, 'Perspectives on the nuclear debate', Bulletin of the Atomic Scientists, Vol.30, No.9, 1974, pp.35-39.

[7] For a criticism of the argument that what is normal is good see G.E. Moore, Principia Ethica, University Press, Cambridge, 1951, p.43 and p.58; D.C. Anderson, 'Policy Riddle : Ecology vs the Economy' in Environment and Society, R.T. Roelofs, J.N. Crowley, D.L. Hardesty (eds), Prentice-Hall, Englewood Cliffs, 1974, p.148.

[8] K. Mellanby, 'An environmentalist's case for the Sizewell PWR', New Scientist, 13 January, 1983, p.87.

[9] Greater London Council, Planning for the Future of London : Minerals Planning, 1982.

[10] The reader is invited to consider whether the following discussion of the application of utilitarian method to planning comprises a form of the naturalist fallacy. See also A. MacIntyre, 'Utilitarianism and Cost-Benefit Analysis', in Values in the Electric Power Industry, K. Sayre (ed.), University Press, Notre Dame, 1977, p.217.

[11] The following section is based upon K.S. Shrader-Frechette, Nuclear Power and Public Policy, Reidel, Dordrecht, 1980, Chapter 6.

[12] US Nuclear Regulations Commission, Reactor Safety Study - an Assessment of Accident Risks in US Commercial Nuclear Power

Plants, Report No.WASH-1400, NUREG-75/014, Government Printing Office, Washington DC, 1975.

[13] See B. Barry, 'On analogy', Political Studies, Vol.XXIII, Nos.2 and 3, 1975, pp.208-24.

[14] This provided part of the advice by the Bedfordshire County Secretary to the Chairman, Environmental Services Committee, 22 Oct. 1976 : 'A limited case presented solidly and well is usually more effective than one presented on a broader front, some salients of which are too weak to withstand pressure', quoted in A. Blowers, The Limits of Power, Pergamon, 1978, p.61.

[15] A. Blowers, 1978, op.cit., p.61.

[16] H. Glennerster, 'From containment to conflict? Social planning in the Seventies', Journal of Social Policy, Vol.10, No.1, 1981 pp.31-51.

[17] For a use of the above type of analysis in the field of the law, see W.T. Murphy and R.W. Rawlings, 'After the ancien regime : the writing of judgements in the House of Lords, 1979-1980', Modern Law Review, Vol.44, 1981, p.617.

[18] For an analysis of the differences between political and scientific arguments see H. Garfinkel, 'The rational properties of scientific and common-sense activities', pp.53-74 in A. Giddens (ed.), Positivism and Sociology, Heinemann, 1974; E.F. Miller, 'Metaphor and Political Knowledge', American Political Science Review, 1980, Vol.73, pp.155-70.

[19] Logical analysis of political arguments merely serves the purpose of suggesting that other factors are at work. For example, Zebroski observed that opponents of nuclear power often interpret intense efforts to reduce nuclear risks as evidence that the risks are great, not as a sign that technologists are responsive to the public's concern : E.L. Zebroski, 'Attainment of balance in risk-benefit perceptions', in D. Okrent (ed.) Risk-benefit methodology and application : some papers presented at the Engineering Foundation Workshop, Asilomar, California, Report ENG-7598, School of Eng. and Applied Science, UCLA, December 1975, pp.633-44. And Nelkin's case history of a nuclear plant siting controversy provides a good example of the inability of technical arguments to change opinions : D. Nelkin, 'The role of experts in a nuclear siting controversy', Bulletin of the Atomic Scientists, 1974, Vol.30, No.9, pp.29-36. Similarly Hall et al., in a number of case studies of different social policies, concluded pessimistically that arguments about policy are only rarely influenced by facts as the major source of evidence : see P. Hall, H. Land, A. Webb, and R.A. Parker, Change, Choice, and Conflict in Social Policy, Heinemann, London, 1975. See also R. Axelrod, 'Argumentation in foreign policy settings', Journal of Conflict Resolution, Vol.21, No.4, 1977, pp.727-56, for a similar conclusion.

[20] For an example and a suggestion that the status and access of participating groups is more important than quality of arguments see J. Simmie, Power, Property, and Corporation, Macmillan, London, 1981, p.188.

15 The underlying assumptions in planning arguments

In the last chapter we investigated some of the logical fallacies which creep into arguments about plans and planning. Another type of criticism of arguments involves criticising the underlying assumptions of the argument used. For example, even if we were to have accepted the logic of the Roskill Commission's decision that Cublington represented the best site for London's third airport, we could still have questioned the underlying assumption (contained in the Terms of Reference to the Roskill Commission) that the site should be within the South East.

So if criticising the logic of arguments contained in plans constitutes the first line of attack, a second line of attack is to question the assumptions upon which those arguments are based.

We shall examine the assumptions underlying arguments by considering the question: 'Should the State recoup land profits?'

ARGUMENT ONE : PRIVATE LAND OWNERS SHOULD KEEP THEIR PROFITS FROM LAND, BECAUSE THEY HAVE A NATURAL RIGHT TO THEIR PROFITS.

The assumption here is 'he who generates wealth should keep it'. The problem with this argument is that land prices rise because of more than merely the efforts of the owners of that land. If a person owns a plot of land on the outskirts of a town, his land may rise in value because the whole town has grown in population and prosperity. So if we truly wish to explore the implications of this assumption, we could say that it is the community which generated the wealth, and therefore that it has a right to take the profit from the land and share it out.

ARGUMENT TWO : THE COMMUNITY SHOULD RECOUP LAND PROFITS BECAUSE IT IS NOT IMPORTANT WHO OWNS THE PLOT OF LAND, BUT WHO OCCUPIES IT.

The assumption here is that one should accept squatters' rights. The problem with this assumption is that if one had such a system, it would, for example, not be worthwhile improving rented housing, because tenants would enjoy squatters' rights. Also it would lead to a situation where the owner of a piece of land or property would be frightened to leave it, in case it was invaded by squatters.

ARGUMENT THREE : PRIVATE LANDOWNERS SHOULD NOT RETAIN THEIR PROFITS BECAUSE OF THE NASTY MEANS SOME OF THEM USE TO MAXIMISE THEIR PROFITS.

This argument was prevalent in the early sixties, and in the 1964 general election Mr Wilson made it the object of one of his strongest speeches, creating the vision of the nasty property developer who was pushing small businesses and poor tenants out of twilight areas in order to enable comprehensive town centre redevelopment to take place. Some landlords used methods such as breaking tenants' windows at night in order to frighten them to leave. The assumption here is that if an end requires a bad means (the nasty methods of getting tenants off property) then the end is bad too. However, this argument is faulty. There are many possible means to any given end. Town centre redevelopment or the operations of the private property sector can be regulated and controlled to ensure that such underhand practices are not carried out. For example, tenants could be given more security of tenure or greater legal protection.

ARGUMENT FOUR : THE EXTENT TO WHICH THE COMMUNITY RECOUPS LAND PROFITS SHOULD DEPEND ON THE EXTENT TO WHICH THIS AFFECTS LAND SELLING AND BUYING ADVERSELY.

One assumption we would need to make concerns the relationship between the percentage of land profits taken by the State and the extent of landowners refusing to sell land. Another assumption we would have to make is about the extent to which landowners would desist from land transactions until a change of government restored the right of landowners to all their profits. These are assumptions which can only be explored by carrying out a profits tax and seeing what effect it has. Another assumption we would have to make is whether such a policy would undermine investors' confidence by the removal of predictableness. Presumably the degree of warning and of compensation is relevant here. Another assumption we would have to make is whether or not recouping land profits was fair. One individual may have invested all his money in land while the next individual may have invested his money in some other asset. The first individual may feel unfairly treated. Another assumption we would have to make would be whether or not recouping land profits was popular. Presumably we would exempt private home sales from our policy since the majority of homes are now privately owned.

ARGUMENT FIVE : THE COMMUNITY SHOULD RECOUP LAND PROFITS IN A MANNER WHICH IS PROGRESSIVE OVER TIME.

Perhaps there would be say a forty per cent profits tax at first and this might rise to one hundred per cent at a stated later date. This would encourage landowners to sell, overcoming some previous objections. But one result of a profits tax which got higher over time would be that private landowners would sell but they would not be prepared to buy. This virtually means that the State is left in the position of having to buy land and to form ever increasing land banks. Thus this argument makes two assumptions. Firstly it assumes that such a large financial outlay by the State is justified. Secondly it assumes that private landowners can obtain a just price bearing in mind that the State becomes a monopoly buyer.

ARGUMENT SIX : THE ECONOMIC COSTS OF THE STATE'S RECOUPING LAND PROFITS CAN BE COMPARED WITH THE SOCIAL BENEFITS.

One problem we will face is that our intervention into the land sector will have economic costs. Either the State will have to buy up large land banks or the taxing of land sales will have interfered with the smooth running of the market in some ways. So there is an economic loss. But the benefits will all be social ones. Profiteering by developers will be eradicated, and land use zoning and control will be governed by more strictly rational principles than before. The assumption is thus that economic costs and social benefits can be compared. Perhaps if the private market develops a town expansion then it will be developed quickly but the standard of design may be at a minimum. If the local authority carries out the development it may be slower for lack of money, but the aesthetic quality may be higher. The problem is to weigh these consequences against one another. At present, if the local authority prevents a developer developing a site in the way the developer wishes, he can serve a purchase notice on the local authority. It means in effect 'I give up - you buy the land'. The local authority, if it is preventing him developing the land profitably, must in law buy the land from him. Unfortunately local authorities currently are not rich enough to buy land often in this way, so the mere threat of a purchase notice means the local authority has often to accept second best. Yet if the local authority had the powers and financial backing to buy large amounts of land and to tax land profits the private land market would not be so fast-moving and efficient as it is at present.

One additional problem about this difficult assumption is that generally the avoidance of harm seems to be more important than the obligation to do good, when it comes to political choice. Suppose the proposal for the State to recoup land profits would greatly impoverish a million people. These people would be small landowners, builders, and building workers. And suppose the proposals would also give a more secure future for a million slum dwellers, for the many tenants of private landlords, and for small businesses in twilight areas.

Now it could be argued that the million people who included the land-owners and those in the building industry could look after themselves. We would be doing good by helping slum-dwellers and others threatened by property developers.

But it seems that politicians act by considering the obligation to avoid doing harm as stronger than the obligation to do good. Generally, the presumption in our society would be against an action which harmed a million people in order to do good to another million people.

This series of examples tries to illustrate that all arguments are based on assumptions. These assumptions are inevitably ones of value. In order to make an argument appear impregnable the assumptions are usually hidden. Yet all arguments have an achilles heel - one or several assumptions which is ultimately justifiable only by a preference for one value rather than another.

We saw in the case study of the West Midlands Structure Plan 1980 that the underlying assumption was that inner urban areas, having more severe problems, should receive most investment. The assumption was that need was important. The Plan however, attempted to hide this assumption by pretending that several competing alternatives had been impartially considered.

Because the planning process is political, it is concerned with the investigation and transforming of values. Values should not be hidden, but should be openly discussed in order that public reactions may be more intelligent: [1].

One unfortunate consequence of hidden assumptions in plans is that such assumptions inevitably influence data collection and forecasting: [2]. General criticisms, for example, have been made about the implicit assumptions made in transportation studies: [3], about the fact that such studies have an in-built bias in favour of the motor car: [4], and about the fact that land use and transportation relationships will not change much in the future: [5].

In order to approach our central topic, that of the values and processes used by planners, and the complex relationship between values and processes, the next chapter will investigate how planning arguments are used in the resolution of conflicts between several participants.

NOTES

[1] 'It is impossible to say how much of the unnecessary slavery of the world is due to the conceptions that moral issues can be settled without conscience or human sentiment apart from consistent study of facts and application of specific knowledge in industry, law, and politics...' : J. Dewey, Human Nature and Conduct, The Modern Library, New York, 1922, p.12.

[2] D.N.M. Starkie, Transportation Planning and Public Policy, 1973 Progress in Planning Series, Vol.1, Part 4, Oxford, Pergamon Press, p.346.

[3] M. Roberts, An Introduction to Town Planning Techniques, 1974, London, Hutchinson, p.384.

[4] M. Roberts, op.cit, p.382.

[5] M.J. Bruton, 'Transport in Planning', in M.J. Bruton (ed.) The Spirit and Purpose of Planning, 1974, Hutchinson, London, p.183.

16 The use of planning arguments where there are several participants

Advocacy is the advancing of arguments on behalf of one participant in a situation where there are several competing or conflicting participants. It is by definition not impartial, but partisan. In such a situation the planner is caught on the horns of a dilemma : he has usually been trained to see the benefits of a comprehensive vision, perceiving and understanding the advantages and disadvantages of a proposal to all groups in society. Yet he is also an official in a local authority which has its own peculiar, partisan point of view: [1]. He has to somehow use his ability to employ the language and vision of comprehensiveness to argue a partisan case.

Such a case should present the strengths (i.e. the strongest arguments) of the planner's local authority. It should also present his opponents' weaknesses (i.e. their weakest arguments). The planner should obviously anticipate what his opponents' arguments are going to be: [2].

Usually, in the British context, an advocacy case should take account of the fact that it is to be read by civil servants in the Department of the Environment. If the advocacy case is presented at the Examination in Public of a Structure Plan, or at an appeal or Local Inquiry, then the Planning Inspector will be one of these civil servants. The advocacy statement should therefore take account of the strengths and weaknesses (or preoccupations) of the Planning Inspectorate, the DOE Division which will make the final recommendation to the Secretary of State for the Environment. It should therefore provide the Inspector with reasons why, if he were to agree with it, he would not be liable to criticism of delay, ineffectiveness, or inconsistency (see table later). And it should bear in mind that the Inspector must be seen to be impartial between conflicting groups.

Impartiality requires more detailed explanation. The Inspector wishes to take a total view of the issues, and so will favour advocacy statements which take the majority of the public into account. He will also applaud arguments of fact rather than of opinion, that is, arguments supported by evidence. He will also incline towards arguments supported by a majority of the groups involved (though this is not always possible). He will become suspicious of arguments which are not logical or internally consistent, such as self-contradictions or circular arguments, or of arguments which are founded upon unjustified assumptions. His suspicion may also be aroused by arguments guided by ulterior motives. We define these as arguments stemming not from a participant's strengths but from his preoccupations: [3], (see table later).

In order to make a publicly-available advocacy statement you also need to be clear about where your authority's interest lies. This can be best dealt with by preparing an internal document, an advocacy strategy. This is not for anybody's consumption but merely is to be read within your local authority. It is therefore not a 'public report' but a summary of 'where we go from here', estimating, in the light of the known procedures and organisational and political relationships how best to further your local authority's interests, (defined in the following table as its preoccupation), over a period of time in the future. The strategy will therefore include, (a) a list of forthcoming or possible relevant events and (b) what to do when and if they occur. In the British context, many of these events will involve interaction between County and District.

CASE STUDY : DEVELOPMENT AT STRETTON-ON-DUNSMORE IN WARWICKSHIRE.

Stretton-on-Dunsmore is a picturesque commuter village about ten miles south-east of Coventry. Here is a summary of the main relevant events which occurred prior to November 1978.

(i) In the original Warwickshire Structure Plan submission in 1971 Rugby, (near to which Stretton-on-Dunsmore is situated) was to expand relatively substantially both in employment and population terms, in order to accommodate migrants and jobs from Coventry. The Minister considered jobs moving to Rugby would be unlikely, leaving a commuting problem. So he scaled down the growth of Rugby to a 'natural increase' rate.

(ii) In doing this he was saying that Coventry should do much more than it had previously done to solve its own population growth problems by finding land both within and on the periphery of the city. Some of the peripheral sites subsequently suggested by Coventry (for example to the south of Coventry) threaten the pleasant rural character of Warwickshire; Warwickshire County opposed this, to the extent that land to the south of Coventry is deadlocked. Both the Minister and Warwickshire have suggested land in the Green Belt on the Birmingham side of Coventry but Coventry feel that this might be the thin end of the wedge in starting a much larger erosion of the Green Belt between Coventry and Birmingham. So this land has been deadlocked too. The only other large area of suitable land for Coventry's expansion is to the east of the city, and in fact all the parties concerned: Coventry, Warwickshire and the Minister agree that this is a good site for peripheral expansion of Coventry. However, this site can only be developed once the line of the Eastern Bypass round Coventry (which will eventually form the eastern boundary of the site) has been agreed. But in 1978 the line of the bypass had not yet been agreed. Because of these factors Coventry had not been able to solve its expansion problem in the 1970s, and pressures have developed to such an extent that builders see it as worthwhile applying for planning permission to build houses near Rugby for Coventry commuters, and also to go through the expensive procedure of appealing against the refusal of such a planning permission.

(iii) This has created a situation where there is a Structure Plan (Warwickshire) which only accepts natural increase (i.e. a population increase only resulting from births in Rugby rather than one due to in-migration) in the Rugby area, and yet where pressure for housing (and for that matter industrial) development has been increasing in the Rugby area as a result of Coventry's failure to expand.

(iv) This type of situation, where the policy (the Structure Plan) is stated one way (no growth except natural increase) and where actual trends are occurring in another way (strong pressures for Rugby to take jobs and especially new immigrant population because of constraints on growth at Coventry) is one of 'policy stress'. The no growth policy at Rugby had assumed growth (of a peripheral nature) at Coventry, but this assumption was wrong. This is the first evidence of how, in the rural area around Rugby, the Structure Plan of Warwickshire was undergoing policy stress.

(v) For the past twenty years Warwickshire County Council has followed a policy of encouraging most population growth in 'Key settlements'. These are those settlements with the transport and other facilities (such as schools and suitable land) considered appropriate for enabling a certain amount of growth. The Warwickshire Structure Plan approved in 1975 provides for future growth in the rural areas of the County at a rate not substantially exceeding that of the population's natural increase. Such growth is to take place, mainly in Key settlements of which 2 categories are defined. Stretton-on-Dunsmore is identified as a secondary category settlement, suited to modest development in the range of 100 to 500 persons. From the approval of the Structure Plan until now, however, no growth has occurred in Stretton.

(vi) When the Minister approved the Warwickshire County Council's proposals for its Green Belt, he indicated various 'white areas' within the Green Belt within which development would be allowed. There is a 'white area' around Stretton allowing for further development.

(vii) So both the Warwickshire County Council's Key settlement policy and the Minister's allowance of 'white areas' within the Green Belt allow for a limited amount of growth at Stretton. However since 1975, when the Structure Plan was approved, several pieces of evidence came to light which, without going into the details here, suggest that both Stretton and Wellesbourne could not really be justified due to their low level of transport and other facilities as Key settlements, while Wolston (which had not been designated a key settlement) could be justified as one. This is the second piece of evidence of how certain facts were accumulating since 1975 to suggest that in the rural area around Rugby the Structure Plan was suffering policy stress. In fact Warwickshire County Council undertook a review of their County Structure Plan Rural Settlement Policy in 1979.

(viii) In 1978 Bryant Homes Limited submitted an application for planning permission for the building of 55 houses on 'white land' in the village of Stretton. The application was an outline one (i.e. an application 'in principle' rather than a 'detailed' application) and was submitted to Rugby Borough Council. Although the application was made in outline, Bryant Homes Limited submitted plans with the application which showed details of proposed access arrangements to Plott Lane (in Stretton), for proposed foul and surface water sewers in Plott Lane, and for a proposed surface water sewer in the vicinity of Church Hall. The fact that these three proposals were on land outside the site referred to in the application raised legal and procedural problems which will be mentioned later.

(ix) It is open to a planning authority, such as Rugby Borough Council in this case, to approve or refuse planning permission. Of if it has given no decision within eight weeks (with certain exceptions) it is in law 'deemed' (assumed) that a refusal of planning permission has been given. The latter course of action was the one Rugby Borough Council chose, subsequent to which Bryant Homes Limited appealed to the Minister (the Secretary of State for the Environment) against the deemed refusal.

(x) The Plans Sub-Committee of Rugby Borough Council considered the application at its meeting on 31 May 1978 and resolved that, had an appeal not been made, the Council would have refused planning permission for the following reasons:-

> '(a) The foul sewage system at Stretton-on-Dunsmore to which the proposed development would drain is overloaded, and work also needs to be carried out to the foul pumping station. It is considered that the proposed development is unacceptable at the present time since it will increase the amount of foul flow within the existing sewerage system.
>
> (b) It is considered that the present proposal is premature in that the County Council are currently undertaking a review of the County Structure Plan Rural Settlement Policy and this will include a re-assessment of the rate of growth in the rural area, the need to accommodate further development and a reappraisal of the scale proposed, at the present time, could be prejudicial to the review of the Rural Settlement Policy and any revised policies and proposals that may arise from this review.'

Besides this Rugby made it plain that the application would also have been refused on several other grounds had the above reasons not been considered the most telling.

(xi) This was not, however, Warwickshire's verdict. At the request of Rugby Borough Council, the Warwickshire County Council's Planning Sub-Committee considered the proposed development of the appeal site on 4 May 1978 and resolved:

'That the Rugby Borough Council be informed that the County Council consider that, until the Key settlement policy in the Warwickshire Structure Plan is reviewed, the appropriate grounds for refusing this application relate to the current problems of foul sewerage provision and the disposal of storm water and that the County Council consider that, given the satisfactory solution of these problems, planning permission should be granted on a subsequent application.'

(xii) So, Warwickshire was saying that the current review of the key settlement policy was not a material (relevant) consideration, while Rugby was saying that it was.. Also, Warwickshire was indicating that even though this application might fall on foul sewerage and storm water drainage problems, a subsequent application, once Bryant Homes Limited had ironed out these difficulties, should be approved.

(xiii) The circumstances under which two planning authorities with overlapping functions can come to opposed conclusions on a case are not uncommon in the planning world. Indeed, it might be argued that the fact that decisions are finally made within them by councillors taking conflicting political interests into account leads one to expect it to be the norm. In this case, certainly, there were 'rural Conservative' pressures within Rugby Borough Council against the application. And, as was pointed out above, Warwickshire was also undergoing a 'wind of change' in its approach to its Key settlement policy, tending it to be more critical of the Key settlement status of Stretton.

(xiv) Because Bryant Homes Limited had appealed against Rugby Borough Council's refusal of planning permission, a public inquiry was held on 29 November 1978. The Inspector's report on the public inquiry agreed with Warwickshire County Council's case and was generally in favour of the appellants, Bryant Homes Limited. However, the fact that the proposals Bryant Homes had made for sewerage, surface drainage and surface water sewerage were on land outside the site on which application was made (and therefore on land outside of Bryant Homes' control) made him decide to recommend dismissal of the appeal (i.e. a recommendation against Bryant Homes). On this last point which swung the Inspector towards dismissal of the appeal there was a further appeal fought in the High Court by Bryant Homes.

At the appeal by Bryant Homes Ltd in November 1978 there were eight principal protagonists:

(i) Warwickshire County Council

(ii) Rugby District Council

(iii) Stretton-on-Dunsmore Parish Council

(iv) Stretton Old People's Club

(v) Coventry Trades Council

(vi) Warwickshire Estate Agents Association

(vii) Warwickshire Branch of the National Farmers Union

(viii) Bryant Homes Ltd, (the appellants).

Warwickshire County Council has for many years successfully defended itself against large scale expansion of Coventry southwards towards the high class commuter areas of Kenilworth, Warwick, and Leamington Spa. At the same time, in order to provide for some local grouping of social facilities, the County, until 1982, maintained a Key Settlement Policy.

Rugby District Council disliked the County's interference in what it considered to be its own affairs. Partly this may have been playing to the gallery for the benefit of its own voters. Partly it may have been a perception of the way things were going in central government thinking on District-County relations. At that time the Conservative Government was considering ways of making local government more cost-effective and efficient. At the time of the inquiry (1979) one of the matters being discussed was the thorny subject of County-District conflicts. These occur, in general, for mainly two reasons. First, Districts would often prefer to be autonomous and therefore not answerable to the County in which they are located. They would often prefer all County functions to be handed to Districts. Secondly, some functions are 'shared' (if this is not too optimistic a use of the word) by both County and the Districts located within it. For example, in the town planning function, the County prepared the Structure Plan, and decided 'major' applications for planning permission to develop land (this development control function was later curtailed to include only minerals and waste disposal applications). The Districts prepared Local Plans for much smaller areas than the Structure Plan, which must be 'in accordance with the Structure Plan', and they also decided (as at November 1979) 'minor' applications for planning permission to develop land (for example, for 20 houses or less). Counties could also prepare Urban Structure Plans, as Warwickshire had done for the Rugby area. These functions are often a bone of contention, with County and District pulling in different directions.

In Rugby District's case, even if it had lost the Bryant's appeal it would still have wanted to develop a general strategy of undermining (where it saw fit and where it had reasonable grounds to do so) and discrediting the County's policies, because it wanted more autonomy and less overlapping of powers with the County. Also, since a vocal member of Rugby District Council was a Stretton-on-Dunsmore resident, it wanted to echo the view of the Stretton villagers.

As mentioned above, the Secretary of State for the Environment (on behalf of his cabinet colleagues) was at the time of the inquiry (November 1979) considering ways of making local government more efficient and less costly, and therefore wished to simplify the planning system. The tide was swinging towards the Districts getting all development controls except for mineral workings and waste disposal.

It was therefore in Rugby District's interest to 'play it long', to create delays, and to discredit and undermine County policies, including the very idea of long term or strategic County Structure Plans. But this had to be done discretely or officials in the Department of the Environment would use such indiscretions as signs of irresponsibility in their battle to prevent any change in the planning system.

The Stretton-on-Dunsmore Parish Council is a broad-based body representing residents' opinions in the village. These opinions concern a general fear that drainage problems would be caused by any large scale development in the village, and also, though most residents were not born in the village, a general fear that house prices would fall if development were to take place.

The Stretton Old People's Club wants better public transport and better social facilities within the village. It represents the oldest and most established village residents and thus has some claim to public sympathy.

The Coventry Trades Council is a body formed from delegates from trade unions in Coventry. It would like to see more homes for the working class family made available in the County. It argued that restrictive planning policies raise land and house prices and that these squeeze working class families out of rural areas.

The Warwickshire Estate Agents Association put forward its aims as the adequate servicing of private development. It felt that in the past individual houses or estate developments had not been properly planned. The problem was not that houses in themselves spoil villages or the countryside, but that they are not properly designed.

The Warwickshire Branch of the National Farmers' Union had a brief from its national parent body to put the arguments against encroachment on to our ever-dwindling stock of good agricultural land. The problem, it said, was that good agricultural land is mostly in the lowland, flat, well drained areas near our cities, where there are also strong pressures for urban development. We already import over half our food needs, and there is a possibility in the event of a growing world population, of food replacing energy as the highly priced commodity of the next generation. Therefore land must be regarded as a national resource, and its allocation seen as a strategic and not a local issue.

Bryant Homes Ltd is a medium-sized building firm with a track record of building houses that people want. Their knowledge of the market had led them to identify the area south-east of Coventry as that where local demand was strongest.

The actual interplay of arguments could now be simulated to demonstrate what we consider to be the best way of presenting each of these participants' cases. Instead however, we shall briefly present a table of each participant's strengths and weaknesses and preoccupations.

TABLE: REASONS FOR RELEVANCE OF ARGUMENTS : PREOCCUPATIONS, WEAKNESSES, AND STRENGTHS : STRETTON CASE STUDY.

Actors	Preoccupations	Weaknesses	Strengths
DOE	<u>EFFICIENCY</u> Reduce complexity of town planning (cost cutting, cost-effectiveness). Reduce District County conflicts.	<u>UNCERTAINTY</u> (i) At present reviewing the functions of Districts and Counties. (ii) Government has its own voters tc think of (many live in rural areas). (iii) Market orientation of new Tory government.	
DOE Inspectorate	<u>EXPEDITIOUSNESS</u> Bring a long case to end.	<u>DELAY LACK OF EFFECTIVENESS INCONSISTENCY</u> (i) Must be consistent with previous decision (precedent). (ii) Must show Minister that appeal system works and that not too costly. (iii) The delay argument by builders.	<u>IMPARTIALITY</u> Impartial decision rules.
Rugby District	<u>AUTONOMY</u> (i) Dislikes the County's interference in its own affairs (voters). (ii) Placate Stretton voters.	<u>IRRESPONSIBILITY</u> (i) 681 houses permitted in rural area of Rugby district in contradiction to Key settlement policy; so why should they be perceived as 'responsible'? (ii) Large proportion of Stretton residents themselves commuting recent immigrants.	<u>POLICY NOT BINDING TILL REVIEW FAIRNESS LOCAL NEED PREVIOUS APPEAL DECISION NOT A PRECEDENT</u> (i) County's Key settlement policy inadequate. (ii) The local need argument. (iii) Change since previous decision-demand in Rugby District slackened since last decision (USP) and provision made principally in Rugby town (not rural area). (iv) Possibility of having powers over all development control in future.

Actors	Preoccupations	Weaknesses	Strengths
Warwick-shire County	JUSTIFY CONTAINMENT The need for policy justification to 'contain' demand for commuter housing in rural part of county, (voters).	INCONSISTENCY Inconsistency in Key settlement policy.	SABOTAGE POLICIES BINDING TILL REVIEW Key settlement policy inconsistency due to District sabotage. Key settlement not 'irretrievably' broken down and thus can wait till review published.
Stretton Parish Council	ANTI-GROWTH House prices might fall if exclusive rural character lost. FEAR Fear that poor servicing or drainage might damage the village physically.	SELFISHNESS Many villagers have moved in recently and now want to 'pull the ladder up after themselves'. IGNORANCE Ignorance of strategic issues.	UNITY-MAJORITY KNOWLEDGE Knowledge of local details (e.g. village floods near village green at least once a year). Will development (with its hard surfaces) increase the run-off and cause more flooding?
Stretton Old Peoples' Club	PRO-GROWTH Growth would lead to an increase in the village. Many old people without a car.	MINORITY LONGEST ESTABLISHED RESIDENTS (Many old people were born in Stretton; many younger people are in-migrants.)	SYMPATHY Old people have a claim to sympathetic consideration of their needs. PRECEDENT The designation of Stretton as a Key settlement was partly in order to concentrate services for those who most needed them - the local population, rather than commuters.

Actors	Preoccupations	Weaknesses	Strengths
Coventry Trades Council	ANTI-PLANNING RESTRICTIONS IN RURAL AREAS which raise prices enabling only commuters to afford property and enhancing exclusiveness.	BIAS Suffers from 'political' bias.	REPRESENTATIVENESS The Trades Council represents the whole of Coventry and its hinterland.
Warwick-shire Estate Agents Assoc-iation	PRO-GROWTH Because this would increase their business.	COMMERCIAL BIAS	STANDARDS Interested in adequately serviced development in rural areas.
Warwick-shire NFU	ANTI-GROWTH Planning restric-tions should be supported because they encourage efficient (i.e. higher density) urban development.	SELFISHNESS Farmers make bigger development gains selling their farms for housing when supply of land is limited by planning restrictions.	NATIONAL CONCERN Land for food is of strategic importance. ALTRUISM Many farmers could make development gains if there were no planning restrictions. Despite this they support the NFU policy.
Bryant Homes Ltd	PRO-GROWTH Because of (a) immediate local business advantage (b) possibility of breaching planning policies elsewhere.	COMMERCIAL BIAS	KNOWLEDGE OF HOUSING DEMAND Company has track record of satisfied customers.

This table sets out in an idealised way the main elements that a debate between the participants would take. However, each participant would probably develop also a private strategy, not open to public scrutiny, of how best to further its interests.

Such a private advocacy strategy could contain several approaches. From Rugby District Council's point of view, obstructionism might seem one obvious element. All Districts in England and Wales collect annual rates, part of which are paid to the County for its own provision of services. This part is called the County 'precept'. Thus there is an opportunity for Rugby District Council to create bad publicity for the County, to complain about the size of the County precept, the lack of need for some of its services, the duplication of planning, the inefficient and remote administration of the County, and so on. This is only one example. Others of a more technical nature include the annual Housing Investment Programmes, the Transport Programmes, progress or otherwise on preparing Local Plans (which should 'conform' to the County's Structure Plan), and several other activities.

Another strand in such a private strategy would concern building up more information on one's own strengths and on the weaknesses of one's opponents. Presumably Warwickshire and Rugby could monitor the delays which each is caused by the other tier authority. Presumably the County would seek further evidence of irresponsibility by Rugby District (further to the 681 houses approved in the rural part of Rugby by Rugby District on 'local needs' grounds). Another example might be that, if the appeal found against growth at Stretton, pro-growth groups might wish to monitor the rolls of the new school. Rolls are falling nationally and if the school were found to be underused, growth could again be raised as a 'live issue' on the argument that it would make greater use of facilities (or prevent their future closure). Under its key settlement policy Warwickshire has very recently built a new school in Stretton and if reversal of Stretton's key settlement policy were to lead to the school's closure then the County would be vulnerable to a certain amount of justified criticism.

CONCLUSION

Besides attempting to provide a structured account of how arguments are best employed in a planning conflict: [4], what other relevant points does this example provide? First that despite public claims to comprehensiveness, planners, to gain prestige with other officers within their own authority and to gain the support of councillors in their authority, are constrained inevitably to take a local authority (and thus partisan) view of planning. Secondly, that if plans concentrated more on the analysis and presentation of arguments and values so as to invite intelligent public reaction, planners would be enabled to develop a clientel of support from interested local people to which councillors and other departments would be forced to take notice. And thirdly, that plans would be more robust to change (since they concentrated on presenting all sides of the case with the strengths and weaknesses of their arguments and underlying values) and planners would find themselves less in the difficult position of defending plans which became out of date and inappropriate.

In order to provide some substance behind these ideas, the next five chapters will suggest that, through the relationship of utilitarian values and a disjointed-incrementalist strategy of articulating those values, planners do indeed explore arguments. These arguments in practice serve as the principal means by which they arrive at, and hence evaluate, decisions. These arguments are wholly based on utilitarian values and on disjointed-incrementalist strategies of articulating those values. And such arguments are open to serious objections. But because the evaluation is often not explicit, and because plans avoid discussion of conflicting issues and arguments, these objections are almost never explored.

NOTES

[1] A.J. Catanese, Planners and Local Politics : Impossible Dreams, Sage Publications, Beverley Hills, 1974, p.24.

[2] No claim is being made that this structure is scientifically testable, rather that it may help the reader have a better idea of the considerations which tend toward a particular party winning or losing a case. The extreme, optimistic view, (that winning can be 'predicted') has been put forward in A. Webb, 'Planning Inquiries and Amenity Policy', Policy and Politics, Vol.1, No.1, 1972, p.65.

[3] B. Barry has suggested a classification of arguments into those involving 'privately-oriented wants' (evaluations with oneself and one's family as their object) and 'publicly-oriented wants' (evaluations which benefit others). The problem with this classification is that it ignores the sometimes selfish evaluations of organisations. Barry's classification assumes an atomist view of society - that political conflict can always be reduced to conflict between individuals. See B. Barry, Political Argument, Routledge, London, 1965, p.12.

[4] For a quantitative approach to this question see I. Budge, 'Representations of political argument : applications within meta-planning', Political Studies, Vol.XXVI, No.4, 1978, pp.439-49.

PART III
VALUES IN PLANNING

17 Utilitarianism: an introduction

We have now considered two important properties of arguments in planning - their logic and the assumptions they make. Also we have seen how arguments are used in situations where there are several conflicting participants - the usual state of affairs in planning. And we have seen how plans sometimes elevate the rational-comprehensive strategy above argument in order to seem more rational and convincing.

We now turn to the dominant method for making decisions used in public administration and planning. This method is utilitarianism. It seeks, in any given choice situation, to find that alternative which satisfies the largest number of people and which discomforts the smallest number of people. It therefore concentrates on evaluating consequences of alternatives. Everyone, as a starting point at least, is treated equally.

Suppose we were considering an application to mine a mineral. The applicant might argue that (a) not allowing his application would leave a competitor in a situation of being a monopoly producer in the home market, that (b) if his application is refused we would need to increase imports of the mineral to ensure supplies and (c) that there is uncertainty about the availability of alternative domestic sources of the mineral at such a high quality. These three arguments are about the advantages of his application to society at large. So if we gave everyone equal points and accorded points for the creation of some kind of 'satisfaction', then he would score a large number of points. Now consider the case of opponents of the application. They might argue that (a) the area is a proposed Area of Outstanding Natural Beauty, that (b) a small number of residents would suffer noise and other disturbance, and that (c) the area would be unavailable in its present use, as an area for walking by a somewhat larger number of people. The first argument is about advantages of refusing the application to society at large, the second and third to smaller groups of people. The 'points against' are thus summed accordingly, depending upon the sizes of the groups. While we may not actually do any numerical calculations, we take the relative sizes of the groups into account in our final decision. To help us in our task, we must take account of whether substitutes exist, or whether the advantage or disadvantage suggested is a unique one. Perhaps there are synthetic materials which do just as well as the mineral itself. Perhaps the commodities which the mineral helps to make can be substituted by other commodities. And considering the disadvantages of mining in the area, just how 'unique' or at least 'rare' is a proposed Area of Outstanding Natural Beauty? How rare is housing of the type to be disturbed? How many other recreational areas of this type exist? The last two questions have to be answered in the local context, since those disturbed cannot be expected to live or enjoy recreation a great distance away.

So we have started, in a very general way, to carry out an investigation of costs and benefits of the proposal to extract minerals. There are several problems with this type of investigation. Despite these problems, this utilitarian approach to making decisions is central to planning and public administration as it is currently practiced.

Although utilitarianism began as a nineteenth century political theory, it has received much attention in the last forty years - particularly since the second world war: [1]. During the second world war many analytical methods to technical problems (such as how to organise a convoy) were developed using operations research. Since that time methods have developed, such as systems analysis: [2], to analyse softer, less quantifiable problems: [3]. Notable among these was the advent of welfare economics and cost-benefit analysis. Both represent more rigorous, modernised forms of utilitarianism: [4]. These economic approaches made great headway within planning and public administration in the sixties. They retained much of the quantitative emphasis and mathematical rigour of operations research, while using traditional economic theory. That theory uses the market as the central feature, a market in which individual man is a rational maximiser of satisfactions operating self-interestedly in a situation of relative scarcity. Problems of choice, are perceived as problems of marginal trade-off or exchange among desired outcomes, attributes, or items of welfare. When gains from some outputs (or items of welfare of some individuals) are achieved at the expense of other outputs (or items of welfare of the same or other individuals) there arises the idea of the production-possibility frontier (or transformation curve) as the area of interest of those combinations of outputs (or individual or group states of welfare) which have the property that no gain in any one output can be achieved without some loss in another. To decide which point on the production-possibility frontier ('efficient set') he prefers to all others, a satisfaction-maximising individual constructs a set of indifference curves or surfaces, on each of which the individual is indifferent between alternative combinations of outputs. The indifference curves are assumed to vary continuously with each output (or item of welfare) so that arbitrarily small increments of any output can be traded-off for sufficiently small decreases of any other.

This continuous ability to trade-off is assumed to exist over the entire range of each output, so that very low levels of one output can be compensated for by very high levels of another output. This assumption is justified within the method by the fact that such trade-offs take place between any two outputs along indifference curves which themselves take account of the declining marginal utility of each output to the individual. The rational individual is thus supposed to choose that point on his production-possibility frontier which lies on that point of intersection of all those indifference curves which is farthest away from zero utility.

Imagine now a situation where there is a large number of such individuals. We assume all have perfect information, that bargaining is costless, and that no individual can independently influence group behaviour. Traditional economic theory suggests that the individuals will produce and trade among themselves in such a way that they all have identical marginal rates of substitution for all goods. This process takes place by means of individuals exchanging goods so as to reach a higher indifference curve. Relative prices between goods serve as a measure of the rates of substitution between alternatives. A market in equilibrium, where marginal rates of substitution are equal is one which gives a 'Pareto-optimal' result such that there may exist alternatives which some individuals but <u>not all</u> individuals would prefer to the Pareto-optimal result. In this sense markets are described as 'efficient'.

Traditional economic theory treats efficiency as the fundamental rule of acceptability. Pareto-optimality may be indeterminate since a large number of such solutions may exist. It is also incomplete since it only allows individuals or groups to compare limited sets of alternatives.

The Pareto rule has been modified by what has come to be called the 'Kaldor-Hicks' criterion, under which a change from one social state to another would be considered desirable whenever those who gained from the change could so compensate the losers that, after compensation, the Pareto rule would be satisfied: [5].

The problem for the planner or public administrator choosing between alternative public projects is thus reduced to the technical problem of measurement so that costs and benefits can be compared within some overall metric such as money: [6]. Usually such costs and benefits are those accruing directly to the decision-maker, so that 'externalities' are ignored. Also, in the spirit of the 'Kaldor-Hicks' criterion, an attempt has been made to separate costs and benefits related to efficiency from distributional and other considerations: [7]. Whatever cannot be included within the common metric is usually put on one side: [8].

There are however value choices to be made, since the relevant items of welfare and their associated weights: [9] must be decided upon. These items can then be entered directly into a 'benefits minus cost' calculation, or constraints can be added in a linear programming problem. In the latter case the determination of what constraints are relevant is also a value judgement.

While often the utilitarian method, and in particular its most rigorous variants from welfare economics such as cost-benefit analysis, are used without much regard for uncertainty, some attempts to deal with this problem have been made. One among these has been the notion of expected utility. If an output has a value, and the decision-maker attributes to it a probability, then the actual value of that output - its expected utility - is the product of value and probability: [10]. Another approach has been to model sequences of outputs to take account of the chain of conditional probabilities thus created - which again modify an output's value in the expected way: [11].

Also within planning, where many factors are non-quantifiable in very precise terms, a less rigorous variant of cost-benefit analysis has been developed. This is the goals-achievements matrix. The various goals of a plan are established at the outset and are given weights for relative importance. Then each alternative is ascribed values according to whether goals have been achieved. Care is necessary to ensure that goals are sufficiently precisely stated so that achievement or non-achievement by any alternative can be established. Also goals must be sufficiently comprehensive in their variety to allow for detrimental side-effects of any alternative to come into the calculation.

Although these methods have received much and careful research: [12], there are many questions of an operational nature still unanswered. It is perhaps for this reason that in practice in planning and public administration the utilitarian method is used in its less rigorous form. One of the main sources of disquiet about the use of analytical methods and policy methodologies in planning and public administration has been that such methods claim to be more 'scientific' than they really are: [13]. Underlying the scientific appearance lie a host of philosophical assumptions or practical omissions. It is therefore to these problems that the following few chapters are directed.

NOTES

[1] H.L.A. Hart, 'Are there any natural rights?', pp.53-66 in A. Quinton (ed.), Political Philosophy, Oxford University Press, 1977; D. Braybrooke and C. Lindblom, A Strategy of Decision : Policy Evaluation as a Social Process, Free Press, New York, 1963, pp.147-244; J.J.C. Smart and B. Williams, Utilitarianism : for and against, Cambridge University Press, 1976; B. Barry, 'The Public Interest', pp.112-26 in A. Quinton op.cit.; L. Allison, Environmental Planning : a Political and Philosophical Analysis, G. Allen and Unwin, London, 1975, Chapter 7.

[2] H. Raiffa, Decision Analysis : Introductory Lectures on Choices under Uncertainty, Reading, Massachussets, 1968; J. von Newmann and O. Morgenstern, Theory of Games and Economic Behaviour, Princeton, New Jersey, 1944.

[3] For example, W. Buckley, Modern Systems Research for the Behavioural Sciences, Aldine Press, Chicago, 1968.

[4] The following account of welfare economic theory is based on L.H. Tribe, 'Policy Science : Analysis or Ideology?', Philosophy and Public Affairs, Vol.2, 1972.

[5] A.K. Sen, *Collective Choice and Social Welfare*, San Francisco, California, 1970; I.M.D. Little, *A Critique of Welfare Economics*, London, 1960. The Kaldor-Hicks criterion does not claim to be a complete ordering of all alternative social states (a social welfare function). It has been shown that such a social welfare function is impossible if we assume individual preferences, transitivity, ability to combine any pattern of individual preferences, non-dictatorial preferences, and independence of irrelevant alternatives : K.J. Arrow, *Social Choice and Individual Values*, New Haven, 1963.

[6] A.M. Freeman III, 'Project Design and Evaluation with Multiple Objectives', in *Public Expenditures and Policy Analysis*, R.H. Haveman and J. Margolis (eds), Chicago, 1970.

[7] But

> 'if individual utility functions were allowed to assume strongly interdependent forms (in violation of the assumption of self-interested rationality), then any attempt to separate efficiency concerns from distributional concerns would quickly collapse; indeed, even the concept of Pareto-optimality could then be rendered vacuous (inasmuch as *every* situation might become Pareto-optimal).'; H.L. Tribe, op.cit.

[8] For example, in the Bedford Urban Transporation Study, 1976, certain costs and benefits could not be expressed in monetary terms and these were investigated separately, see A.T. Blowers, *The Limits of Power*, Pergamon, 1978, p.100.

[9] H.J. Storing, 'The Science of Administration : Herbert A. Simon', in H.J. Storing (ed.), *Essays on the Scientific Study of Politics*, New York, 1962, pp.73-81.

[10] L.J. Savage, *The foundation of statistics*, 1954, Wiley, pp.91-104.

[11] W. Edwards, 'Behavioural decision theory', *American Review of Psychology*, Vol.12, 1961, pp.473-98; W. Edwards, 'The theory of decision-making', *Psychological Bulletin*, Vol.51, No.4, 1954, pp.380-417.

[12] See for example, A.J. Harrison, *Economics and Land Use Planning*, Croom Helm, London, 1977; B. Walker, *Welfare Economics and Urban Problems*, Hutchinson, London, 1981.

[13] Planners 'are taught techniques which are irrelevant to their main task. Gimmicks and gadgetry they have in plenty; the sociological imagination escapes them.' *The Planner in Society : The Changing Role of a Profession*, D. Eversley, Faber and Faber, London, 1973, p.300.

18 Problems of using the utilitarian method in planning: the choice of consequences

see p. 137

The language of promises and ideals is central to the way politicians operate. Yet it is almost, if not completely, absent from the world of planners and public administrators, which is dominated by the impartial application of the utilitarian method. We must therefore ask how politics and administration interact, and how this affects the utilitarian method.

PROBLEM 1 : PROMISES

Most people consider that the fact that they have made a promise is sufficient to put them under an obligation to carry it out, regardless of how this may contribute to the sum of human satisfaction or dissatisfaction. The democratic process involves a constant interplay between voter demands and public expectations on the one hand and speeches and promises by politicians on the other. Public administrators, such as planners, sometimes have to take these promises into account in preparing policies and plans. A good example of this is provided by the railway line between Shrewsbury and Aberystwyth which runs mainly through marginal Parliamentary constituencies. Although the line is grossly uneconomic, its retention forms a strong element in local public expectations, and it would be a rash Parliamentary or local council candidate who did not promise to do all he could, if elected, to fight for its retention.

Does this kind of situation undermine our confidence in the usefulness of the utilitarian method in planning? It does not if we accept that most planning proceeds by a process of disjointed-incrementalism. At each step in the process of remedying dissatisfactions, promises by politicians can be seen as only one of many appropriate means. However, where does this leave long-range and structure planning? As an example consider the following. The West Midlands County Council made a proposal for an East-West Route in Coventry. The proposal remained long-term for some years and money was not forthcoming for its construction. The planning blight on property values and lack of confidence in the area affected was expressed in local dissatisfaction. Eventually the Chairman of the Coventry District Planning Committee announced publicly that the fact that a property was on the road-line would not prejudice any subsequent application for planning permission. He was thus prepared, if permissions were given on the road-line, to support the giving of full compensation should such redeveloped properties be reclaimed for road construction at a later date. This was a cheap promise, since such compensation would have had to be paid by the County Highways Authority rather than by the District. Such a situation, where strategic planning powers are eroded by local political obligations, is not uncommon.

PROBLEM 2 : ARGUMENTS ABOUT IDEALS

At first sight it might seem that the utilitarian method does not make any allowance for 'conservationist' arguments. Such arguments might be in favour of creating or preserving beautiful or rare natural or built environments, or works of art. Such things, though not of great value to the majority, it could be argued, nevertheless represent the 'higher' values and thus should be supported even though a purely utilitarian method might consider them of little value.

These arguments come in several different guises with different underlying motivations. Consider the following criticism of the popular belief that well-being must always consist in expanding wealth and capital rather than a stationary situation. It is an example of the <u>anti-materialist</u> strand in the conservationist argument.

> 'I cannot, therefore, regard the stationary state of capital and wealth with the unaffected aversion so generally manifested towards it by political economists of the old school. I am inclined to believe that it would be, on the whole, a very considerable improvement on our present condition. I confess I am not charmed with the ideal of life held out by those who think that the normal state of human beings is that of struggling to get on; that the trampling, crushing, elbowing and treading on each other's heels, which form the existing type of social life, are the most desirable lot of human kind, or anything but the disagreeable symptoms of one of the phases of industrial progress...the best state for human nature is that in which, while no one is poor, no one desires to be richer, nor has any reason to fear being thrust back, by the efforts of others to push themselves forward.': [2].

Another strand in conservationist arguments is <u>anti-artificiality</u>. Consider the following:

> 'There is room in the world, no doubt, and even in old countries, for a great increase of population, supposing the

arts of life to go on improving, and capital to increase. But even if innocuous, I confess I see very little reason for desiring it. The density of population necessary to enable mankind to obtain, in the greatest degree, all the advantages both of cooperation and of social intercourse, has, in all the most populous countries been attained. A population may be too crowded, though all be amply supplied with food. It is not good for man to be kept perforce at all times in the presence of his species. A world from which solitude is extirpated, is a very poor ideal. Solitude, in the sense of being often alone, is essential to any depth of meditation or of character; and solitude in the presence of natural beauty and grandeur, is the cradle of thoughts and aspirations which are not only good for the individual, but which society could ill do without. Nor is there much satisfaction in contemplating the world with nothing left to the spontaneous activity of nature; with every rood of land brought into cultivation, which is capable of growing food for human beings; every flowery waste or natural posture ploughed up, all quadrupeds or birds which are not domesticated for man's use exterminated as his rivals for food, every hedgerow or superfluous tree rooted out, and scarcely a place left where a wild shrub or flower could grow without being eradicated as a weed in the name of improved agriculture. If the earth must lose that great portion of its pleasantness which it owes to things that the unlimited increase of wealth or population would extirpate from it, for the mere purpose of enabling it to support a larger, but not a better or a happier population, I sincerely hope, for the sake of posterity, that they will be content to be stationary, long before necessity compels them to be.': [3].

Another strand in the conservationist argument derives from culturally imposed duties: [4]. Consider the following:

> 'Our consciousness is ancient, and we need to feel our roots and be reminded of our history... We are the recipients of a glorious heritage of buildings and landscape not contrived on the cheap in response to popular clamour, but raised up, without considering cost, to the glory of God and mankind, and it is up to us to leave behind as large a slice as possible of our inherited riches.': [5].

The above argument falls into that family of arguments which we could call arguments from tradition. Simply put the strongest version of the argument runs that we should do as our forefathers did. The above argument is a weaker one - that we have a link with the past and therefore a duty to preserve continuity with the past: [6]. Preserving architectural continuity with the past is a standard and accepted concept in development control. In the wider context, an interesting example of argument from tradition has emerged as one of the arguments used by the conservation lobby for some American Indian Reservations, on the grounds of protecting the traditional Indian way of life.

All the above types of conservationist arguments share the common property that they hold up an ideal to be valued - whether it is spiritual, traditionalist, or the seeking of naturalness. The concept of the consequences of a decision is as irrelevant to such arguments as it is relevant to the utilitarian method. The justification for this indifference to consequences is that if one believes in an ideal, then one regards doing something (say conserving a pretty village) as morally right, regardless of the consequences (that is, regardless of the cost). Politicians do sometimes make decisions on grounds of principle regardless of cost, as in the decision of the British government to preserve the way of life of the Falkland Islanders at whatever material cost. But in public administration, and in planning, such an approach is extremely rare if not absent. Public administrators and planners all share the utilitarian values of public bureaucrats. These values involve observing impersonal rules and stress the impartial weighing of the consequences of actions: [7]. Thus even when public bureaucrats personally agree with conservationist arguments: [8], they make decisions according to utilitarian considerations.

All the above arguments are examples of where an ideal is held more important than consequences. There is another argument of this type, which used to hold great importance in planning ideas. It is the concept of utopian planning: [9]. Even moderate town planners before about 1950 held some belief that somehow creating the city beautiful, and protecting the countryside, could work through to social and individual betterment. At its most utopian there was the equating of a new civic architecture with a new type of society. Partly this was derived from non-conformist ideas and experimental communities of the nineteenth century: [10]. Partly it derived from sociological naivety about the subtlety of the relationship between society and environment. Partly it was encouraged by the major social experiments of the 1930s in America, and of the 1940s in Britain. Since 1950 however, apart from temporary surges, planning has tended to recede from utopianism.

All the four above arguments from ideals have weaknesses. The most notable and critically damaging weakness of the anti-materialist argument is that it is rejected by the large majority of people. The anti-artificiality argument has more subtle weaknesses, stemming from the difficulty of defining artificiality. One definition may be that what interferes with Nature is artificial. Notable examples are cutting down the tropical rainforests and creating plutonium nuclear fuel. But if we accept this definition, to what extent do we condemn all technology? Another definition is that artificiality involves lack of spontaneity - such as controlling people's movements in particular environments. But such a definition is clearly the result of much reflection and can itself therefore be defined as artificial. Another definition resorts to defining artificiality as that which contradicts 'human nature'. Unfortunately several contradictory theories of human nature exist, leaving no clear answer. The argument from tradition suffers from its unpopular association with reactionary and non-progressive ideas : doing what has been done in the past does not recommend itself to many in the modern world. Visionary arguments were generally based upon a crude version of architectural determinism which is now discredited. They also were developed in an elitist, paternalistic era and are much less credible in a more democratic age when information about environmental change is more available and when the old environmental consensus no longer exists. Moreover the justification for some of the more visionary contributions of the environmental professions, such as modern town centres, high rise flats, and comprehensive redevelopment, have been seriously questioned.

Notwithstanding their deficiencies it must be acknowledged that these arguments are held by significant numbers of people in certain circumstances: [11]. We must therefore ask to what extent the utilitarian method does or does not accommodate them.

Let us consider again the case of extraction of minerals versus conservation of the rural environment. It is the local opposition which the proposal injures. Thus the focus of interest settles on the injury to local groups and individuals. What exactly is the nature of the injury? Can the injury be reduced while still allowing the proposal? Is the inquiry sufficiently serious that compensation is necessary, or is a more appropriate reaction to refuse development? Thus despite the preference of the utilitarian method for the group with the numerically largest constituency (in this case the mining company which claims to benefit tne nation) it is the smaller constituency which takes pride of place in any investigation because it is the injured party. Here is a formulation of this process:

> 'People using the strategy of disjointed-incrementalism manage to fix on reference groups and to shift them according to circumstances. They conserve points of departure without necessarily being conservative in the points referred to. Their working procedure may be described by the following two-part rule : First, some injury or liability to injury must be shown for the burden of proof lies on those who advocate a shift from the reference groups traditionally used. (We may define "injury" broadly enough to include missed opportunities.)
> 'This rule is enforced in practice by the operation of the various features of the strategy. It conforms to the serial and incremental features of the strategy that, in the absence of challenges, the reference groups should be the ones used in the past. The remedial orientation of the strategy determines the sort of challenge that is recognised. Finally, whether or not the burden of proof has been sustained by the challenges depends, not on their having evidence that meets any advance criterion of sufficiency, but on their succeeding in convincing other participants in the dispute that the evidence of possible injury is serious enough to require a shift in reference groups... By refusing to use any more inclusive group as a steady reference, the strategy operates to preserve the autonomy of multiple-interest groups smaller than the general population.': [12].

Thus for the mining company to convincingly argue its case of benefitting the nation by extracting minerals, it must show that (i) substitutes do not exist, (ii) substitute commodities, other than those that need the mineral, do not exist, (iii) alternative sites do not exist, (iv) no more than one other supplier exists, (v) that the Balance of Payments would benefit. This is a not inconsiderable list of arguments to win. On the other hand the local opposition starts with a clear, established case - that a certain number of people stand to lose from the development. So the wider scope of the mining company, though favoured by the utilitarian method, is much more difficult to establish, if we accept the starting point that the utilitarian method is operated within a disjointed-incrementalist environment.

One last point about arguments from ideals, such as conservation arguments. What happens when they are employed? Are they somehow redesigned to appear utilitarian to avoid the weaknesses mentioned above? It seems that this is the case: [13]. Because the utilitarian method is the accepted one in public administration and planning, even arguments concerning conservation use utilitarian language. National Parks emphasise the number of visitors per year. National conservation pressure groups stress the large positive economic effect of tourism and its links with attractive towns and countryside. National ecology pressure groups enumerate the numbers of people likely to be affected adversely from different environmental risks. And international ecology groups stress the damage to the total environmental system from technology and development: [14].

Thus not only can utilitarianism as a method take into account arguments about ideals, it also has the effect of transforming these arguments into utilitarian language: [15].

We have seen in this chapter that there are two objections to utilitarianism which raise clearly the differences between the way planners and the way politicians speak and act on planning matters. One objection is that a politician may approve of a decision because it carries out a promise, even though the decision would not have been arrived at using utilitarian values. The more nearly the decision is arrived at by means of the disjointed-incrementalist strategy, the less significant does this problem become. Thus the instance where this problem is greatest is in the erosion of long-range and strategic thinking by promises prompted by short term and local political considerations.

The other objection is that we may approve of a decision because it accords with a certain ideal value, such as the values of tradition, anti-materialism, naturalness, or utopian planning, rather than by a utilitarian consideration of the consequences of the decision. We have seen that because these ideal values do not have widespread public support in most instances: [16], their justification is usually phrased in utilitarian language - in terms of a decision's consequences: [17].

NOTES

[1] For an investigation of the relevance of ideal to wider public policy areas see C.W. Anderson, 'The place of principles in policy analysis', American Political Science Review, Vol.73, 1979, pp.710-23; S. Stitch, 'The recombinant DNA debate', pp. 180-98 in J. Dowie and P. Lefrere (eds), Risk and Chance; Open University Press, 1980.

[2] J.S. Mill, Collected Works, Vol.3, London, Routledge, 1965, pp. 753-4 quoted in L. Allison, Environmental Planning, G. Allen and Unwin, London, 1975, p.90.

[3] J.S. Mill, Collected Works, Vol.3, London, Routledge, 1968, p.765, quoted in L. Allison, Environmental Planning, G. Allen and Unwin, London, 1975, pp.90-91.

[4] See, for example, the 'just savings' principle in J. Rawls, A Theory of Justice, Oxford University Press, 1971, p.290.

[5] G. Haythornthwaite, 'My case for Preservation', The Listener, 24 February 1966, quoted in L. Allison Environmental Planning, G. Allen and Unwin, London, 1975, p.95.

[6] Policy justifications which argue consistency with past decisions are a type of argument from tradition. (We would suggest such justifications are usually of secondary rather than primary importance used mainly to bolster utilitarian judgements.) Consistency and routinization lay behind Weber's definition of rationality : M. Weber, 'Subjectivity and Determinism', pp.23-32 in A. Giddens (ed.) Positivism and Sociology, Heinemann, London, 1974.
See also P. Saunders, 'They make the rules : political routines and the generation of political bias', Political Studies, Vol. XXV, No.3, 1979, pp.31-58.

[7] M. Weber, The Theory of Social and Economic Organisation, (translated by A. Henderson and T. Parsons) 1947, p.340.

[8] There is some evidence that public opinion has shifted away from materialist towards environmentalist concerns : see R. Inglehart, The Silent Revolution : Changing Values and Political Styles among Western Publics, Princeton University Press, Princeton, NJ, 1977.

[9] R. Madge, 'Planning by ideals - the utopian trap', Built Environment, February 1975, pp.66-75.

[10] W. Ashworth, The Genesis of Modern Town and Country Planning, Routledge and Kegan Paul, London, 1954; L. Allison, Environmental Planning, G. Allen and Unwin, London, 1975, Chapter 3.

[11] Arguments about ideals form part of the Barry classification : 'ideal regarding' principles are those which cannot be said to benefit the arguer or others in a direct sense : see B. Barry, Political Argument, Routledge, London, p.38.

[12] D. Braybrooke and C. Lindblom, A Strategy of Decision : Policy Making as a Social Process, Free Press, New York, 1963, pp.242-3.

[13] L. Allison, Environmental Planning : a political and philosophical analysis, G. Allen and Unwin, London, 1975.

[14] Compare this situation with the richer vocabulary of arguments available in the law : e.g. C.A. Perelman and L. Olbrechts-Tyceta, The New Rhetoric, University of Notre Dame Press, London, 1969.

[15] For a more critical conclusion see L. Allison, 'Politics, welfare, and conservation : a survey of meta-planning', British Journal of Political Science, Vol.1, 1971, pp.437-52.

[16] L. Allison, op.cit., Chapter 7 and 8.

[17] The fact that ideals, though expressed in utilitarian guise, are still important in planning is a criticism of the snobbish, 'higher' values in planning : see R. Bauham, P. Barker, P. Hall, C. Price, 'Non-plan : an experiment in freedom', New Society, 20 March 1969, pp.435-444.

19 Problems of using the utilitarian method in planning: promises and ideals

Another problem we must face in this investigation is : what consequences should we include in any utilitarian decision, from the infinity of possible consequences?

In hindsight we could say that when the government gave the go ahead to large-scale industrialised housing and high rise flats, they overlooked certain important consequences of this decision. Those consequences are now very familiar to us. They include families with small children condemned to live high up tower blocks where lifts are frequently out of order, condensation, difficulties of letting some flats and houses, and poor sound insulation. Similarly in hindsight it is possible to say that the present structural problems beginning to develop in many modern concrete buildings could have been foreseen by means of more careful chemical tests. Such structural problems have been estimated to cost horrendous sums to put right. So when decisions are taken, how many consequences should be evaluated? If we have difficulty answering this question, is not the utilitarian method leading us into making all kinds of risky and regrettable decisions?

> 'It is...a misconception to suppose that when someone ignores various facts about prospective policies, he is always guilty of suppressing evidence, like someone who refuses to look at items of information that are offered him as liable to upset his conclusions. A judge and jury, who must decide the fate of a prisoner yet refuse to look at certain items of evidence which are plausibly claimed to fall within the bounds of receivable evidence as to his part in the crime, create a scandal. The general situation of people evaluating alternative policies,

including people practicing the strategy, is quite different. There...information can be disregarded without creating a scandal about suppression... What is relevant to the evaluator's problem is determined by his conception of the problem, and, in deciding upon that conception, the evaluator decides to disregard certain types of information.': [1].

So if we observe the disjointed-incrementalist strategy then we can do no more than include what appears most relevant at each particular stage with the particular participants that are present. The situation is the same as when we are assessing to what extent we can hold up disjointed-incrementalism as being a better process of decision making than the rational-comprehensive method. The justification reduces to the argument that (a) time and resources to carry out surveys and other investigations are finite; (b) no one can objectively define what the problem is since different participants have different definitions of the problem; (c) means at our disposal for implementing a policy are finite. These difficulties limit either our understanding of consequences or the relevance of some as yet undiscovered consequences.

So long as we adhere to a disjointed-incrementalist strategy then, and subject our decisions and policies to constant review and participation by opposed interests, then new consequences will be allowed to come to light: [2].

How true is this of the examples above? Unfortunately there are several reasons why the disjointed incrementalist strategy is avoided in some important plans and decisions. The creation of the policy to construct high-rise flats involved officials, including planners, in central and local government, as well as local politicians and (most significant of all) construction firms. These construction firms produced costings and time-scales and effectively persuaded central government to press for very large numbers of industrialised and high-rise blocks. The momentum for central government to continue the financial subsidies which effectively encouraged local authority high-rise programmes thus became irresistable. This was despite increasing evidence about problems of high-rise blocks. Incidentally one cannot even explain this in terms of an initial lack of 'public participation'. The first residents to move from slum houses to the new high-rise towers were delighted with their new homes. Similar processes were at work in the government regulation of chemicals used in concrete manufacture. Once the Building Research Laboratory had given an initial go-ahead, central government wanted to interfere as little as possible with this new material which was, it was claimed, to solve so many of our highway, housing, and town centre problems.

One can notice a similar process at work in the planning control of agriculture. When the 1947 Town and Country Planning Act was being drafted, the powerful agricultural lobby (so strategically important during the early 1940s) was able to exclude agricultural buildings from planning controls. Despite a subsequent growth in the rural conservationist lobby, agricultural interests have always been able to maintain this exemption.

Similar cases can be made for the way consequences were not aired in the motorway programme and in the town centre property boom. Hopefully one will not be able at some future date to say the same thing of the development of the nuclear energy programme.

It is tempting to blame past blunders on powerful organised groups in society such as the construction and nuclear power industries. A more worrying question that is of especial significance to planning is whether there are some plans or policies which defy inclusion within the scope of disjointed-incrementalism. It is probably true that experimental high-rise blocks could have been built just as it is now argued that we should have only a limited, experimental, nuclear energy programme. But who decides the time-scale of the experiment? And more importantly it would be argued that considerable economic savings would be foregone by such a wait-and-see approach. Perhaps the minister goes for the selfish political pay-off in nearly every case.

The extent to which such large-scale programmes can be disaggregated into tentative experimental prototypes is of great concern to all those who wish to avoid future expensive failures: [3]. In the case of high-rise and industrialised housing it was argued that the advantages (cheapness, precision and safety of components) of large scale production made an experimental approach unworkable. Whether or not this argument was subjected to much scrutiny is probably irrelevant. The attractiveness of a new method of making even more houses available (and thus surpassing Mr Macmillan's 300,000 in one year) was irresistable to national politicians. And they were egged on by local politicians for whom an instant line of high-rise towers would be both a visible vote-getter and a monument. In the case of nuclear power, it is unclear the extent to which the nuclear power industry wishes to develop a sufficient UK track-record (this means large scale production of plants) in order to get into the world export market - one that is expected to boom in poorer countries unable to pay for oil and less educated about radiation risks.

Closely bound up with this is the fact that some projects are more politically convincing and attractive if they are large scale: [4]. Busy ministers only pay attention to solutions which threaten to go beyond a certain threshold of cost and/or promise to go beyond a certain threshold of success. Urban renewal, urban rapid transit systems, a Channel tunnel or bridge, industrial revitalisation of depressed areas - all carry spectacular voter appeal if also their costs are massive and uncertain.

These questions are worrying. But what relevance do they have for the decisions made by planners, rather than politicians? On the one hand it could be argued that planners, who advise politicians, are necessarily implicated. But this is surely to miss the point. Planners can choose to make their own distinctive criticism of issues such as high-rise and future blunders.

What implications does this have for long-range planning such as represented in Structure Plans? The answer is the conventional disjointed-incrementalist one. Even the disjointed-incrementalist strategy makes use of long-range thinking. But this long-range thinking is speculative and subject to change. It is best subordinated to disjointed-incrementalist decisions. Indeed it is in planners' interests to be distrustful of long-range thinking under some circumstances. Often such long-range thinking can be used by politicians to justify large-scale projects which defy the discipline of disjointed-incrementalism. Was it not wildly exaggerated forecasts of car ownership which justified many disfiguring and useless urban motorways? And was it not the similarly misleadingly high forecasts of birthrates which were used to justify the need for a rapid, industrialised, high-rise housing programme? In this sense the strategy of disjointed-incrementalism offers planners the hope of judicious caution:

> 'By favouring limited, incremental departures in policy, the strategy does, however, improve the chances that the predictions will be reliable. The changes contemplated under the strategy are not only relatively less drastic; they also take place within a range of moves for which the community as a whole possesses a concentration of information. Those using the strategy endeavour to preserve the known benefits of present policies while eliminating the known disadvantages. Because the discussion is focussed in this way, the advantages and disadvantages of all the alternatives brought up can be considered more systematically, so far as it is worthwhile to investigate any of them. The discussion will thus have something like a defined agenda. Whatever information is mobilized will run less risk of being lost from sight because of wild fluctuations in the terms of discussion, a point that no one will undervalue who has ever sat in a committee.': [5].

There are two additional problems about the choice of consequences. One is the question of double-counting. Care needs to be taken that one does not double count. For example, if we had four groups: (i) farmers, (ii) commuters, (iii) tourists and (iv) residents, it can be seen that (i) and (ii) form part of (iv). If we are assessing consequences the consequences either costs or benefits, to these groups will be different. Does this mean that some individuals who are included in two groups should be counted twice? If we say yes we are at least taking account of the different environmentally-relevant roles which they play. But we would in some way be giving such individuals more weight than individuals who belong to only one group. The rule which is usually followed is to avoid double-counting by either simplifying the problem or to carry out partial analyses. Both have their problems.

The other problem is how to make the analysis of consequences accommodate uncertainty. In practice uncertainty is best dealt with by means of a range of possible outcomes rather than by the prediction of a unique and certain outcome. Best current practice usually involves two things:

(i) If an outcome would be substantially affected by a particular contingency, for example, by technological innovation, then a supplementary comparison of alternative plans can be made in terms of this modification, including, for example, several different scenarios of different rates of technological change.

When we have some knowledge of probabilities (say on a scale from impossible-zero-to completely certain-one) it has been argued that the expected value of a consequence is the product of the consequence's value (either benefit or cost) and the consequence's probability.

However there are some occasions when probabilities may be known (say the risk of various types of accident at a nuclear energy plant) and also where the consequences can be evaluated in some way. Imagine that because the risk is so low, the overall (benefits-minus-costs) expected value of a nuclear energy plant is 'better' than a coal mine and coal-fired power station complex. (Let us say that the risks associated with coal have less negative consequences but that their probabilities are higher.) Despite this, it is inconceivable that this calculation would be the last word on the decision. In such an extreme situation, the huge scale of the negative consequences of a nuclear plant accident would probably influence an uncommitted politician much more than any utilitarian calculation. This is because firstly there may be a certain threshold above which the size of consequences (a nuclear plant accident) has political repercussions, and below which (utilitarian savings which are small relative to the size of the economy) they do not. And secondly it may be that the relevant politicians calculate that to maintain or enhance their position it is not necessary to do anything well, but rather to avoid making a politically-embarrassing mistake.

(ii) In practice one may need to 'adjust' the analysis in certain ways:

(a) One can be conservative about our estimate of future events either by overestimating risks or underestimating benefits. But does this not in most cases, merely stretch out the range of alternatives - from worst to best - without altering their relative desirabilities?

(b) We can opt for a flexible and adjustable plan rather than one which is 'optimal' in some way, but runs the risk of being inappropriate. An example here may be the preference for conventional housing (where maintenance costs and customer-preferences are known) rather than for unconventional housing. Another example is the South Hampshire Plan, which envisaged an eventual joining together of Portsmouth and Southampton, and which opted for peripheral growth of the two cities rather than a shining new development between the two cities (involving infrastructure which might eventually not be used). Another example would be to avoid a plan which made assumptions about standards of consumption (as the Milton Keynes plan did about a high growth in car ownership): [6].

(c) We can use safety margins. For example, if two alternatives are nearly the same in the value of their consequences, then we avoid saying that either is better.

(d) We can seek more information (continual feedback and adjustment) or information from more sources.

(e) If we are quantifying, we can add a risk element to the discount rate - deprecating the value of future compared with present consequences. But what if benefits and costs are differently distributed over time as between alternatives?

In conclusion, the problem of choosing what consequences to evaluate in any utilitarian approach to decision making is considerably reduced if decision making follows the disjointed-incrementalist strategy. The problem remains however, wherever plans are presented and justified using rational-comprehensive methods. Although these latter methods increase the public's perception of a plan's rationality, they in fact make it more difficult for the public to see that choosing and analysing a plan's consequences has been carried out correctly.

NOTES

[1] D. Braybrooke and C. Lindblom, A Strategy of Decision : Policy Making as a Social Process, Free Press, New York, 1963, p.234.

[2] S. McConnell, Theories for Planning, Heinemann, London, 1981, p.148 and p.150.

[3] For arguments that experimental prototypes are difficult to design for social policies see D. Schon, Beyond the Stable State, Penguin Harmondworth, 1971.

[4] R.P. Schulman, 'Non-incremental policy making - some notes towards an alternative paradigm', American Political Science Review, 1975, Vol.69, pp.1354-70.

[5] D. Braybrooke and C. Lindblom, op.cit., pp.234-5.

[6] Other examples of flexibility include in-built redundancy in infrastructure - e.g. extra lanes and parking (a costly method), and bus rather than rail systems. Most plans use some kind of sensitivity analysis to judge how much 'objective achievement' changes under altered conditions, and how much this reduces the superiority of the preferred alternative.

20 Problems of using the utilitarian method in planning: reductionism

By reductionism: [1] is meant two things. Firstly the collapsing of process into result. Secondly the finding of a common denominator to which all results can be reduced.

THE COLLAPSING OF PROCESS INTO RESULT: [2].

Utilitarianism interests itself only in the consequences of alternatives. It does not concern itself with the values intrinsic to the political or administrative 'process itself...such as the defining and redefining of substantive human roles, rights, and relationships and structuring their evolution over time.': [3] '...with no independent concern for the procedure whereby those outcomes are produced or for the history out of which they evolve.': [4].

However, it is often of vital concern what kind of process is used to create decisions:

> 'In many areas of human endeavour...the processes and rules of its participants matter quite apart from any identifiable "end state" that is ultimately produced. Indeed, in many cases it is the process itself that matters most to those who take part in it.': [5].

Thus in two ways the disjointed-incrementalist strategy recommends itself here. Firstly in the lack of a central decision-maker and in the plurality of interests that play a part in the discussions, there are several conflicting views of the best procedure which should be adopted. To what extent are rights important? Are there inalienable rights? What do we mean by political representation? Should persuasion and argument be central, or should bargains and exchange? What appeal system should there be? The disjointed-incrementalist strategy encourages such questions and makes procedure an important element in decision-making. Secondly, since there are no major initiatives, but merely a series of incremental remedies and temporary explorations, the element of policy evolution: [6] is central to the disjointed-incrementalist strategy.

FINDING A COMMON DENOMINATOR FOR COMPARING ATTRIBUTES OF ALTERNATIVES.

Utilitarianism and its more modern and rigorous developments in welfare economics and cost-benefit analysis require attributes of alternatives to be comparable in some common metric, usually in terms of money. This has been argued to be the biggest single weakness of the method: [7]. For example, one cost-benefit study even evaluated the conservation value of a fine Norman church in terms of its fire insurance value: [8]. Some have argued that the problems are so large that it is better to carry out a survey of people and get them to give the probability that costs and benefits lie in particular monetary classes, and then to take a probabilistic approach to constructing the common denominator scale.

But any attempt to construct such a scale overlooks three types of problem. Firstly some rights may be inalienable in the sense that they relate to values which have an 'on-off' character and which are deeply evocative and emotional. Such values might include integrity of the body (threatened, for example, by toxins or radiation) or integrity of the community or neighbourhood (threatened, for example, by outsiders, or by a development which will alter local lifestyles and attitudes) or uncertainty (the potential threat of a factory near one's house). Such inalienable rights one might say cannot be properly compensated for. Secondly some values (such as historical heritage or quietness) cannot be properly measured. Thirdly some values relate to global entities (such as a particular type of townscape or landscape) which suffer from small increments of intrinsive elements by a much larger amount than might be expected from the relatively small size of the intrusion. These values will be considered in more detail later.

A similar type of problem which does offer some scope for empirical solution is the problem of non-linearity. Specifying an attribute on a scale on which occur units which can be measured suggests that one end of the scale is favoured by a group and the other end is not favoured. Take the example of noise. We can scale noise in terms of decibels. However, for a whole stretch of this scale changes go relatively unnoticed. Above a critical level, or threshold, discomfort or annoyance is felt (although it must be emphasised that the location on the scale at which the threshold occurs will vary between individuals and between different places). Above another threshold important communal activities such as classroom teaching are disrupted. And above another threshold physical injury to the eardrums results.

The problem of reduction to a common denominator scale is also affected - and aggrevated - by the variety of scales of measurement that are available. Usually we recognise four such scales. The nominal scale classifies and categorises, (say into large, medium, and small, or into urban and rural). The ordinal scale ranks entities (for example, into first, second, and third largest). The interval scale provides equally spaced intervals between entities and indicates the differences or distances of entities from some arbitrary origin, (for example, index numbers of gross national product which start at an arbitrarily chosen base year whose value is usually 100). The ratio scale provides equal intervals between entities and indicates the differences or distances of entities from some non-arbitrary origin, (for example, population size, age of buildings, money value).

Unfortunately information is often available on one scale for one attribute and on another scale for another attribute. We are forced in such cases, if we wish to compare attributes, to go down to the lesser scale in terms of accuracy. The conflict with a desire to render all attributes in monetary terms is obvious: [9].

Another problem is that some attributes of consequences may be more uncertain than others. Say if we are comparing two public projects which have different repercussions in terms of school and water policies. The costs and benefits of new schools will be less predictable than the costs and benefits of new water developments. Consumption of water, costs of supplying water, and costs of purifying water have all remained relatively stable for many years. Whereas changes in educational technology and the politics of education have been unpredictable in the past. So the element of risk in educational expenditure will be higher than in water expenditure.

Another important problem is that costs and benefits are often distributed differently over time. For example, in many planning proposals, the majority of costs (disruption, noise, compensation, construction) are short term, whereas the benefits are long term. Benefits consist often of the fact that something bad (traffic congestion, or urban sprawl, or intrusion in a picturesque landscape) that might have happened has been prevented from happening. Traffic congestion, urban sprawl, and intrusion (which with precedence might lead to more intrusion) grow slowly, so the benefits of preventing them are long term. In cost-benefit analysis, the fact that all values are discounted back to present values is very important. This is because the longer into the future a cost or benefit is, the lower will its present value be. Thus with short term costs and long term benefits, discounting depreciates the value of benefits.

Moreover, the choice of discounting period, though arbitrary, may be crucial to the final result. Similarly the choice of discount rate (the amount by which costs and benefits are devalued the further off in time they are), though arbitrary, may also be crucial to the final result. The analyst thus has to make value judgements. It may be tempting to choose the discounting period and the discount rate to favour one's initially favoured alternative!: [10].

Another problem of creating a common denominator scale can be demonstrated using the planning method of <u>goals-achievements</u>. There are basically two strategies for presenting the final results. The simplest is to leave the results uncoordinated. Unless most objectives have been measured on ratio scales, this method is by far the safest. The second method is to attempt to synthesise the evaluations across different objectives again thus creating a common denominator scale.

We shall call this method the weighted index of goals-achievement. According to this method, weights are assigned to goals-achievement scores. The weighted indices of goals-achievement are then summed and the preferred plan among the alternatives is that with the highest index. This method places the least responsibility on the decision-maker since there is just one final figure for each alternative.

Consider this example:

Goals-achievement by measurement on a nominal-scale.
1 = satisfies objective; -1 = does not; 0 = no effect.

	Accessibility		Community disruption	
	plan x	plan y	plan X	plan Y
group a	+1	-1	-1	0
group b	-1	+1	0	-1

	Weighted accessibility (community weight = 2)			Weighted community disruption (community weight = 1)		
	weight	plan x	plan y	weight	plan x	plan y
group a	3	+6	-6	3	-3	0
group b	1	-2	+2	2	0	-2
		+4	-4		-3	-2

Therefore the result is

plan X = 4 -3 = +1
plan Y = -4 -2 = -6

Choose plan X.

However, the degree of simplification and distortion undergone in order to render an unambiguous result leaves this method open to much doubt and criticism. Two plans may both satisfy a particular objective, so under this scheme both plans would be accorded scores of +1, yet one plan may satisfy the objectives far better than the other plan.

Similar dangers attend the use of ranking methods for coming to an unambiguous answer. Consider the following example:

Alternative Plans	A	B	C	D	E
Landscape	3	1	5	4	2
Noise	4	1	3	2	5
Balance of payments	1	2	5	3	4
Flexibility	2	1	3	4	5

(where 1 = best, 2 = second best, etc.)

What we can say about using this method is that plan B is best on 3 of the 4 objectives listed, and second for the other objective, and that no other plan has more than one first.

But we run into serious danger if we do one of two things:

(1) To say 'therefore plan B is best'.

(2) To add the ranks.

In the first case, we are saying that it is the number of firsts that matters. This is dangerous because the objectives vary in importance. Say if a fifth objective was added:

Alternative Plans	A	B	C	D	E
Number of road deaths	4	5	3	2	1.

How can we equate being best on landscape with being best on the number of road deaths?

Because of questions like this, it is tempting to add the ranks. In the above example the result would be:

Alternative Plans	A	B	C	D	E
Total Rank (5 objectives)	14	10	19	15	17 (lowest = best)

Plan B has the best overall ranking score, yet is worst on the number of road deaths. So it seems that maybe we should make some allowance for the importance we attach to objectives. But even if we attached weights in the objectives there would still be serious objections to the method.

Suppose we attach a high rank to high preference and construct a table like this:

	Rank (5 = best) (1 = worst)					Weight	Rank x Weight				
Alternative Plans	A	B	C	D	E		A	B	C	D	E
Landscape	3	5	1	2	4	5	15	25	5	5	20
Noise	2	5	3	4	1	3	6	15	9	9	3
BOP	5	4	1	3	2	40	200	160	40	120	80
Flexibility	4	5	3	2	1	20	80	100	100	40	20
Total	14	19	8	11	8	Total	301	300	114	182	123

The unweighted table gives plan B a clear lead, but the weighted table gives A a narrow win over B.

However, there are serious flaws in this method. It implies that being worst on Balance of Payments is the same as being second to worst on Flexibility. Yet this information is not available in the original ranked information. The trouble is that the results of an analysis like this are only as good as the information originally put in, and ranked data are low on information.

To give an example:

Alternative Plans	A	B	C	D	E
Maximum Noise (decibels) in residential areas	140	50	55	40	45
Ranked (1 = best)	5	3	4	1	2

Plan A is worst, yet a rank does not say by how much it is worst - in fact the difference is very large.

If we feel we cannot work out the values of certain effects of plans, but can, nevertheless, rank them, then we can go little further after ranking. Even if all our data were ratio data, the previous discussion raises serious doubts about our ability to establish a common denominator scale. The best approach is probably not to attempt one, but to look to the politician or decision-maker to read what he likes into the more complex results, providing he has the determination and interest to probe the doubts we have about the methods we have used. It means more work for him, and possibly reduces any infallible technical status that the planner aspires to. But in the spirit of much of the above this is all to the good.

The best conclusion (with doubts and assumptions about methods) is probably of the form:

Landscape	A easily wins
Noise	B easily wins
Health	A slightly better than B
Flexibility	B much better than A

That is to say, a result which does not attempt to reduce attributes (cost-benefit analysis) or objectives (goals-achievements) to a common denominator scale.

As a final point about the difficulties of reducing cost-benefit attributes into a monetary scale let us consider two examples.

JOURNEY TIME

A frequent benefit of a project is a reduction in journey time. Various devices have been used for placing a value on this. Sometimes valuations are the results of an arbitrary judgement. At other times they are the result of careful observation of people's actual behaviour. In the better studies, it is usually pointed out that the value is relevant only for that particular project in that particular place. To transfer it to some other project in another place would be quite wrong. Often the results of such studies are difficult to use because the methods of travel differ so much - not only in time, but in other factors. There are also such matters as comfort, cost, reliability, personal strain, opportunity to read, opportunity to play cards, and so on. All of these besides time are part of the choice by people choosing a particular method of transport.

These matters can never be accurately valued. A survey made in

Manchester showed wide variations in the valuation by people of journey time. The people who conducted the survey tried to explain the variations in terms of income, age, and other characteristics of the travellers, but these attempts were, in their own words, 'only partially successful'. One important finding was that people who travelled faster and more expensively valued their time saving three times as much as the people who travelled by a slower and cheaper method. But both groups, the high and low valuers of time, had similar income and personal characteristics: [11].

NOISE

With noise it is frequently argued that, for example, people living near an airport who find that noise is a problem will find this adequately reflected in house prices. The greater the nuisance from noise, the greater the fall in their house prices, and so a monetary value can be placed on noise.

A difficulty here is that there is not a perfect market for houses. Even if there were no housing shortage the price effect would not necessarily reveal the cost of the noise. When a buyer comes along and buys a house near an airport, he has not experienced the noise and so he may value the house at £20,000. But the owner of the house has experienced the noise and is prepared to sell for £16,000. Because the estate agent will advise the seller to sell at as high a price as possible, the final selling price will reflect the buyer's valuation rather than the seller's. That is, the valuation will be of someone who has not experienced the noise rather than of someone who has.

Another difficulty is that another effect of a nearby airport is that the seller has to wait longer for a buyer prepared to pay his price. This time again there is no effect on price, for the effect is one of inconvenience and delay.

Also the employment at the airport may be expanding and consequently demand for housing nearby will be rising. This time an increase in noise will be directly related to an <u>increase</u> in house prices.

This chapter has dealt with the problem of utilitarian method which we have called reductionism. This problem has two aspects. Firstly, by only considering consequences, utilitarianism collapses process into results, ignoring the process by which human values are explored and discovered. We have offered reasons why the planning practice of reliance on disjointed-incrementalist methods offers some form of answer to this criticism.

The second aspect of the problem of reductionism is the requirement, in the most rigorous applications of utilitarianism, that all the various decision considerations be reduced to one common denominator scale. We suggest that of all the problems of utilitarianism, this one is the most objectionable and should in practice be avoided at all costs, using partial methods: [12].

NOTES

[1] The following account of the reductionism problem is derived from H.L. Tribe, 'Policy Science : Analysis or Ideology?', Philosophy and Public Affairs, Vol.2, 1971.

[2] H.L. Tribe, 'Trial by Mathematics : Precision and Ritual in the Legal Process', Harvard Law Review, Vol.84, 1971, pp.1381-3.

[3] L.H. Tribe, op.cit.

[4] L.H. Tribe, op.cit.; see also R. Nozick, Anarchy, State, and Utopia, Blackwell, Oxford, 1974.

[5] L.H. Tribe, op.cit.; J. McAuslan, 'Planning laws contribution to the problems of an urban society', Modern Law Review, Vol.27, No.2, March 1974; J. McAuslan, The Ideologies of Planning Law, Pergamon, 1980.

[6] C.J. Orr, 'How shall we say : "reality is socially constructed through communcation"?', Central States Speech Journal, Vol.9, Part 4, 1978, pp.263-74.

[7] For example, R. Gregory, The Price of Amenity, Macmillan, London, 1971, p.296.

[8] Report of the Commission on the Third London Airport : (The Roskill Commission), HMSO, London, 1971.

[9] Moreover the quantifiable aspects of a decision may get more attention than the unquantifiable aspects.

[10] For other problems of discounting see R.E. Goodin, 'Discounting discounting', Journal of Public Policy, Vol.2, No.1, pp.53-72.

[11] J. Parry Lewis, 'Criticisms of Planning Techniques : Cost-Benefit Analysis', Discussion Paper, Department of Town and Country Planning, Manchester University, 1969.

[12] An example of this prescription not being applied is the use of a multi-sector goals achievements matrix in the Coventry-Solihull-Warwickshire Sub-Regional Study 1971 : C-S-W Subregional Study Team, The Report on the Sub-Regional Planning Study, Coventry City Council, 1971.

21 Problems of using the utilitarian method in planning: morally-offensive consequences

Another problem of using the utilitarian method is that some conceivable consequences of utilitarianism offend humanitarian values.

The utilitarian method could justify the removal of an individual's rights: [1], (e.g. to property, etc.) if it were argued that society was better off as a result. In practice however, especially in the restrained and cautious setting of disjointed-incrementalism, the humane values of participants as well as of the statutes reduce this risk, but do not completely eradicate it: [2].

Similarly, assuming we can dispose of the problem of strength of preferences (see later), the utilitarian method could be used to justify making the majority suffer for the increased satisfaction of the minority if it was held that the minority's capacity for satisfaction was so superior to the majority's capacity for suffering. Consider the case of the Roskill Commission on the Third London Airport. The Commission used the utilitarian cost-benefit approach to decide in favour of Cublington as the site for the airport. Strength of feeling among Cublington residents was high however, and after a well organised campaign the government was forced to change the site to Maplin, a marshland area where fewer people would be affected but which was further from London. This extra distance from London would have increased passengers' journey times to the airport and, over the millions of passengers per year, had contributed critically to Maplin's cost in the Roskill Commission's report. If Maplin had been developed, therefore, the strength of feeling of a small, well organised group of Cublington residents would have led to their benefit (no airport at Cublington) being paid for by the increased journey time of a much,

much larger number of people (future passengers). Thus the combination of utilitarian method (the Roskill Commission report) plus disjointed-incrementalism (political pressure from Cublington residents) meant that an unrepresented group (passengers) lost out.

Consider another problem of poorly represented groups. In theory utilitarianism does not take account of benefits or costs to the unborn. Yet proposals such as those for nuclear power stations demand that future generations' safety be considered: [3]. In practice probably these considerations might be poorly represented.

How does the utilitarian method accommodate rules about humanitarian values and justice? Taking just one definition of justice, from the many available, we have :

> 'First each person participating in a (social) practice, or affected by it has an equal right to the most extensive liberty compatible with liberty for all; and second, inequalities are arbitrary unless it is reasonable to expect that they will work out for everyone's advantage and provide the positions and offices to which they attach, or from which they may be gained, are open to all.': [4].
> 'Such "inequalities" are defined as "differences in the benefits and burdens attached to (offices and positions) either directly or indirectly, such as prestige and wealth, or liability to taxation and compulsory services".': [5].

Bearing in mind these rules,

> 'The distribution of such differences among a group of people is, of course, a subject that requires census-like investigation. Balancing differences in one respect against differences in another and determining which combination most nearly works out to everyone's advantage are subjects that invite the use of the (disjointed-incrementalist) strategy.
> 'Far from conflicting with the concept of justice, the strategy already incorporates some of the features required... The census notion calls for counting everyone's fate equally... It is, among other things, to satisfy the same scruples that alternatives are redesigned to include compensation. The strategy does not guarantee that everyone's interests will be consulted. By affording many views an opportunity to be expressed and negotiated, however, it does go some way toward seeing that no one is victimised.': [6].

Yet in situations where powerful groups and interests have a major stake in planning decisions, it is likely that such census-like methods will not be used : we have already discussed the various pressures on government to avoid the discipline of the disjointed-incrementalist strategy in all its aspects. One American example of such pressures is the allegation that scientists and engineers engaged in the nuclear power industry refused to testify to public hearings on safety because they feared cutoff of research support from pro-government funding agencies: [7].

Also utilitarianism, in its bias towards consequences, plays down moral issues. Yet often such issues need to be resolved before consequences can be evaluated. In theory one could make some calculation about the effects of an alternative or of a proposal on freedom, justice, future generations and desires (or needs). But utilitarianism cannot tell us how important such things are. It offers no moral theory for discussing in an informed way the extent to which present economic benefits justify risks to the unborn, or how much economic benefits justify an increase in political power of an organisation with large military interests, one of whose aims is to limit criticism of wider government economic-military policy. To suggest that disjointed-incrementalism, through humane values and political pluralism can offer a complete answer is to miss the point that in practice economic and quantifiable questions inevitably dominate moral ones. Decision-makers, including planners, therefore, cannot escape the responsibility to consider moral choices.

So far, the possibility of compensating minorities (or even, perhaps majorities) is one that has been merely assumed. However, to what extent does compensation justify infringing people's rights? There must be a point at which, even if it is still to the overall benefit to carry out a planning proposal despite massive compensation, the infringement of a group's rights is so great that allowing development is not justified? It is to these questions that we now turn.

COMPENSATION

A suggestion has been made: [8] which, if it were taken up, would revolutionise the practice of urban and regional planning. At present we all (with notable exceptions) have to get planning permission if we want to develop land. For example, if someone wants to build a factory next to a residential area he may be refused permission on the grounds that the land is not zoned for industrial uses or that the factory would cause a nuisance to the nearby houses. Or he may get permission if he can show that there will be no great nuisance.

The suggestion is that we should scrap this system and allow anyone to develop anywhere, and then to work out the disturbance to neighbours afterwards. So if the factory is built next to the houses, and smoke from the factory ruins the washing in the nearby gardens, the local council would work out the cost of disturbance and require the factory owner to pay a disturbance fee to the council. The council would then distribute the fee as compensation to those adversely affected: [9].

After a short time people wishing to develop land would know the 'going rate' in disturbance fees and would tend to seek sites which minimised it (unless other factors became more important - a pithead has to be somewhere within a coalfield for example). This would, it is claimed, lead to a system of minimum disturbance. Houses would generally be in residential areas, factories in industrial areas, and so on. It is argued that this gives the advantages of the free market - developers are the best judges of the best sites - and that it eliminates planning delays.

The economic subtleties and operational problems of this idea do not concern us here. The suggestion does, however, raise in a relevant way the compensation issue. The issue can be summarised neatly in the form of a question. To what extent should individual rights be sacrosanct and to what extent should the state intervene?

As we see from the suggestion above, individual rights are not like islands. They come into conflict. So what we need is a method of dealing with infringements of people's rights. This can be most simply expressed in terms of two extreme viewpoints: [10].

(a) Why should we not permit all infringements of other people's rights provided compensation is paid?

(b) Why not prohibit all infringements of other's rights to which the person whose rights are infringed has not consented in advance?

If we consider the first question it quickly becomes apparent that compensation would be required both for exposure to risk and for actual harm experienced. This is most clearly shown in the way people are paid for doing risky work. An extra element in the wage comprises some 'risk element'. But also compensation is payable over and above this if an accident happens: [11].

But this does not operate with environmental risks. Dangerous chemical plants or nuclear power stations do not pay local residents for their daily exposure to risk. Perhaps local residents do experience fear in such cases. But it would be difficult to put a monetary value to such fear, which would vary from one person to another anyway. And such a procedure might actually increase local public perception of risk and increase public fear. Such residents know they will be compensated if an accident happens but they still experience fear.

So some things (having one's car stolen) do not cause fear (the insurance will compensate for the loss). We can call these 'private wrongs'. But other things, for example, environmental risks, do cause fear, even though we know we will be compensated if an accident happens. We can call these 'public wrongs'. This is the justification for prohibiting such infringements of our rights. The argument for government intervention into <u>public</u> wrongs is the following. There will always be some people who are not victims and therefore not compensated who still are fearful. Thus they are not compensated for <u>their</u> fear. Therefore there is a legitimate public interest in eliminating these infringements.

If we now go back to the suggestion at the beginning of a radically restructured planning system based on disturbance fees, people would never know how and when developments crucially affecting their lives might occur. One of planning's principal aims then, is to reduce this uncertainty and to regularise and make more understandable, necessary environmental change.

Two other reasons exist why allowing all infringements of other people's rights provided compensation is paid could be considered wrong. Firstly there are those values that are intrinsically unmeasurable, in at least some of their important dimensions, and are incomparable with the human satisfactions that are bound to play an important part in any utilitarian analysis. One might include in this category values related to ecological balance, unspoiled wilderness and species diversity. Secondly there are those values with inherently global, holistic, or structural features that cannot be reduced to any finite listing or combination of independent attributes. Here might be included ecological balance, urban aesthetics, and community cohesion.

Bearing in mind the fear which attaches itself to uncertainty, why not prohibit all infringements of other's rights to which the victim has not consented in advance?

Besides the argument about fear, there are other arguments for general prohibition. Suppose the radically different planning system outlined above exists: that is, people can develop anywhere they want to provided they pay appropriate disturbance fees which go to those who lose out from development. Let us say a chemical factory sets up next to some houses. The management of the factory knows how dangerous the chemicals are, and the risks of emissions causing deaths to local residents, and what this would cost the company in compensation. Now suppose an accident occurs and local residents are among the casualties.

We would have to bring in another condition, besides disturbance fees or compensation. We would also have to stipulate that all risks should be insured against to prevent situations where environmental accidents happen at the same time as a company nears bankruptcy. We assume this is possible.

Is the above situation another reason, besides that of the inducing of fear, to prohibit certain classes of land uses being near each other? Or should we prohibit land uses being near to each other when one land user opposes development by the other, for example when the residents oppose the siting of the chemical factory?

The manager who proposes to build his chemical factory may not be able to communicate with some of the owners of the nearby houses - they might be abroad. The manager might then argue that the benefits the nearby house-owners get from living there is small, since they live abroad much of the time. On the other hand, the manager might say, the site is just the right place for his factory. It is close to its basic source of chemicals. There is a skilled population (many without jobs) in the nearby town. The company offers to construct a much-needed new road... and so on. The great benefits of the chemical factory might then persuade us that prohibition is not a good idea.

So our answer to the question 'Why not prohibit all infringements of other rights to which the person whose rights are infringed has not consented in advance?' should be that there are three factors to take into account:

(a) the fear created by announcing the exact nature of the potential infringement of rights,

(b) the shared benefits of such a potential infringement (over and above compensation),

(c) the ease or difficulty of contacting those whose rights may be infringed.

If we therefore do not have an automatic ban on certain classes of land uses being near each other, should we merely step in after an accident has happened, for example by making the company concerned completely financially responsible: [12].

The problem here is that if we penalised all infringements of other's rights which were not consented to in advance, then we would bring large amounts of risk and insecurity into business: [13]. Businessmen and industrialists would not be sure that despite the best of intentions they would not end up being punished for accidents. Insurance companies could easily contest the safety standards which they had required. And were the insurance funds not forthcoming the company, such as that which owned the chemical factory, might be bankrupted by the necessary compensation payments. Under American law the residents in areas affected by the Three Mile Island nuclear accident were able to claim three per cent of their property values from the electricity company : the total compensation figure was reputed to be about half a billion pounds - a financially crippling sum for the company, and one which it was unable to insure itself against: [14]. Even this is an interestingly small compensation figure for such a grievous risk. The fact is that were such compensation procedures to be completely fair they would put a stop to many industrial and technological activities. We could imagine airport authorities or airlines being made responsible for crash victims who were not passengers or crew (say crashes in residential areas - how could one insure against this?) or road haulage companies responsible for pedestrian deaths. Some indication of the difficulties involved in the economics of complete safety is given by the evidence about the condition of many football grounds after the 1985 Bradford City Football Ground fire, by the necessary flexibility used by the Alkali Inspectorate (who must avoid bankrupting firms with onerous emissions rules which are too costly to obey), and the large numbers of known cases (which regularly appear when there is a fire) of hotels which do not (and say they cannot afford to) obey the law on having a fire escape.

Consider for example the following:

> 'Asbestos is a useful material; it provides cheap and efficient insulation against fire. However when milled into fibre it produces dust and this dust is a killer. Expose people to the dust for a long period of time and it will scar their lungs and slowly suffocate them to death; expose them for a short period and they may contract cancer, since asbestos, even in small quantities, is carcinogenic. These facts, at least those concerning asbestosis, have been known for many years. In the UK the Asbestos Act of 1931 specially forbade any level of dust whatsoever in factories. Yet today, in Yorkshire and in London, people employed in the asbestos industry since the Second World War are slowly and painfully dying. Why? Because the legislation regarding the permissible levels of dust was not applied, and because the Factory Inspectorate empowered to enforce the legislation never brought a prosecution. This constituted a "policy of non-enforcement". There was a price for cheap asbestos - human health. Dust could have been prevented in the factories but it was not. Someone, somewhere, was unwilling to pay the true cost of safety....this stands as an example of a political and economic system that is morally blind. Everyone opposes pollution yet we find pollution everywhere...': [15].

Thus we are left with the conclusion that neither extreme is completely satisfactory and that in most cases we must determine for ourselves some intermediate position. If we rigidly allow all infringements of rights provided compensation is paid we have an unpredictable environment where people are not compensated for their fear and uncertainty. If we rigidly penalise all infringements of rights which have not been consented to in advance, and if such penalties involve full and fair compensation, then we are jeopardising economic growth.

So compensation does not in all cases justify infringing other people's rights. This limitation is relevant to us when we are redesigning alternatives within the disjointed-incrementalist strategy. Sometimes compensation will be the best instrument to use. Sometimes prohibition of land uses will be more appropriate. We are forced to rely, not on one hard and fast rule, but upon a disjointed-incrementalist strategy where hopefully most of the above considerations would come to light.

ANAESTHETISING MORAL FEELING

It has been argued that utilitarian methods such as welfare economics and cost-benefit analysis, along with other policy sciences, tend to anaesthetise moral feeling: [16]. This tendency is increased the more the analysis claims to be impartial or scientific. This comes about in a number of ways. Firstly merely naming problems, such as unemployment and poverty, in a detached and analytical way often extracts much of the pain and suffering which is the reality of those conditions. Secondly planning recommendations, in their adherence to 'objective' descriptions of policy (such as that a certain number of households are to be 'displaced' by a new road) distract attention away from the uncertainty, loss of confidence, and perhaps frustration which is those households' true predicament.

The naming of problems by planners and public administrators is, however, only one way in which problems can be identified. Adherence to the disjointed-incrementalist strategy however, allows groups to do their own naming. It also helps them to articulate and perhaps <u>realise</u> that problems arise from, as well as reflect, their obscure status within the political process. And frequent interaction between officials, interest groups, and politicians can bring official language more into line with realities as groups experience them rather than with official, 'objective' categories. These processes have received fresh impetus since the growth in public participation, although it may be that officialdom merely comes to wear a populist mask through which it sees the world with the same eyes.

Much, however, while keeping within the framework of disjointed-incrementalism, depends upon actions and self-perceptions of planners and public administrators changing. The more that techniques are realised to be based upon moral presuppositions and that they are not 'objective', and the more that the planner or public administrator reveals the weaknesses of his methods and the value judgements which he often has to make, then the more will the technical appearance of officialdom be stripped away. This might be a painful experience for politicians as much as for officials, since objective language and unambiguous recommendations often remove morally uncomfortable choices which politicians would otherwise have had to make themselves.

Any conclusion about the moral objections to utilitarianism in planning must start from the position that these objections can never be completely removed. The inevitability that some group interests will be ignored, that prohibition of the infringements of rights are often not properly enforced, and that moral feelings are anaesthetised, are all problems endemic to the utilitarian method.

NOTES

[1] For an analysis of the problem of removal of individual rights in public policy see D. Wikler 'Persuasion and coercion for health', pp.199-234 in J. Dowie and P. Lefrere (eds) Risk and Chance, Open University Press, 1980.

[2] A. MacIntyre, 'Utilitarianism and Cost-Benefit Analysis. An Essay on the Relevance of Moral Philosophy to Bureaucratic Theory', in Values in the Electric Power Industry, K.M. Sayre (ed.), University Press, Notre Dame, 1977, pp.217-37; K.M. Sayre and Goodpaster, 'An Ethical Analysis of Power Company Decision-making' in K.M. Sayre (ed.) op.cit., pp.238-88.

[3] B. Barry, 'Intergenerational Justice and Energy Policy', pp.15-30 in D. MacLean and P.G. Brown (eds) Energy and the Future, Rowman and Littlefield, Totowa, New Jersey, 1983; R. Goodin, Political Theory and Public Policy, University of Chicago Press, Chicago, 1982.

[4] J. Rawls, A Theory of Justice, Cambridge, Mass, 1971, quoted in D. Braybrooke and C. Lindblom, A Strategy of Decision, Policy Making as a Social Process, Free Press, New York, 1963, pp.220.

[5] J. Rawls op.cit., quoted in D. Braybrooke and C. Lindblom, op.cit., p.220.

[6] D. Braybrooke and C. Lindblom op.cit., p.221.

[7] A.M. Michalos, Philosophical Problems of Science and Technology, Allyn and Bacon, Boston, 1974, p.527; S. Novick, The Electric War, Sierra, San Francisco, 1976, p.109.

[8] These ideas are influenced by E.J. Mishan, 'The Spillover Enemy, Encounter, Vol.32, 1969, pp.3-13.

[9] The Council would need to be able to monitor different types of pollution : R.W. Hahn, 'Marketable permits - what's all the fuss about?', Journal of Public Policy, Vol.2, No.4, pp.395-412.

[10] H.L.A. Hart, 'Are there any natural rights?', pp.53-66 in A. Quinton, Political Philosophy, Oxford University Press, 1977; R. Nozick, 'Prohibition, Compensation, and Risk', pp.235-54 in J. Dowie and P. Lefrere (eds) Risk and Chance, Open University Press, 1980; S.I. Benn and R.S. Peters, Social Principles and the Democratic State, G. Allen and Unwin, 1977, pp.88-106.

[11] E. von Magnus, 'Preference, rationality, and risk-taking', Ethics, Vol.93, July 1984, pp.637-48.

[12] This strategy might be based on the argument that a company's right to develop is connected to its duties (about risk etc.). For this kind of argument see W. Kendall, 'The open society and its fallacies', American Political Science Journal, 1960, Vol. 45, No.54, p.975.

[13] D. Duclos, 'Unemployment or pollution? : Attitudes of the French working class to environmental issues', International Journal of Urban and Regional Research, Vol.5, 1981, pp.45-65.

[14] In the USA the Price-Anderson Act limits the liability of the nuclear industry to 560 million dollars in damages for any one

accident, although government estimates of losses for a single nuclear incident go as high as 17 billion dollars. This means that as much as 97 per cent of the damages resulting from a nuclear accident might not be covered : K.S. Shrader-Frechette, Nuclear Power and Public Policy, Reidel, Dordrecht, 1980, p.166.

[15] W.I. Jenkins, Policy Analysis, Martin Robertson, 1978, pp.106-7.

[16] Compare Weber's comment that substantive rationality (discussion of basic values) was disappearing in Western society (relative to discussion of how to achieve given values) : M. Weber, The Theory of Social and Economic Organisation, Hodge, Edinburgh, 1947; M. Weber, The Protestant Ethic and the Spirit of Capitalism, G. Allen and Unwin, London, 1965; K. Mannheim, Man and Society in an Age of Reconstruction, Kegan Paul, Trench, Trubner and Co. Ltd, London, 1944.

22 Utilitarianism: a conclusion

Much of the above discussion, in its reference to the strategy of disjointed-incrementalism, is predicated upon participants holding 'humane' values, so that, for example, individuals or minorities are not made to suffer unduly in order that the decision should benefit the greater number of people. Indeed decisions made according to the description above may in some way be 'wrong', setting aside for the moment the problem of finding what is meant by 'wrong'. Although the above description has implied that in some important respects the disjointed-incrementalist strategy, by making only marginal adjustments to policy, minimises the risk of making mistaken choices, there is still another element which is missing if we want decisions to be self-correcting. For a decision-making system to be self-correcting in some way it must be accountable. Mistaken decisions need to be identified and appropriate actions taken.

Before we go further on this tack let us deal with the last few problems of utilitarianism. They have a particular bearing, in the context of the disjointed-incrementalist strategy, upon the question of accountability.

STRENGTH OF FEELINGS

In the original formulation of utilitarianism, each person has an equal importance in deciding the balance of advantages and disadvantages of alternative policies. It has been realised however, that many people may be indifferent between alternatives and thus that strength of preferences or strength of feeling should be taken account of.

We can do this partly by a technical adjustment. We can accord different weights to different subgroups if we are doing an appraisal based on a preference survey. And if the matter is being discussed in a disjointed-incrementalist process, we can accord prior attention to those groups whose rights are threatened, just as previously we have done when it was claimed that disjointed-incrementalism is open to a shift in reference groups. However we must then accord more weight to biased and partisan opinions.

> 'It is, of course, one of the tasks of mutual discussion to compare and correct these partisan pictures, though it will not usually be felt necessary to correct them beyond the point at which a reasonably harmonious decision on policy becomes possible. Biased though they may be however, they provide the community with information about those hazards and benefits of policy which the different groups belonging to the community most fear and most desire, (allowing that there are some fears and desires that it would be impolitic for a group to disclose). The expectations with which different groups greet policy proposals are not, of course, always well founded. Nor do every group's expectations get a hearing. Some groups are not well enough organised or well enough led to make themselves heard - a familiar and important defect in the interest group process. However, at least those fears and desires about consequences that are expressed must be confronted if the community is to be satisfied that the consequences of the various policies proposed have been sufficiently considered.': [1].

What role should planners play if they suspect that, say, a well organised middle class pressure group is pressing for a proposal which would be detrimental to a less advantaged group?: [2]. There is no specific statutory duty for planners to advance the interests of less advantaged groups. Yet at the same time they can use 'census-type' methods of social surveys, and can use public participation, to try to reflect the views of all groups. It could be that local councillors might prefer them not to, since it would then create an irresolvable conflict. But at least nothing (apart from a desire to maintain good relations with councillors) prevents them from doing so. It is in some ways unfortunate that planning in many local authorities is seen as a technical process which has only minor political implications. This situation is partly a function of the outsider's (lay and non-planning specialists) view of planning as being about the technical detailed control of land use. Partly it can be helped by planners' own self definitions. Having a mainly technical or expert status saves one from being contradicted and criticised. And it helps planners who fear being embroiled in party political disputes at the local council level, and who wish to maintain a position of detachment from local politics. Where such a situation exists, it is easy for the planner who wishes to initiate public participation to represent non-organised views to be 'warned off' by the argument that the issue is 'too political'.

MAXIMISING SATISFACTIONS VERSUS MINIMISING DISSATISFACTIONS

It has been pointed out that the original formulation of utilitarianism, advocating as it did decisions which maximised satisfactions, was unworkable in practice. This was because it was very difficult to see what makes people satisfied, but easy to see what makes them dissatisfied. So it has been suggested: [3] that the utilitarian method should seek to minimise dissatisfactions. This is a sensible suggestion. The implication for plan-making is that instead of attempting to satisfy vague and abstract goals (however well one attempts to define them in terms of objectives) one should instead attempt to solve problems (defined as existing or future dissatisfactions). Much of the ridiculing of Structure Plans is bound up with criticising the vagueness of goals such as 'The maximisation of choice of employment possibilities' or 'The creation of a satisfactory residential environment'. Yet sub-regions do have their own problems which can be ameliorated at the regional or sub-regional level, and it would be better to attempt to define what they are.

If defining problems is easier and more credible than defining goals, why do so many current plans, particularly Structure Plans, use the goals-based approach? One reason of course is the belief by many planners in the rational-comprehensive method and its insistence that a comprehensive statement of goals should be the starting point of the planning process. Perhaps another is the fact that the goals-based approach in its vagueness and its appearance of rationality, is less liable to criticism. This provokes one to ask whether such plans aim to achieve a disinterested investigation of problems, opportunities, and alternative solutions, or whether they aim to achieve other, political objectives. This question will be dealt with in more detail later.

ACCOUNTABILITY

Planners in local authorities have to make their plans acceptable to the majority political party. In situations where one political party is predominant and there is little chance of change, there is a narrow range of alternatives open to planners to consider. This does not represent any moral dilemma since in such a case local elections have provided planners with a clearly defined set of boundaries or constraints within which to define problems and alternatives. Groups whom any such alternatives ignore, one can argue, are groups which are in a minority. Under these circumstances, as indicated above, the planner has a choice about how far he wishes to take a political position and attempt to provide a forum for minority views. Once they have been represented however, the utilitarian method as has been outlined merely suggests that minority views have especial significance only if such minorities have rights which will be infringed by some alternative. The question then becomes whether such infringements are justified.

In situations of no party political predominance, or where a change of political party is likely to occur, the pressure is on planners to attempt to reach a consensus so that their plans will appeal to all or at least offend nobody and so that their plans will survive any changes of local political leadership. Such a consensus is often contrived. It often plays down those issues where disagreement is strongest - perhaps those issues which are most important.

In both types of situation the easiest stance for planning to take is a technical one. Under one-party control, it is tempting for plans to overlook those who stand to lose from what is proposed. Under equivocal or unstable political control, it is tempting to overlook those whose views are extreme or those views are on 'hot' issues.

This is undoubtedly a simplification of the efforts that planners take to be comprehensive, in their initial public participation in the early stages of a plan. It is at the evaluation stage that such groups and issues are dropped from the agenda. Moreover, the current presentation of many plans obscures this. It is possible to read many current plans and to be uncertain about the groups who gain or lose from particular alternatives, about why groups are persuasive or not, and about why some issues are important elements of the plan while others are not. If such matters were included, (and it is admitted that present statutes or procedures do not unambiguously suggest that they should be) then plans would become essentially arguments. Such plans would be much easier for lay people to understand, react to, and participate in.

There is another reason why this change would be beneficial. It does not concern accountability. It concerns robustness. The current type of plan tends to be written to make the process of choice appear justified. It simplifies or ignores conflicts and arguments. When a central tenet of such a plan is questioned or undermined by events, the plan becomes useless or nearly so. On the other hand, a plan which gave conflicts and arguments a central place would be much more robust to change. This is because the major element of change is the degree of influence which groups and organisations have - all with their own place in the conflict and all with their own arguments and preferences.

The reason why plans are presented in the way that they are is because of a deep-seated belief by planners and other public administrators that their proper role is essentially to address matters of fact (such as the public's or politicians' definition of issues), use impartial techniques to provide politicians with alternatives, and to objectively select the best alternative (or at the very least, to objectively illuminate the strengths and weaknesses of each alternative).

Thus matters of value are beyond their domain of responsibility, and choosing what question to ask is for someone else (the politician, the decision-maker). Deviations from this 'ideal' may exist, but usually such deviations are explained by (a) tempering objective analysis with 'wisdom' or 'intuition', or (b) senior planners or officials playing intermediary roles between technocrats (planners, officials) and politicians. Whatever explanations for deviations are offered, however, all will overlook the impossibility of extricating facts from values in planning and policy-making.

> 'Values as perceived by one who holds them are often nothing more than predictions referable to even more fundamental values. Facts as perceived by one who believes in their truth are often inseparable from the values held by the believer, particularly when the facts in question refer to predictions of likely consequences in a highly uncertain environment. Moreover, both the relations within a set of values and the internal structure of a particular value are amenable to much the same sort of disciplined insight and rational inquiry that can characterise discussions of factual questions. Finally, and perhaps most importantly, the whole point of personal or social choice in

> many situations is not to implement a given system of values in the light of the perceived facts, but rather to define, and sometimes to deliberately reshape, the values - and have the identity - of the individual or community that is engaged in the process of choosing. The decision-maker, in short, often chooses not merely how to achieve his ends, but what they are to be and who he is to become. The fact-value dichotomy and the perception of values as fixed rather than as fluid thus impoverishes significantly the potential contribution of intellect to problems of choice.': [4].

Whatever one may say about the ability of planners and public administrators to manipulate councillors: [5], interest groups, and ministers, it seems highly probable that the frequency of interaction between, for example, planners on the one hand and councillors and interest groups on the other, will determine whether or not this fallacious separation of fact and value can be maintained. The greater the contact, the more easily one can see through disguises. Although statutory public participation (whatever its weakness) has proved a move in the right direction, councillors are still part-timers, overawed by technicalities and professional experience. It is mostly councillors to whom planners are accountable, and while councillors are part-time there remains little hope that planners' technical self-perceptions will change.

But even if the technical self-perception of planners gave way to a willingness to make value judgements (and make them openly) there would still be the habit of expecting the decision-maker or politician to provide the questions to be answered. The problem with this passive self-perception is that the questions may be plain wrong, or they may not be the ones that were intended.

> 'And the lesson....is that there must be a system of closely linked and frequent interactions between the decision-maker and his "answering device" which employs to the full whatever capacity can be built into that device for identifying and expressing tacit assumptions and for exploring alternatives not envisioned by the decision-maker at all.': [6].

The responsibility of the planner and the public administrator in this regard is again to make his personal values and assumptions plain to the politician, to be prepared to remedy any oversights that the politician makes, and to throw away any 'rational' or 'technical' props that he may wish to use.

To be realistic, these technical self-definitions are most likely to change if the public and politicians are in a better position to challenge planning ideas. Three major barriers to such a change at the local level are the unresponsiveness of local elections to local issues, the amateur, part time status of local politicians, and the present statutory arrangements which govern the public scrutiny of plans. The undemocratic nature of local elections is most clearly reflected in the acknowledged poor showing of major local issues as election arguments, and the fact that local elections rather tend to reflect the popularity or otherwise of national politicians and policies. In such a situation local councils do not invite public debate on major local issues: [7]. Instead the political aspects of their decisions become impoverished.

With no understanding of any major political ideology which specifically has been created out of local circumstances: [8], decisions are either guided by party political loyalty: [9] (whose definition is evolved only at Westminster) or are 'depoliticised' and made to conform to some notion of rationality created by professional officers: [10]. The heavy hand of Westminster: [11] or professional advice is stamped on many local government decisions: [12]. Moreover councillors often receive no formal training and are only part-timers. The abortive attempt to 'institutionalise' corporate planning in local government at the end of the sixties would have done better to have recognised this fact. Some full-time status and training in corporate planning ideas for councillors might have had more effect than battling against local government departmentalism head-on.

At the level of central government, the barriers to such a change are mainly posed by the unwillingness or inability of planners and public administrators to challenge anything which promises to help economic growth. In the sixties there was the argument that limiting car use might depress home demand for cars, a prerequisite for healthy car exports. The house and road construction industries, the road users' lobby, the agricultural lobby, the nuclear power industry, all use arguments which touch on economic growth. Perhaps the greater the preoccupation with the poor state of the economy, the more are ministers vulnerable to these sorts of pressures. All these arguments can be analysed and criticised. Part of the role of planners and public administrators is to put such arguments under as much scrutiny as possible. Unfortunately technical self-definitions of planners in central government are very durable since they fit into a pattern which serves both professionals' and politicians' needs. Planners emphasise that facts are their province and that their role is to answer questions. Unwittingly many of their techniques and answers provide sufficient 'cover' for politicians to present them as the result of 'objective' analysis, as inevitable conclusions for which they have no responsibility. Some of these 'inevitable' conclusions come in the form of large scale projects which lock politicians into a system of commitments over which they have little control.

NOTES

[1] D. Braybrooke and C. Lindblom, A Strategy of Decision : Policy Evaluation as a Social Process, Free Press, N York, pp.235-6.

[2] For example, A. Blowers, The Limits of Power, Pergamon, 1978, Chapter 5 : 'Councils in Conflict - Transport Planning in Bedford', pp.77-109 at p.81.

[3] B. Needham, 'Concrete problems, not abstract goals', Journal of the Royal Town Planning Institute, Vol.57, No.7, 1971, pp.317-19.

[4] L.H. Tribe, 'Policy science : analysis or ideology?', Philosophy and Public Affairs, Vol.2, 1972.

[5] W.H. Cox, Cities, the Public Dimension, Penguin, Harmondsworth, 1976.

[6] L.H. Tribe, op.cit.

[7] J. Gyford, Local Politics in Britain, Croom Helm, London, 1976.

[8] P.J. Dunleavy, Urban Political Analysis, Macmillan, London, 1980, p.135.

[9] B. Wood, 'The Political Organisation of Local Authorities', p.16-22 in Party Politics in Local Government : Officers and Members',

Policy Studies Institute and Royal Institute of Public Administration, London, 1980.

[10] N. Collins, C.R. Hinings, and K. Walsh, 'The officer and the councillor in Local Government', Public Administration Bulletin, Vol.28, p.34-50, 1978; K. Newton, Second City Politics : Democratic Process and Decision-Making in Birmingham, Oxford University Press, London, 1976, p.146.

[11] E. Page, 'The marginalisation of local political elites in Britain', Environment and Planning C, 1984, Vol.2, pp.167-176.

[12] R. Hambleton, 'Planning systems and policy implementation', Journal of Public Policy, Vol.3, No.4, pp.397-418.

PART IV
EVALUATING PLANNING

23 Political and administrative uncertainty in planning

It is a common view of the planning profession that it is in a state of identity crisis. The profession came into being largely by borrowing practitioners from other professions. Also in order to get all party support for major planning legislation: [1], planning had to offer varied and sometimes contradictory themes. And major planning problems, or at least their priority, change rapidly and induce differential changes within the profession: [2]. Also the political values of planners vary: [3], and this influences whether or not their professional aims are physically-based or oriented towards socio-economic considerations, whether they consider economic efficiency or equitable distribution to be important, and the value they place on public participation. We shall now explore some of these dimensions of uncertainty which contribute to the difficulties which the profession experiences: [4] in the creation of a strong and durable identity.

PHYSICAL PLANNING VERSUS SOCIO-ECONOMIC PLANNING

The extract from the 1968 Town and Country Planning Act in Chapter 11 above illustrates unambiguously the much-widened definition of material considerations in current planning: [5]. Yet the courts have been slow to accept this change. And, because planning law combines two sometimes incompatible principles - the protection of private property rights and the furthering of the public interest - contradictory rulings have emerged from the courts:

> 'From the perspective of the planners, there has been, since the 1968 statutory reforms in development planning, a decided if not always consistent trend in the direction of expanding

> the scope of material considerations from the primarily physical amenity factors to economic, social, and other similar factors. By doing this, development control has been and is being brought into line with development planning. In ideological terms, what has happened is that the planners have expanded the scope of the public interest to embrace a wider area of decision-making than was previously within their sphere and have, as a corollary, cut down the sphere of decision-making guided solely by private property considerations.
> 'What has been the courts' response to this? Until the second half of the 1970s the courts were unwilling or unable to advance beyond either general statements .. which were not too helpful, or specific decisions whose guiding principles seemed to be that what was good for, or relevant to, the interests of the private landowner determined the scope of material considerations. It was certainly the case that this might on occasions involve the consideration of social factors but the overriding concern was that the relevance or irrelevance of any particular consideration was tested by reference to private property rather than public interest-oriented factors. More recently, however, there is evidence of judicial recognition of more explicitly public interest considerations being relevant to planning applications but how far this will go, to what extent it supercedes the more private property-oriented approach or runs parallel to it, leaving planning authorities in doubt which approach the courts will adopt in any case, is as yet unclear...
> 'Correspondingly, it becomes increasingly necessary from a "safety" point of view to disguise or dress up a relevant social or economic factor as a physical factor so as to lessen the chances of a successful judicial challenge. Such confusions and dissemblings cannot but harm the planning process.': [6].

The second way in which this dimension of concern causes difficulties for planning professionals comes from the fact that other officials in other departments in local and central government perceive planning in its older, physically-based role. This would not be a problem except that the newer, wider scope of planning: [7] inevitably leads planners into making judgements on matters considered by other departments to be their own "territory".

Moreover the planning profession is itself divided as to how far social and economic questions are a relevant concern. Older planners tend to be more conservative about this, younger planners tend to favour a wider definition of relevance. And individual political values add an extra source of unpredictability: [8].

RULE OF LAW VERSUS THE BARGAINING OF PLANNING CONSENTS

Part of the legitimacy for planning comes from its promising to provide a predictable environment: [9]. Yet in reality plans are not strictly complied with. This more realistic view was recognised in the 1968 statutory reforms - for example, Local Plans are to show only 'preferred' land uses (an explicit admission that others might be acceptable).

Many local authorities enter into agreements with developers whereby the developer gets his permission (which is not strictly acceptable) in return for providing land, buildings or roads for community use. This gain to the community is termed 'planning gain'. In a recent questionnaire study of 87 local authorities one half admitted to achieving planning gain: [10].

Sometimes applications are amended so as to incorporate a use additional to the one for which planning permission was initially sought. Some local authorities attempted to control the actual use in a development, and even the identity of the user. For example, shopping was provided at street level in a development where formerly only office fronts were proposed. Or residential units were included in office developments. Or space was provided for members of a particular trade. These amendments were incorporated using amended applications, or section 52 agreements, conditions, or local acts.

Some cases involved the developer dedicating land and sometimes even buildings to the local authority - for example, for public open space, or for a sports or community centre, or 'amenity deck'. Others involved the developer agreeing to provide a public right of way over his land. Still others agreed to provide infrastructure (sewers) and others involved extinguishing a non-conforming use.

The uncertainty arises, not about the beneficial results of this bargaining of planning consents, but about whether it contradicts other widely-held views about planning. One such view might be that plans act to control official discretion. Another might be that of distributive justice - that like cases be treated alike. Another might be that planning provides a predictable environment, where developers can know in advance the probability of receiving planning consent or refusal: [11].

EXPLICIT VERSUS IMPLICIT DECISION-MAKING

Although the widely held view of planning is that it is a process of making public statements of plans and decisions, many decisions on planning matters come from implicity-held ideas rather than from explicitly-stated ones. Sometimes this is because a plan cannot foresee all contingencies. For example, a large new industrial complex is proposed in a town where no large industrial zoning exists. The economic benefits for the town may cause the planners to rapidly alter their planning conceptions of the town, even if these are not stated in the plan.

COMPREHENSIVE VERSUS PARTISAN DECISION-MAKING

Although one of planning's aims is to be comprehensive, the fact that other departments and organisations make bargains and take partisan positions often means that to be effective planners must adopt a similar stance in some situations. A housing department may frame its housing investment strategy with no regard to the social services or education department, or it may act without formal collaboration to avoid unpleasant dealings with the other department. An area health authority could close an old people's hospital without warning or discussion with the local authority. In order to exert at least some influence, planners may find they need to bargain or negotiate with other bodies or departments whose aims are essentially partisan. Or in order to open up a dialogue or conduct joint planning exercises planners may find themselves making compromises about how strictly they should adhere to a comprehensive view.

SYSTEMS PLANNING

During the sixties there was a growth in what could be called systems ideas in planning: [12]. The example was provided by systems analysis, which attempted to understand the basic goals of an organisation in order to see if they were achieved. These ideas were used in an abortive attempt to reform central government. They also influenced the movement (largely a failure and in many cases discontinued) of corporate planning in local authorities: [13], which attempted to see the inter-connectedness of the different services provided. There was for a short time a willingness to reconsider the basic goals of government: [14]. The housing crisis and poverty were 'rediscovered'. Planning, programming, and budgeting systems began to be used in some central government departments. And dissatisfaction with the planning system resurfaced with the Planning Advisory Group's: [15] criticism of over-detailed plans. The 1968 Town and Country Planning Act was the government's answer to this criticism, providing for more conceptual and less physically based plans. There was also criticism of the lack of a voice for the poor and disadvantaged: [16]. The advent of statutory public participation procedures were considered by some to be a positive answer, although the need to provide an extra check on a more decentralised planning system was certainly a powerful motivation. There were also warnings of racial violence in the inner city areas, answered by an Urban Aid Programme aimed at providing funding to community groups, although the small level of funding suggested it was more of a symbolic gesture than a deliberate attempt to solve the problem of racial and other social tensions: [17].

The systems challenge failed because it threatened too much conflict. Corporate planning in local authorities, and central government reform, were aimed at breaking down departmental barriers and removing departmental thinking: [18]. Such a challenge was bound to be resisted: [19]. Also since the mid-seventies governments have been concerned to reduce public expenditure, using public expenditure guidelines, cash limits, and expenditure planning as financial rationing devices. Inevitably the result was to further weaken any corporate thinking: [20], and to cause departments to reduce cooperation and retrench.

The main justification for the systems view of planning - that is, corporate planning, has now disappeared. True, many plans, especially Structure Plans, begin with statements of goals and objectives, but these now seem inappropriate since such wide-ranging aims cannot be achieved in any integrated or comprehensive sense: [21]. Also Structure Plans include policies of other relevant agencies but these are included more as an attempt to be comprehensive than making a claim to coordinate through actively influencing those agencies.

The only positive legacy of systems planning is the wider definition of material considerations to include social and economic matters and the quality and breadth of social science training of planning personnel. But, apart from the greater ability to comprehensively judge private sector applications for planning permission, these advantages are rendered less effective by the strength of departmentalism in local and central government.

SPECIFIC VERSUS AMBIGUOUS PLANS

The specificity or ambiguity of a plan is determined by the precision with which targets or locations are specified and in the subtleties of wording implying the degree of intended flexibility of that part of the plan: [22]. Often there are pressures from interested parties - residents' groups, other agencies, developers - for more specificity. Thus a residents' group may wish to know why its area has been designated an action area without any clear statement of the kind of action intended. Or a developer may be interested in the statement (in the plan) that major residential sites will only be located in certain specified locations. What, he asks, is meant by 'major' sites?

The disadvantages to the planning authority of increasing specificity is that they will thereby increase the chances of the plan becoming inappropriate: [23]. This can happen in three main ways:

(a) Most planning statements which claim to be specific must be justified at least partly through making predictions of what their effects will be. These predictions will be based upon some set of assumptions about the future operating environment of the planning authority. These assumptions are rapidly going to be undermined by unexpected events. For example, a county population policy may be based upon rapid provision of housing, both private and public, in one of the Districts. At the time the plan is prepared central government strongly supports council house building, but shortly afterwards the central government policy changes and council house-building terminates. If the housing is for workers at a nearby industrial complex or new airport, there will soon be a shortage of unskilled and semi-skilled workers. The alternative might be for the plan to be ambiguously worded and guarded about such a rapid development.

(b) The more specific the plan attempts to be, the more easy is it for opponents (developers, residents' groups, other planning authorities) to criticise it as not meeting their specific requirements in their particular location. For example, a Structure Plan may have a policy that hotel developments only take place in existing settlements, since only there can be found the full range of supporting services (transportation, labour force, shopping centres) required to service such developments. If however, a developer finds that such services exist somewhere else that is a profitable location for hotels (a regional airport, a motorway intersection, an out-of-town shopping centre) he has a good chance of breaching the policy.

(c) The more specific a plan attempts to be, the more will responses to public pressure be a cause for the policy becoming out-of-date. Control of a local council might change, and with it a complete change on one or more important strands of policy - away from a policy of encouraging the motor car, for example, towards encouraging public transport. Or a key proposal may be successfully resisted by a pressure group.

These disadvantages of plan specificity mean that ambiguity is one of the important components in plan design. The dilemma is that ambiguity reduces the intended influence of a plan. The problem is that either the plan becomes so bland that it proposes little or nothing, or that its ambivalence can be manipulated by its opponents to their own ends.

THE OVERLAP OF DISTRICT AND COUNTY FUNCTIONS

Another source of uncertainty in planning comes about from the overlap of plan-making functions between the two tiers of local government.

The county planning authority may if it thinks appropriate include the following in its written statement of the Structure Plan:

> '...the existing structure of the area to which the plan relates and the present needs and opportunities for change.'

The district planning authority, on the other hand, may if it thinks appropriate include the following in its written statement of the Local Plan:

> '...the character, pattern and function of the existing development and other use of land in the area to which the plan relates and the present needs and opportunities for change.': [24].

THE DIFFICULTY OF DEFINING AESTHETIC QUALITY

Planners have the responsibility for maintaining and improving the quality of the environment. This inevitably means that they have to make judgements about what is or is not aesthetically pleasing. One of the reasons for the creation of a planning profession separate from architecture after the Second World War was that it was believed that if architects were required to vet the schemes of other architects, there would not be the same element of detachment and criticism. However, while in the early years of planning (1947-67) many planners were architect-planners or trained (in planning schools) by architects, the same cannot be said today. The orientation of the majority of today's planners is a social science one. Design has played only a small part in their training. Even before this change, however, architects complained that their schemes were judged by bureaucrats who had few of the skills or sensibilities of architects. The design values of planners were claimed to be conservative, traditionalist, and unoriginal. Since the advent of social and economic planning ideas in the sixties, moreover, the relative importance of aesthetic quality has declined, as the planner's repertoire of material considerations has widened.

Moreover the means at the planner's disposal have declined since the early years of planning legislation. In the late forties the nationalisation of development rights and the need to reconstruct war-damaged cities created an optimism about the ability of planners to create a new civic architecture. The withdrawal of such nationalisation in 1951, and the removal of local authorities' ability to buy land cheaply from the private sector in 1959, eroded this confidence and placed planning in its modern, negative role of aesthetic critic of predominantly private sector schemes. This negative role is beset by difficulties. Developers can serve purchase notices if they can show that the local authority is preventing them from making a reasonable return from developing land. And the areas in greatest need of aesthetic regeneration - the older parts of urban areas - were largely developed prior to 1963 and thus have existing use rights - removable by planners only through public acquisition or expensive compensation. Also aesthetic ideas have greatly changed - partly because of changes in public opinion, and partly because of architectural fashions changing. For example, Victorian architecture has changed from being (in the fifties) an ensemble of poorly-correlated styles borrowed from earlier times, to its present popularity. And the ability of planners to control aesthetic changes is much less under the Town and Country Planning Acts than if the local authority had greater resources with which to own land.

Now, we could ask, does the difficulty in defining aesthetic quality arise from the subjectivity intrinsic in such a definition, or does it rather arise because the relevant question in modern planning is what level of environmental quality is the lowest that the public will find acceptable, so that we can share the social and economic benefits of modern development? Modern development uses cheaply constructed materials employed in rather regular, predictable ways. Some argue that this is not so, that in every new development era the 'modern' has been criticised, and that current developments will eventually become aesthetically harmonious with what has gone before. This kind of question, while important, seems unanswerable largely because aesthetic tastes change so fast. It may be that poor design leads to low expectations. It may be that uniform design reduces public expectations of variety. It is probable that a development and construction industry which has learnt what is the least, in terms of architectural care and expense, that planners find acceptable will use such a baseline in all its future design decisions: [25]. Because the planner's powers of aesthetic control have been weakened: [26], and are increasingly being weakened by the promotion of other, newer, considerations, does not this undermine any claim he has to be able to authoritatively define what is meant by aesthetic quality? and does it not reinforce the belief that there exists a lowest common denominator in terms of architectural care and expense beyond which developers do not have to venture?

Inevitably the impoverishment of this lowest common denominator has been greatly increased by criticisms of the subjectivity with which planners judge aesthetic matters. This is because planners have reacted to such criticisms by attempting to quantify or at least standardise aesthetic control. Preferred building materials, preferred distances between buildings, preferred street architecture, even preferred architectural styles, have all become more uniform. And this uniformity has gone hand in hand with a parallel standardisation of modern construction. Variety, surprise and individuality in buildings and spaces have consequently declined. Such a process has hardened public attitudes to new building and in some cases has prevented the construction of architecturally innovatory buildings.

Compare this process with what happened two hundred years ago. Then a new house or public building would increase the local status of its owner or of the local inhabitants. The aim was to be individual, yet not to outrage local feelings. The richer the patron, the more cosmopolitan the materials and style would be. Often materials were local. Streets were socially mixed and often included a variety of different uses - shops, warehouses, houses and so on. Industrialisation and urbanisation processes since then have eroded most of these sources of variety and social meaning. New sources have had to be recreated intellectually through architecture's concepts. But a new kind of harmony has not been generated. Planning has only been partly responsible for this. True, it has shifted part of the developer's task from artistic problems towards dealing with bureaucracy. And it has provided a lowest common denominator definition of what is aesthetically acceptable. But other reasons exist too. The old aesthetic consensus, created and handed down by a refined aristocracy has disappeared. Materials and construction methods are more uniform and less durable. The huge benefits of technology and development are so much greater than they were, so that aesthetics occupies a position of dwindling importance in our criteria.

The above seven dimensions of difficulty of the planning task mean that the planner is faced with the problem of imposing some kind of order and coherence in a situation continually undermined by irreconcilable conflicts and unresolvable dilemmas: [27].

The principles that offer some kind of hope and which serve the simultaneous symbolic functions: [28] of simplification, distraction and transformation are the principles of rationality and efficiency. Simplification occurs because the very fact that planning embodies these principles means that order and coherence become magically attainable. Distraction is the process by which evoking the principles of rationality and efficiency serves to take attention away from all the nagging uncertainties of plan-making and planning decisions. Transformation takes place by convincing participants and onlookers that the principles are of greater weight than any uncertainties, that the attempt is worth any underlying risk, and that to aim for an ideal matters more than becoming preoccupied by time-consuming and energy-sapping difficulties.

It is important to realise here that rationality and efficiency have not wholly materialised as stage devices created by a planning profession in identity-crisis. Rather, these magical principles have also evolved out of the need of the mass public and politicians for symbols, and the realisation by the planning profession that, though these principles do not relate to any workable process of planning, they form the backbone of the public image of what planning is about: [29]. Thus the symbiosis of planning profession, mass public, and politicians is complete: [30]. This is why, despite their observation of the disjointed-incremental policy and institutional environment, and the fact that both Structure and Local Plans fit this process strategy quite closely, many planners find the rational-comprehensive strategy so deeply ingrained. Often therefore, plans are created in a disjointed-incrementalist strategy, and yet are dressed up as products of a rational-comprehensive strategy. We must now therefore examine more closely the factors that make for such a satisfactory circle of on the one hand public expectations of planners' rationality, and on the other hand planners' need for order and coherence.

NOTES

[1] J. Backwell and P. Dickens, 'Town planning, mass loyalty, and the restructuring of capital : the origins of the 1947 planning legislation revisited', Urban and Regional Studies Working Paper No.11, University of Sussex, 1979; G. MacDougall, 'The state, capital, and land : the history of town planning revisited', International Journal of Urban and Regional Research, Vol.3, 1979, pp.361-80.

[2] For evidence of the effects of fashion in planning see A.H. Thomas, 'An Analysis of Changes in Planning Education, 1965-1975', Unpublished PhD Thesis, University College London, 1979; M. Hebbert, 'The Evaluation of British Town and Country Planning', Unpublished PhD Thesis, University of Reading, 1977.

[3] D. Donnison, The Good City, Heinemann, London, 1980.

[4] E.R. Alexander, 'After rationality, what?', Journal of the American Planning Association, Vol.50, No.1, 1984, pp.62-9.

[5] J. Jowell and D. Noble, 'Structure Plans as instruments of social and economic policy', Journal of Planning and Environment Law, 1980, pp.466-80.

[6] P. McAuslan, The Ideologies of Planning Law, Pergamon, URP Series Series, Vol.22, 1980, p.179.

[7] For investigations of social planning as a part of town and country planning see D.V. Donnison and D. Eversley, Urban Patterns, Problems, and Policies, Heinemann, London, 1973; R. Williams, 'The idea of social planning', Planning Outlook, Vol.19, Autumn 1976, pp.11-19. For criticisms see F. von Hayek op.cit., and J. Jewkes, Ordeal by Planning, MacMillan, London, 1948.

[8] We suggest that not all planners would agree with Paragraph 49 of Town Planning and the Future, Royal Town Planning Institute, November 1976 : 'Planning must be partisan in its defence of freedom and social justice....it must help to absorb or to initiate changes in social structures..' (quoted in S. McConnell, Theories for Planning, Heinemann, 1981, p.142). See also E. Howe and J. Kaufman, 'The ethics of contemporary American planners', Journal of the American Planning Association, Vol.45, July 1979, pp.242-55.

[9] F. von Hayek, The Road to Serfdom, Routledge and Kegan Paul, London, 1944.

[10] J. Jowell, 'The limits of law in urban planning', Current Legal Problems, Vol.30, 1977, pp.63-83.

[11] P. McAuslan, Land, Law and Planning, Weidenfeld and Nicholson, 1975, pp.31-3.

[12] The ambitious stance of the systems view of planning is summed up by the description of the planner as the 'helmsman of the city' : J. McLoughlin, Urban and Regional Planning, 1969, Faber, London, p.75. See also F. Stuart Chapin, 'Taking stock of techniques for shaping urban growth', Journal of the American Institute of Planners, May 1963, p.81.

[13] The Bains Report : The New Local Authorities, Management and Structure, HMSO, London, 1972.

[14] E.g. Central Policy Review Staff, A Joint Framework for Social Policies, HMSO, London, 1975.

[15] Planning Advisory Group, Report on the Future of Development Plans, 1965, HMSO, London.

[16] Report of the Committee on Admin. Tribunals and Enquiries (The Franks Report), 1957, Cmnd 218. Skeffington Report on People and Planning, 1969, HMSO.

[17] J. Edwards and R. Batley, The Politics of Positive Discrimination : an Evaluation of the Urban Programme 1967-77, Tavistock, London, 1978.

[18] J. Skitt, Practical Corporate Planning in Local Government, Leonard Hill, Leighton Buzzard, 1975; J.D. Stewart, The Responsive Local Authority, Charles Knight, London, 1974.

[19] A.T. Blowers, 'Checks and balances, the politics of minority government', Public Administration, Autumn 1977, pp.305-16; Royal Town Planning Institute, Planning and the Future, a Discussion Paper, November 1975.

[20] J. Dearlove, The Reorganisation of British Local Government : Old Orthodoxies and a Political Perspective, Cambridge University Press, London, 1979.

[21] B. Needham, 'Concrete problems, not abstract goals', Journal of the Royal Town Planning Institute, Vol.57, 1971, No.7, pp.317-9.

[22] For a fuller account of this problem see J. Friend, 'The dynamics of policy adjustment and design in an intercorporate field', Paper for Synposium on Interorganisational Decision-Making and Public Policy, International Institute of Management, West Berlin, June 1975.

[23] For a classification of planning environments and appropriate responses in terms of this problem see R. Axelsson and L. Rosenberg, 'Decision-making and organisational turbulence', Acta Sociologica, 1979, Vol.22, No.1, pp.45-62. For other discussions on the subject of planners' reactions to accelerated change see A. Faludi, Planning Theory, Pergamon, 1976, Chapters 7, 8, 9; D.A. Schon, Beyond the Stable State, Penguin 1971; D.A. Hart, 'Ordering change and changing orders - a study of urban policy development', Policy and Politics, Vol.2, No.1, pp. 27-41.

[24] P. McAuslan, Land, Law and Planning, Weidenfeld, 1975, p.200.

[25] For example, many new developments do not involve anybody fully trained in design : A.R. Beer, 'Development control and design quality : Part 2', Town Planning Review, Vol.54, No.4, 1983, pp. 383-404.

[26] P. Booth, 'Development control and design quality, Part 1 : Conditions : a useful way of controlling design?', Town Planning Review, Vol.54, No.4, 1983, pp.265-84.

[27] For analyses of town planning ideologies from the point of view of the psychological and socio-psychological perspectives of planners, see D.L. Foley, British Journal of Sociology, Vol.II, 1960; M. Douglas, 'Environments at risk', pp.278-96 in J. Dowie and P. Lefrere (eds) Risk and Chance, Open University Press, 1980; R. Glass, 'The evaluation of planning - some sociological considerations', International Social Science Journal, VII, 1959, pp.393-409.

[28] G.M. Dillon, 'Policy and dramaturgy : a critique of current conceptions of policy making', Policy and Politics, Vol. 5, 1976, pp.47-62.

[29] See also R. Darke, 'The Dialectics of Policy Making. Form and Content', pp.194-210, in P. Healey, G. McDougall, M.J. Thomas, Planning Theory : Prospects for the 1980s, Pergamon, London, 1982, p.203.

[30] P. Saunders, Urban Politics : A Sociological Interpretation, Penguin, Harmondsworth, 1980, p.224.

24 The symbolic uses of rationality in planning

We can identify, from the beginnings of management science methods being used in government, through operational research, systems analysis: [1], welfare economics, to corporate planning, what could be termed a rationalist tradition in government: [2]. Planning has been infected by this tradition: [3], along with other branches of government. Purpose is one of the predominant characteristics of this tradition: [4]. Rational activity has been defined by the tradition to be behaviour which is purposeful, and which strives to achieve an independently conceived end. Goal directed behaviour is then a model of rational action. Goals not only determine behaviour, but they also offer a standard by which to judge achievement, and by which those responsible can be held accountable. Already some of the underlying assumptions are beginning to show. Firstly there is the theory, either understood by the mass public or easily communicable to it, that government action should proceed according to the rational-comprehensive strategy - a central decision-maker carrying out a chronological sequence of tasks : goals, then alternatives, then evaluation of alternatives using goals. Secondly there is the belief in the accountability of the decision-maker. Both are myths, but, more importantly, both fit in with how the mass public thinks or can be persuaded to think.

Also, rational activity aspires to an objective knowledge, unaffected by personal bias or political dogma: [5]. It requires that decision processes and their justification be explicitly stated: [6]. It condemns departmentalism, institutional inertia, and secret bargains, and advocates the use of novel analytical approaches to planning problems. While all of these things have highly favourable connotations for the mass public: [7], they are unattainable either because the world of government institutions resists such changes or because no knowledge on social or political matters can ever be objective: [8].

Also the rationalist tradition takes on a particular view of political activity which has several important weaknesses. Firstly there is the idea that politics is a matter of resolving problems as evidenced by 'felt need': [9]. Individuals or groups who experience some kind of felt need represent a political problem which must be resolved. Yet in reality resources are allocated only after individuals or groups have shown that they have the ability to exert sanctions on society if such resources are withheld. However, it is very useful for politicians to portray this view of 'felt need'. They direct public attention towards groups and individuals who can receive popular sympathy but who receive no significant benefits in return, and whose political ineffectiveness is unchanged by such dramatic gestures: [10].

Secondly there is the idea that the political process can in some way be made perfect. The idea assumes that the only aim of plans is to solve problems, and that there are no problems to which there exist no solutions. Thus there exists an ideal way of organising the planning process so that it meets the systems view of goal attainment. From the point of view of the technocratic version of organisation theory this idea is associated with the existence of a 'one best way' and with optimisation. We shall show later that the idea is grotesquely simplistic: [11].

The third distortion of the real nature of political activity perpetrated by the rationalist tradition is the idea that politics can be made uniform: [12]. The idea assumes that a perfect planning process can be imposed at national and local levels. The idea also led to the systems view - that the planning process was systematically ordered in a mistaken way and required to be drastically remodelled.

In making the setting of goals the fundamental and primal activity in the policy process, the rationalist tradition assumed a political consensus existed as to how the resources necessary for welfare and security were to be exploited, mobilised and allocated. However, the values of welfare and security are highly ambiguous. They are shared by all, but their interpretation varies. Planning and policy making can in reality do little more than explore the conflicting elements of these values. They cannot satisfy the conflicting demands which such values have generated. And these processes of exploitation, mobilisation, and allocation and these values have been subjected to the interpretations, coordinating activities, and direction of planners. Associated and equally ambiguous values have also been generated and largely internalised. One such value has been the value of efficiency. Another has been the value of order. Both have undergone continuous transformation as the planning environment has changed. Initially efficiency was associated with harmonious land use distributions which minimised nuisance to neighbours and which minimised communication requirements. As physically-based concepts of planning changed to social and economic ones, it became associated with a smooth-running and appropriate distribution of local authority services. On the other hand order was initially associated with orderliness: [13] with zones of homogeneous land uses from which non-conforming uses had been expelled and with the uniform application of space and density standards: [14]. As urban change and the control of development became more complex and more difficult, with the removal in the fifties of local authority powers to buy land cheaply, the concept of order became detached from the act of control, and associated with the act of understanding. Order in planning came to mean producing a sufficiently robust and dynamic understanding of how urban and regional change fit into an ordered pattern: [15].

The rationalist tradition has brought with it an associated value system about the specification and application of formalised managerial techniques. These techniques directly mirror the intellectual assumptions of the rationalist tradition. More significantly, these techniques have been offered as the necessary stage props: [16] of the managing of the corporate state - most significantly the way in which the ordering of values and priorities, and their achievement, can best be guided in the inter-connected policy areas of modern government.

Some techniques can serve to add justification for adopting a particular definition of political accountability: [17]. For example, it has been claimed that the goals achievement approach in planning is flexible enough to allow residents' groups and other affected parties, or local councillors, to feed in their own values (goals and objectives and their relative importance, and even the extent to which different alternatives achieve them). However what is often overlooked is that use of such a technique determines the planning process to be followed - in particular a chronological sequence of logically separate tasks of the kind found in the rational-comprehensive strategy. One political advantage of this is to limit public or councillor participation to carefully designed and located windows into the planning process, and to limit the range and therefore potential unpedictableness of the questions that might be generated. It also serves to perpetuate the mythical conception of the planner carrying out the commands of politicians and public, and of his role as being merely to answer questions which others can ask.

Most techniques serve to limit the expression of conflict: [18]. The goals achievement approach depends upon consensus of goals completely: [19]. Linear programming can allow only one definition of the objective function to be optimised. In theory, it is possible to sample survey a wide variety of opinions and use them to take a probabilistic approach to cost-benefit analysis, although the use of this approach is extremely rare. Such techniques are politically useful in that they create the impression of political consensus: [20] and unless someone is directly involved or a member of an active pressure group such an impression will be a convincing one. Thus the necessity for politicians to placate losers or to produce intricate justifications for decisions in terms of overall advantage is removed: [21].

Another way in which such techniques are politically useful is that they produce a self-contained political process with a well-defined beginning and end. There is a sense of inevitable progression through the process: [22]. Participants all begin the process as it were afresh. There are few opportunities to bring up politicians' broken promises or sins of omission from the past. And the lack of any discussion of the reasons why problems exist (failure of past policies perhaps) is comforting for officials too.

Planning forecasts also have their political function. An interesting question about the use of forecasts is the extent to which the planning horizon is the determinant of the length of the forecast rather than the degree of certainty of the forecast being the determinant of the planning horizon. One study of employment projections concluded that they could only be made for local areas with any confidence one year ahead: [23]. Regional employment projections suffer lesser, though still serious, problems. While one must have long term planning, it seems strange that the current planning system predicates plans based on surer projections (Local Plans) upon plans based on less sure projections (Structure and Regional Plans). Part of the explanation must lie in the rationalist belief that the overall pattern should determine the growth and change of the component parts, rather than the overall pattern being continuously adjusted to organic change in the parts (that organic change being informed by, but not determined by, the overall pattern).

Although we have attempted to show earlier the intense difficulties of evaluating plans and decisions afterwards, this procedure has its political usefulness. (The procedure fits in with the rational-comprehensive strategy and its rationalist assumption that logically different tasks can be chronologically separated.) The political usefulness of deferring evaluation till after the plan is finished is of course that it puts off many difficult questions until after the crucial decisions have been taken. The onus of responsibility is thus taken off planners at the time of agreeing the plan, for providing many of the value justifications of the type discussed earlier. And since review is less politically crucial, this can be undertaken in the privacy of the planning office rather than in front of the public: [24]. The act of relegating the most searching questions to the status of an epilogue of the planning process thus enormously simplifies the act of choosing between alternatives: [25]. And because departments in both local and central government are in a sense competing with each other for the scarce attention and time of politicians, such a procedure greatly increases the likelihood that a plan will be agreed by them, rather than being discussed and deferred ad nauseam.

We have suggested above that the actual way in which all types of plans are produced by planners fits the disjointed-incrementalist model far more closely than it does the rational-comprehensive one. But in the interface with politicians or public the plan is given the appearance of being the product of the rational-comprehensive strategy. There are a number of reasons for this. Partly it comes about because of the exaggerated expectations of both politicians and public that the planning process, indeed all government processes, can be made rational. Partly it suits the requirements of planners and public officials to present their plans and policies in an understandable and clear way, and the rational-comprehensive strategy has the advantage over the disjointed-incrementalist strategy that it is both understandable and clear. Also it is a much surer instrument by which officials can control politicians and the public since it limits the type and timing of political and public participation in the planning process.

This discussion thus gives a clue to the main role which these techniques, methods and strategies perform. That role has been a dramaturgical one: [26]. Dramatury is defined here as a preoccupation with creating and using symbolic and stylised representations of reality so as to propagandise and sustain a given intellectual, organisational or social order. Because of the ambiguities which are inherent in these representations, they have in practice operated so as to give symbolic and dramatic effect to the rationalist tradition with which planning is now implicated. Their principal effect has been to formalise, symbolically, a rationalist rhetoric, and provide the legitimating symbols of rationalist planning debate.

Dramaturgy has arisen for a number of reasons. In the first instance the primary aim of the rationalist view of the planning process is to provide a fully explicit description of matters relevant to a plan, with all elements of fact and assumption in the foreground and with few elements of historical development and of psychological perspective. This mythical aim is exemplified and symbolised by the techniques, methods and strategies that are used. While the rationalist tradition seeks to justify decisions by means of these techniques, methods and strategies, the mythical nature of such a justification is shown by the fact that they do not represent principles for guiding action: [27]. They can only operate when the substantive issues of planning have been dealt with. To attempt to argue otherwise would be to commit the naturalistic fallacy (see chapter 14).

In this regard then, techniques, methods, and strategies display two of the characteristics of myth : standard motivations and recurring themes. The standard motivations are the need for justification, and the need for control. The recurring themes include plan-making as a productive process, the means-ends concept, the centralisation-decentralisation dilemma, the requirement for plans to be coherently orchestrated, the resistance to change by large government organisations, a belief in progress.

Secondly the dramatic and symbolic effect of these techniques, methods, and strategies has also been of the kind associated with cathetic symbols. They have evoked predictable responses from politicians and the public, such as the deference given to scientific method and quantification. They have also brought legitimacy for decisions associated with them because they appeal to shared and highly favourable values.

Thirdly planners and other policy makers not only have a large amount of formal authority and discretion, but they have to deal with conflicts of an irreconcilable nature. Imposing order and coherence on these dilemmas brings its own tensions and ambivalence. Such tension and ambivalence have to be tolerated. The myth of rational action and its associated techniques, methods, and strategies is an indispensible part of any effort to maintain order and coherence in the face of such conflicts and dilemmas.

NOTES

[1] On the intellectual and psychological satisfactions provided by systems, and on the symbolic significance in the politics of pollution, see M. Douglas, 'Environments at Risk', pp.278-96, in J. Dowie and P. Lefrere (eds) Risk and Chance, Open University Press, 1980.

[2] In Oakeshott's words, 'rationalism...has become the stylistic criterion of all respectable politics' : M. Oakeshott, Rationalism in Politics and Other Essays, Methuen, London, 1962.

[3] E.C. Banfield, 'Ends and means in planning', International Social Sciences Journal, Vol.XI, No.3, 1959; M. Meyerson and E.C. Banfield, Politics, Planning, and the Public Interest, New York, The Free Press, 1955; J.M. Simmie, Citizens in Conflict, Hutchinson, London, 1971; J. Friedmann, 'Planning as a vocation', Plan, Vol.6, No.3, p.99-124.

[4] For example, the definition of planning as 'the process of strategic choice' : J. Friend and W.N. Jessop, Local Government and Strategic Choice, Tavistock, London, 1969, p.97. The most common example of this view is the view of the planner as a rational allocator of resources.

[5] This aspiration is unrealistic in that, even in natural science, the scientific process is social in the forming of consensuses and the outlawing of rogue theories : Z.A. Medvedev, The Rise and Fall of T.D. Lysenko, trans. by I.M. Lerner, New York, Columbia University Press, 1969; D.R. Bewen, 'Objectivity as a normative concept', Journal of Politics, 1977, Vol.39, pp.201-10.

[6] The rationalist tradition has even infected the study of political processes:

> 'Impressed by the accomplishments of modern natural science, and seeing in it potency, many students of politics have emulated its language in the hope of matching some of its achievements. Professional political science has shown an increasing tendency to restrict itself to language which is literal, static, and intersubjectively uniform. The goal seems to be a political vocabulary with clear observational predicates, stripped of the multiple meanings attached to words of conventional discourse.'

E. Zashin and P.C. Chapman, 'The uses of metaphor and analogy - toward a renewal of political language', Journal of Politics, Vol.36, 1974, pp.290-326 at pp.293-294.

[7] For an investigation of situations where policy justification may, or may not, be needed, see P. Hall, R. Land, A. Webb, and C. Parker, Change, Choice, and Conflict in Social Policy, Heinemann, London, 1975, Chapter 15.

[8] J. Watkins, 'Imperfect rationality', pp.167-230 in R. Borger and F. Cioffi, Explanation in the Behavioural Sciences, 1970, Cambridge University Press.

[9] For an example see Royal Town Planning Institute, Planning and the Future, A Discussion Paper, November 1976, p.1.

[10] This is why we reject the idea that 'need' and 'real income distribution' should be the principal motives of planning. Such an aim would fit nicely into the rationalist tradition. See S. McConnell, Theories for Planning, Heinemann, 1981, Chapter 6.

[11] Even the scientific method upon which the rationalist-comprehensive strategy is based has been shown to be simplistic. In reality, scientific breakthroughs have very often been made despite methodology, the methodological mask being readjusted after the breakthrough. T.S. Kuhn, The Structure of Scientific Revolutions, University of Chicago Press, Chicago, 1970; A. Kaplan, The Conduct of Inquiry, Chandler, San Francisco, 1964.

[12] In planning this has been associated with the idea of a rational generic planning process. Such an idea has been vague enough not to be measurable or testable in any way; in this lay its usefulness to practitioners : see E. Reade 'If planning is anything, maybe it can be identified', Urban Studies, Vol.20, 1983, pp.159-71.

[13] J. Simmie, Power, Property, and Corporatism, Macmillan, London, 1980, pp.165-6.

[14] See for example the application of such values in Oxford in the 1940s and 1950s; J. Simmie, op.cit.

[15] D.A. Hart, 'Ordering change and changing orders - a study of urban policy development', Policy and Politics, Vol.2, No.1, pp. 27-41.

[16] J.M. Simmie, Citizens in Conflict, Hutchinson, London, 1974, p.121.

[17] A. Rapoport, 'The use and misuse of game theory', p.16-32, in J. Dowie and P. Lefrere (eds) Risk and Chance, Open University Press, 1980.

[18] One way of suppressing conflict is by the statement of extremely vague goals which everyone will agree with but which have very little explanatory power : Greater London Development Plan, Report of the Committee of Inquiry, HMSO, 1973, p.27.

[19] Either subgroups are not defined in the population (e.g. the Coventry-Solihull-Warwickshire Sub-Regional Study, 1971) or else a central decision body (a mixture of planners and local councillors) puts weights on sub-groups.

[20] One example of this is the setting forward, in a plan, of a universally applicable set of goals, and then a process of 'deduction' of objectives from these, giving the appearance of a logically-defensible and value-neutral process. See N. Lichfield, P. Kettle, M. Whitbread, Evaluation in the Planning Process, Pergamon, Oxford, 1975, pp.201-2.

[21] Increasing the degree of rationality by more planning often fulfils the same symbolic role as research often does - to prevent the need for action. For example, basic governmental reform in the USA is often sidestepped by adding on extra efficiency exercises (e.g. cost effectiveness studies) : G.A. Daneke, 'Whither environmental regulation?', Journal of Public Policy, Vol.4, No.2, pp.139-51.

[22] The reader may care to consider the extent to which such beliefs represent a 'historicist' position. See K.R. Popper, The Poverty of Historisism, Routledge, 1976, pp.1-54; K.R. Popper, The Open Society and its Enemies, Vol.2, Routledge, 1977, Chapter 25.

[23] K. Allen and D. Yuill, Small Area Employment Projections, Macmillan, London, 1977.

[24] In many cases such reviews of planning's effects actually discourage searching questions : D.E.C. Eversley and M. Moody, The Growth of Planning Research since the Early 1960s, SSRC, London, 1976.

[25] 'Very often the visible issues are the safe ones and issues which do not reach the political agenda are more important'; A. Blowers, 'Much Ado About Nothing : A Case Study of Planning and Power', p.140-60, in P. Healey, G. McDougall, M.J. Thomas, (eds) Planning Theory : Prospects for the 1980s, Pergamon, Oxford, 1981 at p.143.

[26] G.M. Dillon, 'Policy and dramaturgy, a critique of current conceptions of policy making', Policy and Politics, Vol.5, No.1, Sept. 1976, pp.47-62.

[27]

> 'These evaluative ideas are for their part empirically discoverable and analysable, as elements of meaningful human conduct, but their validity can not be deduced from empirical data as such. The "objectivity" of the social sciences depends rather on the fact that the empirical data are always related to those evaluative ideas which alone make them worth knowing and the significance of the empirical data is derived from those evaluative ideas. But these data can never become the foundation for the empirically impossible proof of the validity of the evaluative ideas.':

M. Weber, The Methodology of the Social Sciences, Free Press, 1949, p.111; see also H. Albert, 'The Myth of Total Reason : Dialectical Claims in the light of Undialectical Criticism', pp.157-94 in A. Giddens, op.cit., p.158.

25 The political functions of plans

Two of the weaknesses of the rationalist tradition in planning are that it encourages the view that one should judge a decision or plan by whether or not it is implemented and that it treats plans as large-scale decisions. This view interlocks with the prescription that the most hyper-critical type of plan-evaluation, called plan review, should take place as the final stage in the planning process. Plans are viewed as proposed solutions to problems, and all problems are seen as amenable to solution. In some cases the view seems to fit in with reality, as in the construction of a motorway network, or in the phasing of new housing, or in the balancing of the various elements of a new town. New towns would seem to be a perfect example of where it is possible, afterwards, to evaluate the effects of the plan. But the political functions of new towns have varied considerably since their inception. At the beginning they were limited examples of land reform and the recouping, by the community, of land profits. In the late fifties and sixties they became an easy instrument for the speeding up of house building in what came to be known as the 'numbers game'. And in the late seventies they became one of the vehicles for privatisation and subsidisation of the central exchequer: [1].

It is therefore worthwhile looking beneath the surface of plans to understand their political functions. What follows is an inventory of possible functions which plans can perform. Some simple plans perform one only : these are easier to evaluate but also more liable to lose political support. More commonly plans perform many political functions simultaneously.

INDIRECTNESS

Sometimes it is necessary for plans to have a publicly acceptable aim as a cover for a purpose which is less acceptable or which is not shared by all. Or an organisation may publish a plan through an indirect channel to cover itself in some way.

For example, the 1980 Code of Practice on opencast coal mining published by the Association of Metropolitan Authorities is a means by which individual local authorities can attempt to influence the National Coal Board. If such influence were exerted directly by any local authority, this would involve making the concession that there is a possible case for open cast operations in its area. Such a Code of Practice may also help local planning authorities to avoid inviting the interest of mining companies consequent on the production of mineral subject plans.

Also key settlement policy can play the function of indirectness. While it focuses attention on growth and rational justifications for concentration in a small number of centres, it performs, implicitly, its chief function in many cases of minimising a shire county's population growth from in-migration.

CREATING CONFIDENCE IN AN AREA

With the increase in the new, developmental, entrepreneurial planning, promotion is becoming an increasingly important objective for planners. Plans which 'enable' by smoothing the way for private sector investment, are particularly relevant here. Design Briefs, Small Firms Packages, GIAs, HAAs, and Conservation Area Plans are all examples of plans with a promotional component.

SYMBOLIC REASSURANCE

Often the aim is to show that 'something is being done'. The stock criticism of such plans (for example, the Urban Aid Programme, the Inner Cities Partnership Schemes, and Regional Policy) is that they do enough to reassure but not enough to achieve what they claim to achieve: [2].

The easiest way to reassure without the commitment of scarce resources is to collect information. For example, the introduction of land registers of publicly-owned urban wastelands pacified the Conservative critics of public land ownership in the early eighties without committing the government to irrevocable action.

Another way of providing symbolic reassurance is to change the names of spending programmes without significantly altering the level of funding. For example, the Inner Urban Areas Act 1978 inasfar as it relates to Designated Districts, drew on resources which were previously largely available in another form. (This worked to planners' advantage, since it put directly or indirectly into their hands, money and leverage with other local authority departments, and it enabled planners to take the initiative to do positive things.)

COUNTERING CRITICISM

Partnership, liaison, and consultation are all methods of drawing the teeth of potential critics. It is perhaps no coincidence that public participation in planning was introduced after a period of intense public criticism of planning proposals, nor that Inner City Partnerships (bringing potentially critical local authorities in closer contact with central government) have come about at a time of redistribution of resources away from the older connurbations towards the faster growing and economically more viable shire counties. The process is as follows. The under-resourced area is promised money only in return for scaled down demands, in the form of a plan. The plan thus implicates the local authority, and forces it to defend central government financial stringency.

MONITORING RATHER THAN PROPOSING

Some plans do not, despite the wording of the legislation, predict or propose, but simply monitor a fast changing or unpredictable situation. This is sometimes a very sensible thing to do. There is now a growing category of planning situations which are unpredictable, yet which demand, by their importance, staff resources to monitor them. For example, guidelines for oilfields and gasfields are of this type, as those published in 1981 by Dorset County Council reveal: [3]. Another example is that of the West Sussex Structure Plan 1980, which openly acknowledged that it was beyond the ability of the planning authority to control the extent to which air traffic would be increased at Gatwick. Yet this would be the single most important cause of increased labour demand in the county, possibly leading to the need for additional housing land. For this type of situation then any claim that the plan is 'rational' has to be finally abandoned as impossible and inappropriate.

GENERATING COMMITMENT BY OTHERS

A good example here is the Glamorgan Heritage Coast Plan 1976 which, although an inventory of many detailed environmental improvements, aimed to create goodwill and understanding between the Countryside Commission, South Glamorgan County, Ogwr Borough Council, Mid-Glamorgan County, and the Vale of Glamorgan Borough Council. Countryside Management Plans provide another example of this type of plan.

Often such plans aim to act as a generator of ideas or as a catalyst. They are therefore (unless inventorying past achievements or decisions) vague. Also such plans aim to leave plenty of room for action by those bodies they seek to commit. They tend therefore, when making prescriptions, to make them at a fairly abstract level - many development or design briefs on cindarella sites demonstrate this characteristic. Also such plans tend to be incremental. For example, the fact that payment of grants must be supplemented by private sector investment means that Industrial Improvement Area Plans can only be tentative documents.

Also plans can be used directly to engineer commitment by others. For example, chief executives who wish to proceed by ad hoc decisions can be partly outflanked by plans. Also districts can be partly constrained by structure plans.

BACK-COVERING

It is quite commonplace for officials or politicians to publicise their reservations or even criticisms of plans despite their official endorsement of those plans. An example is the acceptance of central government house improvement funds while at the same time warning of the impending need, in the future, for a renewed clearance programme: [4].

BARGAINING COUNTER IN DEVELOPMENT CONTROL

In the traditional, regulatory role of planning departments the role of a plan as bargaining counter is crucial. In those authorities where the old pre-1968 development plan was well thought out and largely still relevant, there has been much less motivation to draw up local plans. Moreover the problem of site-by-site outdatedness of an old development plan is often got round by means of supplementing with a whole array of informal plans, design briefs and decisions relating to what in effect are site-by-site amendments. The bargaining counter function of a plan inclines it towards being incrementally formed and changed : the traditional pattern of informally amending and supplementing the development plan. In this organic process the impreciseness of planning concepts is crucial. For example, the difficulty of defining and implementing a policy of 'meeting local needs' (a difficulty made worse by central government spending cuts) allows wide scope for negotiation.

CREATING FAIRNESS, CONSISTENCY AND PREDICTABILITY

This traditional political objective is currently somewhat on the defensive, as non-conforming industries are given longer term or permanent permissions in residential areas, as recreation uses are encouraged in the urban fringe, and as jobs gain priority over the environment.

MAKING EVERYTHING LEGAL AND ABOVE-BOARD

Because of the new, promotional, entrepreneurial planning, there is an increase in the type of plan which describes what has already happened, in order to show that money was spent honestly. The need exists in such cases, to publish a plan as a kind of audit to justify the payments and resources used for 'enabling' purposes.

BID FOR RESOURCES

Plans and their related documents are powerful tools for arguing for more resources from central government. Mid-year population estimates (mainly revised according to housing statistics) are used by local authorities in arguing for more block grant. Structure plans and their sometimes optimistic population projections have often been used in a similar way. With the possibility of compensation funds being available under Sections 32 and 41 of the Wildlife and Countryside Act 1981, plans which would ultimately lead to management agreements with farmers and landowners obviously have a similar significance, since there is a somewhat limited central pool of money, and allocation is on the basis of first come, first served. Also sometimes plans include scenarios of the future. Such scenarios can include convincing warnings of what may happen (loss of confidence in an area leading to urban decay, increasing urban crime and racial violence, increasing land speculation in the absence of firm policies, and urban riots). These warnings are unusual attempts to persuade local councillors and national politicians to provide more resources.

ARENA FOR DEBATE

When the planning environment becomes so complex and turbulent that any hope that a plan can achieve coordination has to be relinquished, then a plan takes on the political function of stimulating debate. Unlike the other political functions of plans, however, this is a residual one which planners hope will not be necessary. Because of this the plan usually is presented to politicians and the public in a rational-comprehensive form. Policies on which consensus exists are given greater weight and specificity than policies on which conflicts exist. The existence of conflict is usually played down or ignored altogether. This was the case, for instance, with the Bedfordshire Structure Plan 1976. It would be far more useful for such plans not to make specific proposals, but to attempt to illustrate and analyse the arguments on all sides, to suggest where the current balance of advantages lie, and to suggest where the source of uncertainty lie (strength of opinion may change, political control of councils may change, statutory undertakers may make different policies) and the implications of the balance of advantage changing. To take just two examples, a study on the implementation of development plans found that the 'bending' of public sector programmes in line with plan policies did not occur through the agency of plan policies: [5]. And another study on the role of local plans in 'facilitating' development found that local plans only had an impact where private sector demand for sites already existed: [6]. In such cases, and in cases where conflict exists, plans containing several viewpoints might provide a more appropriate forum for the eventual resolution of ideas.

THE EFFECT OF A PLAN'S POLITICAL FUNCTION UPON HOW IT IS PRESENTED

With the exception of the last-mentioned political function whose presentation has already been discussed above, we are now in a position to relax somewhat the hard and fast generalisation that, although the planning process is in reality nearer to the disjointed-incrementalist strategy, plans are actually *presented* to politicians and the public as the result of the rational-comprehensive strategy. Four exceptions emerge when we consider the political functions of plans. We would expect that if a plan's main political function was to monitor, rather than propose, then the tentative and temporary nature of what the plan represents would tend planners to present the plan as if it were part of a disjointed-incrementalist strategy. This tendency would be greater if there were several dimensions of uncertainty rather than one. Similarly if a plan's main aim was to generate commitment by others, then the explicit assumption of several decision-makers other than the planner would again tend to influence presentation in the same direction. Similarly plans which invite bargains must be undogmatic and tentative and if this was the only political function of a plan we would expect to find the same tendency. Back-covering usually takes place by means of asides and is usually accompanied by plenty of other material to serve to disguise it. It is, therefore released in a seemingly haphazard way rather than calling attention to itself as the central theme of a document. We can therefore suggest that it would not be given the importance necessary to present it as a product of the rational-comprehensive strategy.

NOTES

[1] Even the 'technical' justification for plans can change quite radically over relatively short periods : e.g. R. Newman, The Road through Christchurch Meadow, Oxford Polytechnic, 1980; also M. Camina, Bowthorpe, Centre for East Anglian Studies, University of East Anglia, 1980.

[2] J. Edwards and R. Batley, The Politics of Positive Discrimination; an Evaluation of the Urban Programme : 1967-77, Tavistock, London, 1978; for planning practitioners' views about the Inner City Partnership schemes see G. Shaylor, Seminar Report, Town and Country Planning Summer School, Report of Proceedings, 6-17 September 1980, University of Exeter, p.59.

[3] County Planning Department, County Hall, Dorchester, Onshore Oil in Dorset, 1981.

[4] For example, while Coventry is officially pursuing a housing improvement policy this did not prevent one senior Council official from warning that the low funding of the programme from central government threatened to create the need for a massive slum clearance programme within 15 years : Coventry District Council, Planning Committee, 10 January 1979.

[5] P. Healey, J. Davis, M. Wood, M. Elson, The Implementation of Development Plans - a report to the DOE, Feb. 1982, Dept of Town Planning, Oxford Polytechnic.

[6] R. Farnell, Local Planning in Four English Cities : Concerns, Conflicts and Commitments, Gower, London, 1983.

26 The forms and meanings of political language in planning

When asked about its politics, an opinion sample will tend to emphasise and reemphasise various themes. Such themes may tell us very little about political processes. But such themes will probably tell us a lot about the hopes and fears of the people sampled and of their need for reassurance. These hopes and fears will usually be rationalised in the form of a system of beliefs. Such beliefs are important in that they serve the function of political cohesion.

Such beliefs will usually tend to include the following. There is the belief that the public determines what government decides; the evidence given is elections, and consultations with the public: [1]. Also it is generally believed that public officials, including planners, carry out the will of politicians, and therefore the will of the public; the evidence usually offered is that our laws require them to do so. Also it is generally believed that a government (central or local) which satisfies public demands wins political support. Also government has the power and the information to get the results which people want.

However the real situation is rather different. What people get from local and central government is usually what public officials, including planners, decide to do about their problems, rather than what statutes or political speeches would suggest should be done: [2]. Public officials, including planners have considerable discretion in practice to respond or not to respond to demands made upon them: [3]. It is impossible in practice to legalistically specify in advance what they should do. There is therefore wide leeway for policy interpretation in practice: [4]. This public belief that what administrators do has been specified already by politicians, helps to legitimate administrative (including planning) decisions.

Also it can be rarely known what concrete future effects will come from public policies: [5]. But laymen dislike uncertainty, and so they substitute the personality of politicians for impersonal and unpredictable forces. They want to believe that politicians and bureaucracies have the power to influence future events. They therefore pay great attention to the promisory gestures that politicians make. Usually such gestures are vague, but much can be read into them to provide symbolic reassurance: [6].

The achievement of a political goal by a group leads to claims for more of the same kind of benefit and not to contentment. Pássivity and contentment can only be created by symbolic reassurance, periodically renewed: [7]. Politicians create symbolic reassurance by dramatising their ability to deal with political problems even when these are beyond their control: [8]. Because the forces which politicians claim to be able to control are so impersonal and threatening to the public, it is prepared to view these gestures as valid and convincing: [9]. This happens even when the public does not share the politician's values - it is sufficient that he be regarded as strong and effective. It also happens even when the politician does not provide any tangible benefits, compared with promising gestures and symbolic reassurance: [10].

Reassurance is conveyed in three ways. Firstly rhetorical speeches: [11] justify regulatory programmes and plans as protecting widespread public interests. Secondly administrators use legal language which commands enforcement, by its appearance of precision and its containing confident commands. Thirdly judicial and administrative hearings maintain the appearance of a rational weighing of evidence: [12]. Such reassurance is created, and political conflict reduced, by a variety of different language forms which characterise local and central government.

These different language forms do not convey meanings by themselves: [13]. It is the social setting of political language which creates its meaning. And in particular it is from the responses of the audience that we can understand its meaning. For example, naming can usefully be viewed directly as a form of knowing: [14]. To speak of the need for nuclear power in terms of reducing the power of coal miners to strike is to place it in a category of <u>political control</u>. To argue that nuclear energy is cheaper than coal-derived energy is to place it in the category of <u>economic benefits</u>. The evaluation of each of these statements will be quite different: [15]. So language is not just another kind of activity. It is the central feature of the relationship between a speaker and his audience: [16].

We will now deal with those meanings of political language used in planning associated with its forms or styles: [17]. These are more persistent and stable than the connotations of language content, and also more complex. Most of the time we are not aware that the meaning of language is contained in its form. But in a real sense the 'medium is the message'.

What formal properties does political language in planning have? We shall show that the following stylistic elements are relevant : commands; definitions, statements of premises, inferences, and conclusions; and descriptions of the role and status of the originating agency and of the audience.

We can distinguish four distinctive language styles in planning. These are the hortatory, legal, administrative, and bargaining language styles. They deal with authority, persuasion, and participation; with whether people see themselves as in control of, or controlled by, events; and as a party to political status and benefits, or as excluded from them: [18].

We shall see that the meanings of each language style for unorganised and uninvolved mass publics (revealed by their responses) are often the opposite of the meanings each style has for those intimately involved. This has direct relevance to any understanding of how it is possible to maintain widespread acceptance of the need for planning and public agreement of its main aims in the face of continual evidence of conflict on particular planning issues and of large amounts of discretion by planners and politicians.

THE HORTATORY LANGUAGE STYLE IN PLANNING: [19].

Hortatory language is most in evidence in appeals to particular audiences for support of policies, in public statements by politicians, in those planning debates which reach the public view, in public statements by the courts and by planners, and in local council and Parliamentary debates on planning issues. The language style is directed at the mass public.

The stability of recurrence of the central terms of this language form comes about as a direct result of the instability and ambiguity of their content. The terms commonly employed, such as 'public interest', 'needs': [20], 'strategic importance', 'amenity', and 'balance of net benefits' all mean different things to different people: [21].

The hortatory style consists formally of premises, inferences, and conclusions. The conclusions are usually in the form of promises or threats and amount to appeals for public support. Generality of appeal is the style's most useful feature.

Even if we disagree with a particular appeal for support of a planning idea, and in spite of the ambiguity of the terms employed, each example of the use of the style is accepted as valid evidence of the need for widespread support of planning policies and planning decisions. Thus the key meanings of the style are popular participation and rationality. Whatever the particular planning issue involved, the use of the language style bolsters the belief that the public has an important role in planning decisions. Moreover the public values gestures and postures consistent with rationality. So the most intelligent use of this language style conceals the emotional appeal using the disguise of intending to define the issues.

Consider the following :

'West Midlands County Council Structure Plan, 1980: [22].
...The Preferred Strategy.
Urban regeneration - the Priority Areas.

3.13. The Strategy has the principal aim of regenerating the older urban areas of the County in order to improve the quality of life for the people who live and work there. The Plan designates these as "Priority Areas" as shown in the key diagram. These are the areas with large numbers of houses in unsatisfactory condition, industrial dereliction, decaying shopping centres and large tracts of derelict waste land. They also have related socio-economic problems including high levels of unemployment. The Plan, therefore, proposes that the main emphasis of policies should be towards creating employment opportunities, improving housing conditions, restoring derelict and waste land and generally providing a better quality of environment in these areas.

'3.14. The overall aim is that these policies should be complementary and that the objectives set out in para. 3.1 should be mutually reinforcing. In certain circumstances, however, there may be conflicts, particularly where essential developments are likely to have an environmental impact. In such cases, it is intended that the adverse environmental impact should be minimised by appropriate means and this will involve the cooperation of the private sector. Indeed, the success of the Strategy will depend on a commitment to the Priority Areas by both the public and private sectors working together in partnership to ensure that their respective aims are achieved.'

The extract above contains the following arguments : premise 1 (problems of various kinds exist in the inner areas), inference 1 (these, it is implied, can and should be solved), conclusion 1 (designate inner areas for most investment); premise 2 (solution of problems comes from investment, investment depends upon both public and private sector), inference 2 (success depends upon commitment of both sectors), conclusion 2 (an implied appeal for such commitment). These chains of reasoning therefore are an appeal for support.

The ambiguity lies in terms used (e.g. 'policies should be complementary') but more importantly in the statements that 'environmental impact should be minimised' (if the inner areas have a poor residential environment, how can more factories and warehouses help that environment?) and that 'success of the strategy will depend on a commitment to the Priority Areas by both the public and private sectors', (in view of substantial land release to industry in greenfield sites why should the private sector wish to provide investment in inner areas, since many sites are insecure to vandalism, have uncertain subsoil conditions, and suffer from congested access?).

Again, let us look at this example from the Barlow Report :

'The Urgency of the Problem of London and the Home Counties.

426. The disadvantages under all three heads - social, economic, and strategical - and the problems which arise in consequence, present themselves with special insistence in the case of London and the Home Counties. It is not only that the mere size, spread, and growth of this great conurbation tend to accentuate the various disadvantages present in greater or lesser degree in other conurbations, but also the trend of migration to London and the Home Counties is on so large a scale and of such a long-term character that it can hardly fail to

increase in the foreseeable future advantages already shown to exist. For instance, the attractive pull of the Metropolis and the growth in the density of its population and of that of some of the centres on the periphery are enlarging the Metropolitan target and rendering it more vulnerable to aerial attack. In the view of those who have given evidence before the Commission - a view with which we find ourselves in complete accord - the circumstances are such as to demand that steps be taken without delay with the object of checking its further growth.
'....428. The Commission unanimously accepted the following nine conclusions :
(i) In view of the nature and urgency of the problems before the Commission, national action is necessary.
(ii) For this purpose, a Central Authority, national in scope and character, is required.
(iii) The activities of this Authority should be distinct from and should extend beyond those within the powers of any existing Government Department.
(iv) The objectives of national action should be:-
(a) Continued and further redevelopment of congested urban areas, where necessary.
(b) Decentralisation or dispersal, both of industries and industrial population, from such areas.
(c) Encouragement of a reasonable balance of industrial development, so far as is possible, throughout the various divisions or regions of Great Britain, coupled with appropriate diversification of industry in each division or region throughout the country....': [23].

The argument is of the form : premise (concentration in centres), inference (this concentration has disadvantages, no existing Government Department deals with industrial distribution), conclusion (national action through a new Authority is required).

The ambiguities are chiefly in 4(c), where 'a reasonable balance of industrial development' has held different connotations for different sections of society. The established interests of private and international industry have maintained a different view of this phrase from the one implied by the Royal Commission. Those interests have succeeded, in the years since then, in considerably diluting its original intended meaning.

The last example relates to public statements by a local councillor. It shows that such statements always appeal to the concept of popular participation - that councillors have their constituents uppermost in their minds when taking decisions :

> '"Nobody mentions rates in Hammersmith", one councillor loudly argued at a Labour group meeting, "People want services. They are not concerned with the level of rates, and, after all, when did the Labour party last lose an election here by putting up the rates?"': [24].

The extract shows the crude level of generalisation that many politicians use in public statements. The terms 'services' and 'level of rates' are not defined. They belie the greater attention to detail that councillors use when making decisions away from the public limelight.

The emotion that political argument about planning generates helps the individual to feel that there is a wholeness about society's approach to planning and that he is a participant in it. If the content of hortatory language draws different responses (of interpretation, of interest) from groups involved directly in the planning process, the form of this language style draws out similar responses from the mass, uninvolved public. By reinforcing the mass public's view that the public participates in the planning process it promotes their acceptance of planning policy: [25]. Thus temporary conflicts on passing planning issues serve to promote consensus on the fundamental aims of planning, by the mass public. They do this while simultaneously providing access to the planning process for small organised groups such as developers and representatives of the industries supplying urban and regional infrastructure.

THE LEGAL LANGUAGE STYLE IN PLANNING

The second language style in planning is the legal style: [26] evidenced in planning legislation and case law. While the lay public may interpret such language using dictionary definitions, these definitions are almost irrelevant. In reality, such definitions are almost completely ambiguous in meaning :

> '...the law relating to land use planning (and by land use planning I mean to embrace town and country planning, housing, road building, compulsory purchase, compensation, and community land) lacks objectivity and neutrality so that far from being the "golden metawand" of planning with all other aspects in a state of disarray, the law, its administration and official interpretation (via circulars and ministerial decisions as much as by cases decided by the courts) is itself a major contributory factor to the continuing disarray of planning.
> '...The judicial position at the moment then is, as it has been for some time, in a state of uncertainty. This is in part due to changing conceptions of planning slowly working their way through the system from central government to local authorities and back up again through inspectorial and ministerial decisions to the courts; and in part due to different ideologies at work in the courts which make for varying degrees of receptivity to the changing and widening conceptions of planning. The courts both reflect and contribute to the current crisis of identity in planning; reflect it because their differences mirror the differences in the planning world between the older and now largely outdated approach of the physical planners (architects and engineers by training) and the newer, more modern approach of the social science-oriented planners (educated in economics, geography, planning, sociology, as well as in urban design), and contribute to it, because...a casual decision reached on the basis of no or inadequate argument or no or inadequate understanding of the process of planning can for a time, until reversed or dissented from, overthrow long-standing practices and policies of the DOE and the local planning authorities. Equally, the inability of the courts and the lawyers to give some consistent and clear guidance on the scope of material

considerations is itself a stimulus to further judicial involvement in and muddle on the topic. As the courts are unable to give clear guidance, it is always likely to be worth-while challenging a ministerial decision when factors other than the traditional physical amenity ones are overtly taken into account in arriving at a decision adverse to a developer': [27].

It is this ambiguity which gives public lawyers and planners their political and social function in this sense, since unambiguous laws and rules would call neither for interpretation nor for argument about their meaning. Whether a statutory standard is phrased in terms of a widely accepted value ('strategic importance') or as a requirement to seek a particular goal ('the maintenance of a good physical environment') it means what public lawyers and planners do about it: [28].

So the dictionary meaning of the legal language style in planning has two main political functions in regard to the mass, uninvolved, public. It gives the public some reason for assuming that laws and rules are applied mechanically and automatically. Also it provides a vocabulary for organised groups to express themselves on planning issues in a way which reinforces this public view.

In terms of syntactical form legal language consists almost entirely of definitions and commands. These create an impression for the uninformed public of great precision. Public ridicule of legal language typically represents it as a series of nonsensical synonyms. But above all the impression given by legal language is that it must be obeyed, since it issues from popularly elected institutions. Reinforcing this popular view is the idea that statutes reflect the public will, and, being precise and unambiguous, are implemented mechanically by the courts and planners.

However, what meaning does legal language have for those directly involved in planning decisions, such as planners, public lawyers, developers, and representatives of public bodies? The most important attribute of meaning is flexibility, affected by changing circumstances, altered needs, and different interests. Thus for lawyers and their organised clients the most useful characteristic of legal language in planning is its ambiguity. In any particular planning dispute participants will make different interpretations of any relevant legal documents available.

For example :

> '<u>Town and Country Planning Act 1968 Section 1</u>
> (iv) A local authority shall, for the purpose of discharging their functions under this section of examining and keeping under review any matters relating to the area of another such authority, consult with that other authority about those matters.'

What does 'keeping under review' mean? Does it mean that if a structure plan is completed or renewed first by one county, and that if it has carried out extensive surveys relevant to matters in an adjoining county whose structure plan is not yet completed or renewed, and if it has attempted to liaise with that county, that it can justify policies, at the examination in public, which <u>prejudice</u> policies of the adjoining county's structure plan? What is the scope and content of the 'matters relating to the area of another such authority' which can be so reviewed? On these points the legislation is totally empty. Thus faced with a specific case, the planners and lawyers of one local authority will proceed as if the law is ambiguous, and expect other local authorities to do likewise.

However, when faced with an abstract discussion of law, public lawyers empowered to make <u>public</u> interpretations proceed as if the law has a clear meaning. For example, in the Fawcett case where a local planning authority attempted (eventually successfully) through a planning condition, to ensure, in a green belt, that only farm workers should occupy certain cottages :

> '...Lord Denning likewise supported the condition and rejected a prima facie powerful argument for the appellants that "the statute gives the planning authority power to say in what <u>way</u> property is to be used but no power to say by what <u>persons</u> it is to be used. I cannot subscribe to this proposition for a moment. I should have thought that a planning authority could very reasonably impose a condition that cottages were to be reserved for farm-workers and not let to city dwellers : for this would help to preserve the green belt."': [29].

Thus the behaviour of those empowered to make public statements on changes and interpretations of planning law is a means of providing symbolic satisfaction to the mass public (the law is precise and must be obeyed), and of providing conflict resolution between opposing interests (the law is guided by opposed principles which have varying degrees of importance depending on the case). A language form which brings this result is therefore very useful.

THE ADMINISTRATIVE LANGUAGE STYLE IN PLANNING

The language style of planning decision notices, and the more specific development control-oriented rules found in development plans, and of central government circulars and memoranda resembles that of planning statutes in some respects; but in two major formal elements (originator and audience) and in public response the styles are very different: [30]. Here, as in planning statutes, confident commands and precise definitions are evident. But instead of coming from a popularly elected body, this kind of language issues from planners. Instead of constantly asserting that the public will is being carried out, the administrative language style is addressed to an audience in the form of instructions which must be complied with. Here there is a very real sense of the ability to help or hinder, and this authority can be sensed from the wording of such instructions.

For example, conditions on a planning permission may be of the following form :

> '(a) That the use of the site for a motor car repair workshop is limited to between the times of 9 a.m. and 6 p.m. from Mondays to Fridays, and use of the site for this purpose should not take place on public holidays.
> (b) Noise levels shall not exceed 80 dba at the periphery of the site.
> (c) That the boundary of the site bordering Green Lane shall

have a brick wall 2 metres high.'

The imperative mood runs throughout the condition, and the clear statement of times of permitted activity, limits of permitted noise, and height of a required wall all give the impression of great precision.

The public response is in the form of anger at the arbitrary nature of much development control and ridicule of administrative jargon. Thus the public meaning is one of a closed group acting with arbitrary authority, using an incomprehensible language. Developers and pressure groups often engage in such criticisms, but they only find this approach effective because they strike a public chord. Sometimes politicians find it useful to join in such denunciations to show that they reflect public feeling. Such cases reveal that the use of administrative language sometimes undermines the public myth that planners merely carry out the public will. Thus the public myth is reinforced by the general authoritative tone and precision of administrative language, and undermined by the apparent arbitrariness of particular cases. This leads to public ambivalence about, and uncertain popular support for, decisions issued in the administrative language style.

However, the popular conceptions of the administrative language style differ markedly from the response of groups directly involved in the planning process. These are the organised groups, often developers, who have most to gain by attempting to influence it. In this sense the planner has authority only so long as he is sensitive to the web of groups with access to him. The planning policy that :

'Major office developments shall occur only in established centres'

will bring forth strong pressure from office developers for more precise and more favourable interpretations of the terms 'major' and 'established'.

Developers have potential to exert strong sanctions - the refusal to invest, and the serving of purchase notices as well as going to appeal with an army of lawyers. And other organised groups can exert sanctions too. An example of planners' response to such pressures is the greater reluctance to take enforcement proceedings against Asian small businesses in Coventry, since some wards have high proportions of Asians, and since councillors wish to avoid any accusation of racial bias. Here is not personal despotism by planners, but resource manipulation in response to group pressures.

Yet in public such a relationship is expressed in terms of a battle : between planners and property speculators in the sixties, between house-builders and conservationist shire counties in the eighties, between risky technologies and ecology groups, between efficiency-oriented farmers and conservation groups, between shire counties and inner cities (competing for grant), between developers and protectors of old buildings. This appearance of battle serves to give dramatic expression of the anxiety in the public's mind - that there will be a risk from nuclear energy, that concrete and tarmac will cover everything, that the countryside as we know it will disappear, and so on. Government's response is often to create symbolic reassurance by creating new institutions (the Countryside Commission, the Sports Council, the Civic Trust, the Urban Aid and Inner Cities programs, the Commission for Racial

Equality) or by elevating the status of existing ones (for example, the creation in 1970 of the giant Department of the Environment from the preexisting Ministries of Housing and Local Government, and of Transport, to symbolise the emerging importance of 'environment'). The act of creating such bodies rarely leads to tangible, rather than symbolic, benefits, and when they do (for example, the National Trust) it is because influential groups are able to make use of them (for example, via the law on death duties and transfer to the state of stately homes and land).

The same kind of analysis comes from considering central government circulars and memoranda. Here is a circular warning that caravan licences were being issued by local authorities with excessive numbers of conditions attached, and asking local authorities to

> 'review their practice in this respect and to consider what is the minimum that need be included (rather than the maximum that can be included) in the licences they issue.': [31].

The imperative mood is again present, but what is significant here too is the ambiguity of terms such as 'review',and 'minimum'. While the Ministry has the last word should an appeal to it be made by a dissatisfied applicant, it also depends upon the compliance of local authorities for its coordinating and policy-revision functions to have any effect. It thus leaves wide room for interpretation by local authorities in most of its policy advice.

The significance of the difference between the public response and the reaction of involved, organised groups to the administrative language style now begins to appear. The public response, which is largely one of anger and ridicule, encourages inaction by planning authorities and other bodies (the Alkali Inspectorate, the Health and Safety Execute, local health authorities) responsible for environmental regulation. The reaction of organised groups often encourages the same thing. There are thus endemic factors which reduce the likelihood that planning authorities and other similar bodies will deliver the tangible benefits (protection of the environment, reduction or elimination of environmental nuisance and risk) which politicians promise and which legislation transforms into law.

THE BARGAINING LANGUAGE STYLE IN PLANNING

The use of bargaining language, like hortatory language, involves an attempt to gain support: [32]. But while hortatory language appeals for political support, bargaining language offers a deal. A public reaction is to be avoided and not sought. A resolution of incompatible differences is sought in the form of a quid pro quo, not through any expression of premises, inferences, and conclusions.

The bargaining of planning consents: [33] is one example of the use of bargaining language in planning. For example, the Centre Point skyscraper office block was given permission in an area of London (the junction of Tottenham Court Road and Oxford Street) which at the time was subject to plot ratio, density, and building height controls which prohibited such a building. However there was a need for highway engineering works on the site which the local authority was disinclined to pay for on such an expensive central site. The developer got his permission in return for the provision of this highway construction.

The inexactness of planning law on the subject of inter-county coordination of structure plans and on 'conformity' of local plans with structure plans offers other examples where two parties may have incompatible interests: [34] and the ability to sanction each other, and where bargaining language becomes the appropriate language style for the resolution of conflicts.

Bargaining often has unsavoury connotations to the public: [35] and can only be rendered respectable by means of being presented as the rational devising of means of achieving laudable public goals: [36].

Because by its very nature bargaining takes place in private, and because the nature of bargaining language is never publicised to the mass, uninvolved public, the significant formal element conveying meaning to the public is the setting. Privacy and secrecy are aspects of the setting which evoke public suspicion about the extent to which group interests are being included or excluded: [37]. More often than not, the public assumes that the public good is being served. Such assumptions can, however, be seriously questioned: [38]. In the case of the bargains that planners and developers made on town centre redevelopment schemes in the sixties and early seventies, the official publicity emphasised the solving of traffic problems, the provision of safe shopping environments, and so on. Although it was obvious to the public that developers wanted profits, it was much less obvious to them that planners wanted the power and status within their council consequent on the control of large scale developments and the favour of councillors wishing to expand shopping hinterlands and put their town 'on the map': [39]. Thus the way in which bargains are presented to the public serves, like the other language forms in planning, to promote social harmony and quiescence: [40].

To the bargainers themselves, the meaning of the quid pro quo is clear: [41]. It is nearly always in the form of a written contract or in the conveyance to the local authority of a gift of land, buildings, property rights, or money.

CONCLUSION

When these language styles are put together an interesting observation emerges. The difference between the meaning of each style for the mass, uninvolved public on the one hand, and for involved, organised groups on the other, grows smaller as one goes from the hortatory to the bargaining style. At the same time, the involvement of the mass, uninvolved public gets progressively smaller. The inescapable inference must be that meanings conveyed to the mass, uninvolved public are always different from the meanings conveyed to direct participants in the planning process, but the mass uninvolved public gradually disappears as a factor as one moves toward the language styles most associated with the allocation of tangible, rather than merely symbolic, benefits. The significant political function of the hortatory language style is to reassure the mass public so that involved and organised groups can deal with planners: [42] while at the same time not disturbing the appearance of political consensus. This comes about because the hortatory, legal, and administrative language styles serve to confirm in the public's mind the myth that planners carry out the public will. And the legal and administrative language styles enable organised groups to use such language to serve their own ends: [43]. In the case of bargaining, organised groups, politicians and planners avoid any response by the mass public while at the same time sharing a clear understanding that bargaining is taking place: [44].

In specific situations political conflict in planning is usually resolved using more than one language style. It is through administration and bargaining that organised groups chiefly obtain tangible benefits rather than merely symbolic ones. But these are the activities which use language forms that generate most public suspicion. These two language forms are therefore nearly always used in conjunction with hortatory or legal language styles. This makes it easy for the public to underestimate the importance of the two less popular language styles and overestimate the importance of the two more popular language styles: [45].

Moreover, the greater the failure, the clearer the denial of tangible benefits to the public expecting them, and the more intense the resort to hortatory and legal language. The resort to hortatory language in much of the extracts from the West Midlands Structure Plan cited above tends to reveal that those responsible for working on it were aware of the severe problems of implementation which the Plan faced, despite the commitment by the councillors to regeneration of inner urban areas. Both issues and the use of the rational-comprehensive strategy provide hortatory justification. Similarly the Bedfordshire County Structure Plan 1976, while it faced problems of implementation of equally severe proportions, had the additional problem of a County Council with minority control, and of central issues about which there was conflict. Its hortatory tone is just as intense. In the Bedfordshire Structure Plan, however, the rationalist tradition and the rational-comprehensive strategy form an even more obvious feature. The rational planning process replaces substantive issues as the sole element of hortatory style. Statements about goals and objectives form initial premises; the reaction to these in the form of a large number of alternatives generated, form the central inferences; and the evaluation by planners and politicians against the goals and objectives in choosing a preferred solution forms the conclusion. In this way <u>form</u> (the rational planning process) can be emphasised as receiving widespread public support, and <u>content</u> (the substantive issues on which no consensus exists) can be played down.

Thus consideration of the forms and meanings of political language in planning helps us to find which groups are participating in the planning process and with what effect. It means that we must continually ask questions about political tactics and symbolising rather than assuming that plans are authoritative declarations of policy which will later be transformed into subsequent resource allocations: [46].

NOTES

[1] P.J. Dunleavy, <u>Urban Political Analysis</u>, Macmillan, London, 1980.
[2] K. Newton, <u>Second City Politics : Democratic Process and Decision Making in Birmingham</u>, Oxford University Press, London, 1976.

[3] A. Samuels, 'Structure plan examination in public', Journal of Planning and Environment Law, March, 1975, p.137.

[4] H.A. Simon, Administrative Behaviour, New York, 1958, p.81.

[5] M.C. Poulton, 'The limits to and effective use of evaluation methods', Environment and Planning B, Planning and Design, Vol. 10, 1983, pp.179-92.

[6] D. White, 'The parrot language of politics', New Society, 2 October 1980, pp.8-10; R.M. Merelman, 'Learning and legitimacy', American Political Science Review, Vol.60, 1966, pp.548-61.

[7] M. Edelman, The Symbolic Uses of Politics, Chapter 3, Harper and Row, N.York, 1966.

[8] 'The most intense dissemination of symbols commonly attends the enactment of legislation which is most meaningless in its effects on resource allocation', M. Edelman, 'Symbols and political quiescience', American Political Science Review, Vol. 54, Sept. 1960, pp.695-704 at p.697.

[9] Because public opinion is so difficult to define, people commonly imagine majority support for their views : see J.M. Felds and H. Schuman, 'Public beliefs about the beliefs of the public', Public Opinion Quarterly, Vol.40, 1976, pp.427-48.

[10] This applies not only to party politicians, but to leaders of political and moral movements as well : see R. Wallis and R. Bland, 'Purity in danger : a survey of participants in a moral-crusade rally', British Journal of Sociology, Vol.30, No. 2, June 1979, pp.188-205 at p.203.

[11] For an analysis of the use of suggestion and association in rhetoric speeches see F. Burwick, 'Associationist rhetoric and Scottish prose style', Speech Monographs, Vol.34, 1980, pp.21-34.

[12] For a sceptical view on this process in planning see T. Hancock, 'The Big Decisions - Who Decides?', Town and Country Planning Summer School, Report of Proceedings, 6-17 Sept., 1980; also R. Kemp, 'Planning, legitimation, and the development of nuclear energy', International Journal of Urban and Regional Research, Vol.4, 1980, pp.350-71.

[13] A.J. Meltsner, 'Don't slight communication : some problems of analytical practice', Policy Analysis, Vol.5, No.5, 1979, pp.367-92.

[14] C. Mueller, The Politics of Communication : a Study of the Political Sociology of Language, Socialisation, and Legitimation, New York, Oxford University Press, 1973.

[15] Thus the ability to name and classify is connected with political power : 'one may hypothesise that the greater the number of alternatives available, the greater the amount of power the given group possesses. From this point of view the fortunate interest which can redefine an issue expands its own possibilities for action', T.A. Smith, The Comparative Policy Process, Santa Barbara, California, 1975, p.171.

[16] An example of the importance of naming is the implications of setting up a transportation study in an area. Such a study will start from the initial premise that there is a traffic problem concerning accessibility and congestion and adopt an investment or management solution, irrespective of the smallness of the problem relative to other areas.

[17] The importance of language in planning has been emphasised by N. Taylor, 'Planning theory and the philosophy of planning',

Urban Studies, Vol.17, 1980, pp.159-72.
[18] K. Prandy, 'Alienation and interests in the analysis of social cognitions', British Journal of Sociology, Vol.30, No.4, Dec. 1979, pp.442-74.
[19] M. Edelman,op.cit., p.134-38.
[20] G. Smith, Social Need, Routledge and Kegan Paul, London, 1980; D. Watson, 'Making reality intelligible : the relation between philosophical analysis and the study of social policies', Journal of Social Policy, Vol.12, No.4, 1983, pp.491-514.
[21] S. Chase, The Tyranny of Words, New York, 1938, p.137.
[22] West Midlands County Council, Structure Plan : Report, (as submitted to DOE) 1980.
[23] Royal Commission on the Distribution of the Industrial Population : Report, January 1940, CMD 6153, HMSO, pp.200-1.
[24] W.I. Jenkins, Policy Analysis, Martin Robertson, 1978, p.251.
[25] Plans often contain hortatory passages about the limited powers of planning authorities to carry out proposals. These serve to lessen public fears about arbitrary bureaucratic power. Laymen and non-planning specialists tend to criticise planners for having too much power while planners themselves tend to think that their powers are limited.
[26] M. Edelman,op.cit., p.138-42.
[27] P. McAuslan, The Ideologies of Planning Law, Pergamon, URP Series, Vol.22, 1980, p.2 and p.179.
[28] C. Perelman, The Idea of Justice and the Problem of Argument, Routledge and Kegan Paul, 1977, pp.11-35.
[29] P. McAuslan,op.cit., p.164.
[30] M. Edelman,op.cit., p.142-45.
[31] Ministry of Housing and Local Government, Caravan Parks, Circular 2/62, Para.3, 1962.
[32] M. Edelman,op.cit., p.145-59.
[33] One factor which increases the attractiveness of bargaining to developers is that should they decide to go to appeal, there is only one in four chance of success : G. Dobry, Review of the Development Control System, HMSO, 1975, p.61.
[34] R.A. Dahl and C. Lindblom, Politics, Economics, and Welfare, New York, 1953, Chapters 10, 11.
[35] J. Simmie, Power, Property and Corporatism, Macmillan, London, 1981, p.187.
[36] For the details of how such formulae are jointly agreed, see I.W. Zartman, 'Negotiation as a joint decision-making process', Journal of Conflict Resolution, Vol.21, No.4, December 1977, pp.619-38.
[37] P.M. Blau, Exchange and Power in Social Life, New York, Wiley, 1964.
[38] One avenue of evaluation of the Welfare State has been to study which groups benefit and in what way. Surprisingly, it is the less needy, though more demanding and articulate, who benefit most : J. Le Grand, 'Who benefits from public expenditure?', New Society, 21 Sept. 1978, Vol.45, No.833, pp.614-18.
[39] For example, a study of agreements between car manufacturers and dealers shows how two strong organisations can strike deals which ignore unrepresented interests : see S. McAnley, Law and the Balance of Power, 1966, (referred to in J. Jowell, 'The Limits of law in public planning', Current Legal Problems, Vol. 30, 1977, p.83). On his Tolmers Square case study, Jenkins suggests a similar kind of process : '...Yet the Council rarely

sought to mobilise grass-roots opinion...policy may be explained by the inactivity of political authorities, in particular through the deliberate exclusion of some groups from the policy process.': W.I. Jenkins, Policy Analysis, Martin Robertson, 1978, p.12.

[40] M. Edelman, 'Governmental Organisation and public policy', Public Administration Review, Vol.12, Autumn 1952, p.276-83; G.Y. Steiner and S.K. Gove, Legislative Politics in Illinois, Urbana III, 1960, p.77.

[41] For the importance of clarity and trust in bargaining see W. Korpi and M. Shaley, 'Strikes, industrial relations, and class conflict in capitalist societies', British Journal of Sociology, Vol.30, No.2, June 1979, pp.164-87.

[42] J.M. Simmie, Citizens in Conflict, Hutchinson, London, 1974, p.136.

[43] M. Eisenberg, 'Private ordering through negotiation : dispute settlement and rule making', Harvard Law Review, 1976, p.637.

[44] The bargain, of course, may amount to no more than an agreement to disagree. This was the case in the bargain made between Bedford District and County Councils over car parking in Bedford. See A. Blowers, op.cit., at p.90-91.

[45] An extreme reliance on trading (the bargaining language style) to the exclusion of argument (the hortatory language style) suggests a dislocated and disjointed political culture. When such a situation exists an 'individualistic' ethical system is pursued to the exclusion of a 'relational' system of ethical values. D. McRae Jr, 'Scientific communication, ethical argument, and public policy', American Political Science Review, Vol.65, 1971, pp.40-50.

[46] For an example of this naive view see : R.S. Bolan, 'Community decision behaviour : the culture of planning', Journal of the Institute of American Planners, Vol.35, September 1969, pp.371-94.

27 Evaluating planning

Besides theorising about why and how planning decisions come about, it is also necessary to evaluate them. Theories about why and how are difficult enough. They involve tremendous simplification of reality, and they reveal their author's own biases and prejudices. But when we come to evaluating planning we move onto even more dangerous ground. At the start we must decide what is important, relevant, and good. Is it a smooth-running and efficient planning system? Is it one which is well-informed about how its intervention affects land development processes? Is it one which is aware of the value implications of the assumptions being made? Is it one which leads to a 'better' quality of environment? These four questions demonstrate not only the variety of interpretations of what 'the effect of planning' means, but they move, from the first to the fourth question, from more easily to less easily answered questions.

The first question was asked by the Parliamentary Expenditure Committee: [1], and is continually asked by the DOE and the private sector land development lobby. The emphasis is upon efficiency and delays in the land development control process. Fairly precise measures are possible to answer this question, and it it relatively easy for administrators and planners in the DOE and local authorities to implement any findings that emerge from research prompted by this question.

The second question represents a considerable increase in difficulty for research from question one. It was asked by a DOE-sponsored study in 1978. It investigated current research on planning intervention into the land development process, but concluded that little had been done to find what the role and responsibility of public sector planning should be: [2]. This conclusion, together with its suggestion for a greater theoretical content (other than operations research) in future studies led it to suggesting research which considers political and ethical values.

Such values are the subject of the third question : what are the values used in planning? Again, the level of difficulty providing an adequate answer increases. Moreover any answers that might be found are much less usable by the DOE and local authorities - indeed they bring in value conflicts and question accepted assumptions. Such research is thus troublesome for practitioners to deal with. Yet there is a small though significant academic interest in investigating this question.

Question four, 'does planning lead to a "better" environment?' is the most difficult one to answer. It seems to have been abandoned not only by research sponsors such as the DOE but by academics too. The reason must be because of the lack of consensus that exists, the realisation that answers are subject to fashion, and that the public must have a say. Indeed the public does have a say - many opinion polls include detailed questions on environmental matters and national politics increasingly reflects the importance given to environmental matters.

So answers to the first two questions are beginning to emerge, although even a question as seemingly straightforward as the effect of planning intervention on land development raises questions of value. The last two questions are most definitely under researched. It is clear, therefore, that much of what planners do is done in a research vacuum. Yet this does not prevent plans and decisions being made. What happens is that planners merely make assumptions. This is a very dangerous situation, bearing in mind the wide range of matters with which they deal.

The increasing scale of difficulty of the four questions is explained by referring to the problems of policy evaluation after-the-event which were raised in Chapter 9. As one moves from the first to the fourth question the number of variables increases, their measurability declines, and the value-content of them rises.

RESEARCH METHODS IN PLANNING

Much research done in planning has a short-term view, is influenced by topical interest: [3], and is used by practitioners to justify existing fashions, rather than as an objective basis of reform. Such research is understandably popular, and being topical, it attracts a wide readership and is thus suitable for publication in journals. Longer-term research, which attempts to take a more objective view, is more difficult and less likely to attract financial sponsorship, and is less productive of publications bearing in mind the effort expended. Since the switch from new-build to housing improvement in 1969, hundreds of journal articles have appeared on the subject of housing improvement. Yet none has attempted to establish if such a programme is cost-effective. Seventeen years have elapsed since 1969. Many houses 'improved' since then have had to be repaired yet again. And eventually a sudden switch back to clearance and new-build may be required, with all the expense and upheaval which that creates. The data exists (though the reluctance of Public Health Departments in local authorities to release such data is understandable) and other data on house prices and household characteristics could be collected relatively easily.

Research on planning is difficult. Not only must one choose what kind of research is to be done - suggested by the four questions at the start of this chapter - but also there are the inevitable difficulties inherent in evaluating policies after they have been discussed, decided, and implemented (see Chapter 9).

There are also the many difficulties inherent in any social science research. Planners work in teams, local or central government departments, and belong to a profession, all of which carry their own blinkered view of the world. They have personal and intellectual differences of opinion with colleagues and the public. Their decisions have implications for people, for jobs, for leisure opportunities, for accessibility, and so on. Any research which attempted to come to terms with such complexity would always have to be aware of the questions : 'Why was that meaning given to that action at that time?' The question is how to interpret what is going on in as 'objective' a way as possible, or at least to reflect the meanings of those observed as accurately as possible.

Arriving at 'objective' conclusions is therefore difficult. One useful stance to take is a comparative one. A planner says that a decision is 'good'. But good compared to what? Such questions can often help gain useful insights. It could be argued that the low densities of new residential areas in Brittany provide a superior quality of environment to that found on new estates in Britain. Does the land and infrastructure saving in higher density estates in Britain justify this difference?

Another important factor in research is replication. Can the researcher be sure that another researcher would come to similar conclusions? Or are the research findings the result of personal bias? Moreover, each researcher is prone to define things in slightly different ways, making comparison of studies difficult. The Government Social Survey is an example of a data source where definitions remain fixed so that one can estimate trends over time in an accurate way.

One possible way of generating statistics about the effects of planning which would remain comparable over time and space might be to produce legislation to force local planning authorities to monitor effects of planning (those effects having been narrowly defined) and to publish, annually, those statistics. Thus it would be possible for each local authority to estimate the proportion of average house prices taken up by land prices. If such statistics had started to be published ten years ago, and were now suggesting that in some areas local authorities were too restrictive in their planning policies, local newspapers would be ensuring that these facts were widely known. The comparison with recent pressure on state schools to publish exam performance (and thus to give parents some basis for choice of school) suggests itself. It would go some way to push the planning profession in the direction of public accountability. Other statistics could also be collected. For example, in respect of industrial planning permissions, the average distance from a factory to the nearest group of more than ten houses, for different categories of potentially dangerous industrial process, would, over a ten-year period, show whether safety standards were being maintained.

In estimating the reliability of a research study the question of how the sample has been determined is of central importance. Only from random samples can one estimate exact boundaries of confidence within which the results can be safely generalised. However, the greater the policy relevance of the research, the more that other sampling frameworks become necessary. If one was comparing three types of landowner, for example, one would want three equally-sized groups of respondents. The respondents would perhaps be randomly chosen within their group but the sample would not be fully random. This is an example of a quota sample. Another example is where one wished to interview an equal number of residents in several different residential areas. The last main type of sampling method is purposive sampling. A researcher wishing to investigate 'best practice' of some aspect of planning might approach a reputedly good planning department. Only random sampling can give confidence intervals and allow statistical inference. Quota sampling is cheaper but prone to errors. Purposive sampling is only of use for case studies, where the value of deeper insights outweighs that of generalisability.

In natural science, intervention is often tested by comparison with a 'control group' on which no intervention is used. Thus a group of patients may be given either a drug or a placebo. If both give the same result, the drug has not had the desired effect. Creating control groups in planning research is usually difficult or impossible. One might study residents within a General Improvement Area and those outside it, to see the effect of housing improvement policies. But usually the two types of area are different - that is why one has been declared a General Improvement Area.

The perfect research design includes four main ingredients. It is fully controlled - through random sampling - and thus reliable. The researcher participates in the process he is observing and thus gains insight. The data are collected, codified and analysed using recognised scientific methods. And the research is carried out with the full knowledge of those who are being observed. Such perfection, however, is never attained, though the best studies make a valiant attempt.

Some questions to ask of any research on planning are the following. Was there a pilot study? How long and carefully-done was it? Could the questions have suggested the answers? (respondents might guess what the researcher's hypothesis was and give answers to fit this hypothesis). Could the environment have influenced the answers? (answering questions in a planning office might make the respondent give the 'official' line). Were the answers codified? Were the interviewers trained? How much control was there over the form of the answers? Who was being interviewed? (a developer might react adversely to a planning researcher).

Answers are no good until the questions have been properly thought out. This involves the researcher examining his underlying assumptions.

For example, one might wish to investigate the effectiveness of development control in preventing the development of retail warehousing. But a better question might be, why is retail warehousing usually thought to be bad? There might be strong pressure on councillors from the local town centre shopkeepers. Also developers of retail warehouses might have broken an unspoken code held by the development control officer. Such development does not fit in with his existing land use categories making it easy to label the developer a 'cowboy'.

Often one might wish to construct causal explanations. Yet such an approach is extremely difficult due to the number of variables involved. This particularly affects the attempt to establish the effects of a planning policy. Care needs to be taken that all relevant variables are being measured, though this is usually impossible.

The weight put on evidence in any planning research is of crucial importance. When one is referring to documents, for example, selection is bound to be subjective. Moreover, statistics should be treated with care. Clerks in planning departments record various kinds of statistics, and may be insufficiently aware of the meaning of the categories they are fitting cases to. Such categories may be ambiguous and thus the statistics recorded may depend upon the clerk who is doing the recording.

Always there is the danger in planning research of subjective interpretation of events. For example, one may be trying to find out why sites in inner cities remain vacant for so long. If one favours planning and the public sector one might seek evidence of market irrationality or property speculation. If one favours the private sector one may criticise planning delays, or uncertainty created by planning policies.

Interpretation can be made on a variety of levels. Particular land development processes could be seen as purely economic and explained by means of relationships between demand and supply. Inner city vacant sites might be seen as due to a lack of demand. Or a behavioural approach might be taken. Owners of vacant sites might hold inflated, unrealistic estimations of the value of their land.

Usually where evidence is put forward which supports existing opinion, there is no scrupulous examination of evidence. Where policy is contradicted, there is always a search to explain away the results. There is, for example, much evidence on the lack of effect of school quality, and the importance of a poor environment on eductional attainment. This is a good case for improving education by better housing and environment and welfare services rather than more teachers and better schools. Yet such heresy challenges existing opinions and structures, and is therefore explained away: [4].

The usefulness of planning research to policy makers can be greatly exaggerated. Research avenues and reporting of research findings are influenced by topicality and the availability of sponsors. Topicality leads to superficiality and results which are soon forgotten as policy issues change. Sponsors, such as the DOE, have short term objectives related to making existing policy more effective rather than instigating fundamental reappraisals. Because of all the difficulties mentioned above, there is little chance that research can solve complex topical planning problems. Yet such research is usually better than guesswork. The 1938 national population projections warned about population decline, while the 1969 projections created panic about over-population. No noticeable increase in accuracy came about in the interim. But at least such predictions focussed attention on the long-term implications of such trends. A problem often encountered in planning is that, although generally the assumption is made that demand eventually equals supply, often supply creates demand. Certainly a historical investigation of mistaken predictions, their assumptions, and their political uses at the time they were made, would be a worth-while piece of planning research.

CURRENT RESEARCH IN PLANNING

Much current research has a short term orientation and concerns procedures. Much does not evaluate or question policy, but concentrates on the questions of 'fine-tuning'. Procedure is of paramount importance - how to increase efficiency, what information needs local authorities have in order to deal with the problem of vacant sites in inner areas, how to improve the public inquiry system, and so on. The orientation to the short term is reinforced by the preoccupations of the main sponsoring body - the DOE (reinforced by the private sector land development lobby). Much research is done on identifying demand and supply of land and buildings and seeking to predict problems in the development process as a result of private-public sector relationships. Other research deals with local authority standard operating procedures and their improvement - the need for local authorities to collect data on land ownership, and on the costs of holding land, the need for consistent and predictable funding in urban renewal, the effectiveness of Green Belts during house-building booms, and so on. Such research is usually an ad hoc response to topical issues: [5].

Little research is done on the effects of policies: [6]. Since 1973 no work has materialised on the effect of planning restrictions on housing and land costs. Little systematic and comparative work exists on the effect of key settlement policies on the problems of rural accessibility, house prices, and 'rural gentrification'. No research has yet appeared questioning the current government view that planning acts as a barrier to technological and industrial innovation. Little research is done on the precise effects of families living in high-rise flats.

Historical work is even more sadly neglected. An important and relevant question surrounds the factors which lead to planning decisions which can now, with the benefit of hindsight, be called mistaken. Despite the considerable difficulties which exist with respect to access to relevant documents, there is a rich field for investigation here. The influence of fashion, the opportunity to boost one's own career or or help one's section's influence, the effect of powerful commercial interests, are all possible factors in such cases as the development of high-rise housing, industrialised housing, and of many urban motorway projects. Often the reasons for the ending of a policy would be as interesting as the reasons for its initial acceptance. A greater knowledge of the past would also be useful for developing more foresight. Potential mistakes, unhealthy influences, and fallacious arguments may recur, and if they do they would be recognised more clearly.

The major role of planning research should, however, be less to produce suitable evidence for decision makers than to investigate the gap that exists between the assumptions they make and the reality itself.

Bearing in mind the susceptibility of the profession to changing fashions one example of an assumption-challenging topic is the question of jobs versus the environment. How much have development control officers and local councillors (and others involved in appeals and inquiries) become less sensitive to the needs of the environment compared with economic imperatives? Do recent industrial developments have a more detrimental impact than those of ten years ago? Despite the massive operational problems such questions are important and relevant ones to ask, since they offer the possibility of identifying the influence of politics and fashion, and the extent to which planning principles are negotiable. They relate also to historical inquiries into the changing nature of planning and might serve to question the belief that there has ever been a core of inalienable and fixed principles motivating it. How much does such flexibility of principles help or hinder the profession, and what political interests are being served?

The question of changes in professional values leads to a need for an even more fundamental questioning of assumptions. This comes in the form of the following question. What precisely is the effect of the dominance of utilitarianism in planning? Does it tend to drive out open discussion of the more subjective aspects of environmental quality for example? Or is the decline of such aspects more a result of the increasing significance of economic criteria since the 1968 Town and Country Planning Act and since the days of full employment, and of the declining consensus about how to define such aspects? And since utilitarianism gives no help as to how to resolve moral issues, what happens when these issues arise in planning? Does its strength lie in the fact that by using utilitarianism the planner is able to avoid moral issues?

Investigations of the strengths and weaknesses of utilitarianism in particular planning issues would illuminate significant aspects of planning. If utilitarianism has the problems suggested in Chapters 17 to 22, what biases does it introduce, and who are the gainers and who are the losers as a result of these biases? If utilitarianism drives out laymen's considerations of what is right and good, does it give preference to other professionals and organisations over claims by (particularly uneducated) laymen? And what is the influence of utilitarianism upon the planner's ethical sensibilities? Does he express such ethical sensibilities in utilitarian terms, in terms of consequences, or do such sensibilities become blunted?

The suppression of arguments about environmental quality also raise a number of issues. Environmental quality is the bread and butter of development control work. Experience and intuition on this matter often guide development control officers in their decisions, followed by an ingenious process of justification. But what is meant by environmental quality? How do practitioners define it? And are such definitions always the same as public preferences? Comparing a typical modern estate of semi-detached houses with its equivalent, by prices, from the 1930s, two differences seem important. The earlier version often has a tree-lined road, and the houses are at a lower density. Why have these admirable qualities disappeared? And why do internal space standards and quality of building decline, for houses of the same price, after the mid-sixties? If it is the effect of planning controls on housing land availability and density, this is a very basic effect affecting large numbers of people. The public, if it was asked, might be critical. Thus assumptions made by planners need to be tested against the wishes of the public. Such effects, if they exist, might not be known to planners in which case there would be a disparity between their assumptions and reality.

We have seen how the presentation of plans is stage managed using methods and techniques derived from the rationalist tradition. It may be that the method of utilitarianism, in always assessing consequences in terms of the collective or majority good, is most useful to large organisations of industry and government rather than to the individual or small group, who cannot lay such claim to knowing the public interest. In this sense utilitarianism can serve as an instrument of control, as well as a language by which powerful interests communicate with each other. This allows the official, upper-class definition of environmental quality, involving such values as good taste and ecology, to survive under the cloak of the public interest. It also controls the impulse towards vulgarity, speed and built-in obsolescence which are the accompaniments of modern economic growth and consumer satisfaction: [7].

NOTES

[1] Public Expenditure Commitee on Planning Procedures, House of Commons, 1977, HMSO.
[2] S. Barrett, M. Stewart, J. Underwood, The Land Market and Development Process : a Review of Research and Policy, Centre for Advanced Urban Studies, University of Bristol, March 1978.
[3] S. Barrett, M. Stewart, J. Underwood, op.cit., p.41.
[4] M.D. Shipman, The Limitations of Social Research, Longman, London, 1972, p.146.
[5] S. Barrett, M. Stewart, J. Underwood, op.cit., p.15-49.
[6] E.J. Reade, 'The Theory of Town and Country Planning', p.43-58 in P. Healey, G. McDougall, M.J. Thomas, Planning Theory : Prospects for the 1980s, Pergamon, Oxford, 1982.
[7] D. Eversley, The Planner in Society : The Changing Role of a Profession, Faber and Faber, London, 1973, p.278.

Index